A Clinician's Guide to Delivering Neuro-Informed Care

IƟ13Ɵ6Ɵ1

This neurodiversity-informed handbook provides clinicians with a way to think, talk, and write about the autism spectrum brain style in positive, descriptive language that is tailored to the needs of individual clients.

Each chapter provides readers with compelling and instantly recognizable ways to reveal the autistic brain's strengths and differences, reframe behavioral patterns using neuro-affirming language, and link those descriptions to practical, positive supports. The book includes a glossary of descriptive terms and multiple examples of autistic Brain Style Profiles that hold the client's lived experience at the center, guiding clinicians to provide individualized assessment and support across the life span.

This book is an ideal resource for clinicians who wish to reframe diagnosis into a strengths-based narrative and partner with clients to support self-determined needs.

Marilyn J. Monteiro, PhD, is a licensed psychologist and author with over four decades of clinical experience in autism assessment and therapy across the lifespan supporting individuals.

"Dr. Monteiro's work embraces an empirical measurement approach while providing a unique phenomenological understanding for each person. Implementing a straight-up theory structure she calls the Descriptive Triangle, Monteiro provides annotated case narratives which illuminate diagnosis and assistance for people with ASD. Managing to straddle both DSM diagnosis and personalized care, this short, user-friendly manual is an indispensable guide for clinicians."

John Z. Sadler, MD, *Professor of Psychiatry and the Daniel W. Foster Professor of Medical Ethics, UT Southwestern Medical Center, Dallas*

"I had known Marilyn Monteiro personally and professionally for many years when I asked her to work with an incorrectly diagnosed nephew who was in crisis. As I read *A Clinician's Guide to Delivering Neuro-Informed Care: Revealing the Autism Story*, I was reminded of how quickly she connected with my nephew and how in sync she was with him. Her approach changed his thinking from 'something is wrong with me' to accepting and understanding how he processes and interacts with the world. With her continued guidance, he transformed from being resistant, depressed, and insecure to becoming an independent, happy, and self-confident young man. This book spells out her approach for clinicians to have the same success with their clients. Her approach to evaluating and working with autism is not the traditional approach we clinicians were trained in—it is the approach we should all be using."

DeAnn Hyatt Foley, MEd, *parent, presenter, and educational diagnostician*

"*A Clinician's Guide to Delivering Neuro-Informed Care* authored by Marilyn J. Monteiro, PhD, is an indispensable resource for clinicians committed to neuroaffirmative care. The chapters offer an innovative, empathetic approach to understanding and honoring the unique neurodivergent experiences of autistic individuals. This guide transforms assessments into meaningful narratives, empowering both clinicians and clients. Grounded in expertise and compassion, Monteiro's work sets a new standard in autism care, making it an essential tool for any professional seeking to deliver truly person-centered support."

Dr. Diana Goldsmith, *Clinical Director and Clinical Psychologist at Foundations Child and Family Therapy, Central London*

"Reading *A Clinician's Guide to Delivering Neuro-Informed Care: Revealing the Autism Story* is like getting to be in the room watching, listening to, and learning from a master clinician as she supports her clients, enriched by case examples and the MIGDAS framework. It's like receiving personal mentorship from a seasoned expert, making it a valuable resource for any professional committed to authentic, compassionate care."

Donna Henderson, PsyD, *Neuropsychologist and co-author of* Is This Autism? A Guide for Clinicians and Everyone Else *and* Is This Autism? A Companion Guide for Diagnosing

"I believe Marilyn Monteiro's new book is a 'must-have,' not just for everyone who assesses autism, but for all clinicians who work with Autistic clients. Her ability to align with, and support, the energy cost of Autistic styles of communication is both ingenious and profound. An example is the use of a 'pause button' to gently scaffold conversational topic transitions. Even something as simple as checking for permission and readiness before asking a question shows a deep and compassionate recognition of the Autistic need for mental preparation. Her book consists of accounts of interviewing, assessing, and supporting various Autistic child and adult character composites. These profiles are written in a way that slowly reveals the characters' stories and how their brains experience the world. Monteiro models a tender approach of report writing that captures the beauty and spirit of her clients, illustrating the kind of report I would love to read about myself or someone I love. This is the first book I would recommend to all clinicians and family members who want to learn kind and nurturing ways to connect with Autistic persons."

Helen San, MA, LPC, LAC, *Autistic Licensed Professional Counselor*

A Clinician's Guide to Delivering Neuro-Informed Care

Revealing the Autism Story

Marilyn J. Monteiro

Routledge
Taylor & Francis Group

NEW YORK AND LONDON

Designed cover image: © Getty Images

First published 2025
by Routledge
605 Third Avenue, New York, NY 10158

and by Routledge
4 Park Square, Milton Park, Abingdon, Oxon, OX14 4RN

Routledge is an imprint of the Taylor & Francis Group, an informa business

ISBN: 9781032874166 (hbk)
ISBN: 9781032858395 (pbk)
ISBN: 9781003532576 (ebk)

DOI: 10.4324/9781003532576

Typeset in Optima
by Newgen Publishing UK

This book is dedicated to the clinicians who have supported and encouraged this work over the past four decades and to the clinicians who will take this approach and make it a part of their autism conversations moving forward.

Contents

x   *Contents*

Foreword

At the heart of Marilyn Monteiro's *A Clinician's Guide to Delivering Neuro-Informed Care: Revealing the Autism Story* is a deep respect for and celebration of humanity. It encompasses the highest ethical principles applicable to psychologists—to protect the rights, dignity, and humanity of those we serve. Monteiro deftly bridges the gap between clinical theory and real-world application, offering a comprehensive guide that is both deeply informative and profoundly human. This humanity is embodied in Monteiro's strengths-based approach, emphasizing the unique patterns of strengths and differences that characterize the autistic brain style.

The joy of Monteiro's book is her laser-beam focus on the autistic individual's orientation and navigation of the world. They are the narrators and main characters of the autism story. She intentionally centers neurodiversity, while at the same time decentering neurotypicality. Through case examples, Monteiro engages with autistic people in an empowering way that gives them agency to understand themselves, their patterns of behaviors, and provides them with strategies and tools necessary for optimal functioning. The inclusion of personal stories and detailed profiles brings the theoretical concepts to life, making the book both engaging and relatable.

There are several factors that will make this book an instant industry leader for autism assessment and diagnosis. The book is meticulously structured, beginning with foundational concepts and progressing through detailed case studies that span the entire lifespan—from young children to adults. Monteiro's use of the Descriptive Triangle provides a clear and accessible framework for understanding the complex interplay of language, social relationships, and sensory experiences in autistic individuals.

Monteiro explores the clinician's role in telling the autism story, encompassing ways to think about, analyze, and write about people with autism. The core of Monteiro's life work fully shines here. She has been at the forefront of the reimagination of test report writing, urging clinicians to move from the traditional deficit-based model to an approach that is both strengths-based and compassionate. Monteiro's dedication to empowering clinicians is evident throughout the book. She provides a wealth of tools and resources. These practical supports are designed to enhance the clinician's ability to create individualized, effective, and compassionate care.

This book is a gift to the clinical community, offering a road map to more effective and empathetic care. Although I refer to her formally in this foreword, Marilyn Monteiro is a mentor and friend. As such, I am honored to recommend this book, which I consider to be a call to action for clinicians to adopt more neuro-affirming perspectives.

Linda Fleming McGhee, JD, PsyD

Acknowledgments

This book represents a lifetime of autism conversations. I am so very grateful to have had the opportunity to partner with so many autistic individuals and their families who shared their autism stories with me over the past four decades. They shaped the way I think, talk, and write about the autistic brain style. My life's work has centered on working together with autistic children, adolescents, and adults to reveal and support their individual lived experiences. It's been a journey filled with deeply moving, extraordinary, and memorable moments. I am appreciative of the many colleagues around the world with whom I've connected throughout the years through my training workshops. Their encouragement to write this book helped get me here. I was happy to be able to work together with the editors at Routledge UK on this timely book, and am glad to have lived long enough to have this work finds its place in the autistic clinician community and the broader neuro-informed autism assessment community. I am ever appreciative of my partnership with my colleagues at Western Psychological Services, the publishers of the MIGDAS-2, as we've worked together for almost two decades. Most of all, I am grateful to my family for all of their love and support every step of the way.

An initial conversation

Revealing and supporting the autism story

Welcome to our time together. This clinical guide is for you and was written to support you in the important work you do with autistic individuals and their families. After a lifetime of revealing and supporting autism stories, the first and foremost drive behind writing this book was to show and tell you ways to truly listen to, appreciate, respect, and share each individual's autistic story and lived experiences in your clinical practice. In other words, this book places a purposeful focus on the importance of providing a place where the individual's autism story is revealed, explored, and understood in ways that are meaningful for that person. Revealing the autism story in a strengths-based way is a powerful process. The words we use during the diagnostic and support process are profoundly life changing and truly make a difference. In this book, we'll explore specific ways to support autistic individuals as you spend time with children, adolescents, and adults to reveal and support their autism stories. This is your guide to delivering neuro-informed care. In the chapters ahead, we'll explore the deeply absorbing and multifaceted experience that characterizes the partnership between autistic individuals across the lifespan and neuro-informed clinicians like yourself.

We'll start with an introduction to a strengths-based way to think, talk, and write about the autism life stories that are revealed through assessment and support conversations in clinical practice. This includes an introduction to the visual framework and descriptive language that forms the basis for the MIGDAS-2 qualitative autism assessment system, or the Monteiro Interview Guidelines for Diagnosing the Autism Spectrum (Monteiro & Stegall, 2018). It also includes a way to bridge the gap between the use of the strengths-based descriptive framework and the *Diagnostic and Statistical Manual of Mental Disorders* (5th ed.; DSM–5; American Psychiatric Association, 2013) medical diagnostic criteria.

Part I of this book focuses on *revealing the autism story* across the lifespan. Starting with young children and their families, moving on to children and adolescents, and then on to adults, you will participate in the process of thinking, talking, and writing about autistic individuals in a strengths-based way. This includes learning how to develop individual Brain Style Profiles that describe the autistic brain style pattern of strengths and differences across age and ability levels. In each chapter, we'll also discuss connections between the autistic brain style and other forms of neurodivergence.

Part II of this book focuses on *supporting the autism story* across the lifespan. We'll explore a descriptive framework to structure the way you go about organizing your support recommendations for individuals across the lifespan. Then we'll revisit the cases discussed in Part I and connect those stories with ways to think, talk, and write about positive supports that are a fit for each individual and their family. We'll structure ways for you to incorporate the use of the positive supports for the autistic brain style across age and ability levels into your clinical practice.

The case stories in this book reflect representative autistic children, adolescents, and adults the author has partnered with in her assessment and support roles over the course of four decades. Each story told in this book was created from multiple experiences. The stories were designed to provide the reader with the opportunity to participate in authentic autistic lived experiences in the context of assessment and support clinical conversations.

As a clinician, whether you are at the start of your story or you have acquired a deeply layered range of experience, I welcome you to explore these autism conversations and adapt the information you absorb into the important work you do in your clinical practice. You will find that the autistic individuals and their families you support in this way will resonate with this approach and appreciate how you share their stories in empowering ways. Let's get started.

References

Autism Spectrum Disorder 299.00 (F84.0). (2013). *Diagnostic and Statistical Manual of Mental Disorders* (5th ed.). American Psychiatric Association.

Monteiro, M. J., & Stegall, S. (2018). *Monteiro Interview Guidelines for Diagnosing the Autism Spectrum: A Sensory-Based Approach, Second Edition (MIGDAS-2)*. Western Psychological Services; Torrance, California.

Introduction

Laying the foundation: the Descriptive Triangle

The words we use in diagnostic and therapy work are powerful. This book is about changing the way we think, talk, and write about the complex, multifaceted, and unique autism spectrum brain style as it presents itself in the children, adolescents, and adults who come to us for assessment and therapy. When we shift our thinking and our language away from labeling deficits and toward exploring patterns of brain style strengths and differences, it allows us to provide a setting that invites individuals to share their singular worldview with us. When we are receptive to hearing the lived experiences of our clients, we become better able to recognize, appreciate, and describe their unique patterns of strengths and differences. This in turn leads us to explore not only the form of the individual's patterns of living but also to understand and describe the function of their routines. This powerful process of describing patterns and their function fundamentally changes the therapeutic conversation. Instead of emphasizing a diagnostic label, the conversation focuses on describing the individual's profile in instantly recognizable and accessible terms. A common language is shared through a framework that establishes a context for understanding the individual's worldview and behavior patterns. When the individual story is revealed in this positive, descriptive way, the label of autism or autistic has a profoundly empowering context. The words we use support individuals in the development of their narrative of personal agency as they are given a framework and descriptive words to help others understand and appreciate their worldview.

Here are examples of the words we want to hear from parents and adults:

Our child is not a label or a category. The way you approached her diagnosis reflected an appreciation of our daughter as a unique individual. That was reassuring to us and helped us understand what the diagnosis means for our family moving forward.

DOI: 10.4324/9781003532576-1

Identifying my autistic brain style as an adult was life changing. Having a written report that describes me has helped others in my life really understand how I think and to take my point of view instead of assuming why I say and do the things I do.

So how do we start the process of shifting the conversation toward strengths-based descriptive language? It begins by using a visual framework to reveal the autism spectrum Brain Style Profile of strengths and differences. The Descriptive Triangle provides a visual context to guide the way we think, talk, and write about each individual's way of being in the world. As we build the individual's story using the Descriptive Triangle, we reveal their singular story while also telling the autism spectrum brain style story. The emphasis shifts from focusing on the diagnostic label to describing the individual's lived experience in recognizable language. When the most compelling story for the individual fits the Descriptive Triangle pattern, we have described the person first while setting the context for the diagnostic name to their story.

I developed the Descriptive Triangle as a way to provide a context for parents as their children completed the assessment process to determine whether the autism brain style pattern of strengths and differences was their most compelling diagnostic story. I wanted to establish a space in which we could focus on telling the child's story first so we would have a common language and a context for the diagnostic label as it applied to the individual child. This Descriptive Triangle forms the basis for the qualitative interview process developed by this author to support clinicians in their autism diagnostic work (Monteiro & Stegall, 2018). The Descriptive Triangle takes the diagnostic criteria (the *Diagnostic and Statistical Manual of Mental Disorders* 5th ed.; DSM–5; American Psychiatric Association, 2013; the *Individuals with Disabilities Education Act*, 2004) and reframes the language from deficit-based labels to strengths-based descriptions.

Let's walk through how you might reveal the autism story using the Descriptive Triangle and its associated descriptive language. The story begins by depicting the unfolding narrative to come: describing the individual's patterns of strengths and differences in three key areas. We start by drawing the triangle with the three points and the words "patterns of strengths and differences" in the center of the triangle. Notice that the triangle refers to patterns, setting the stage to describe recurring features. This is followed by the reference to strengths and by contrasting strengths with differences. The use of the word "differences" is deliberate. By eliminating the words "deficits" or "weaknesses," we tell a story of inclusivity rather than other-ness. Everyone has a pattern of strengths and differences and most notably in the expression of their brain style. When we are presented with the information that someone is about to discuss our pattern of strengths and weaknesses, the contrasting terms generate anxiety. It becomes more challenging to absorb the discussion of strengths because we are waiting to take in what is wrong. It leaves us feeling vulnerable, and not in a good way. When the language is reframed to contrast strengths with differences, we are generally more receptive to processing and absorbing the information. This specific framework of exploring patterns of strengths and differences more accurately characterizes the lived experience of neurodivergence. So we set the stage to tell the story of the individual's patterns of strengths and differences. The autistic brain style diagnosis is based on patterns, and we are laying the foundation to reveal the individual's patterns of strengths and differences. The Descriptive Triangle process of revealing the autistic brain style is depicted below in a series of progressive triangles.

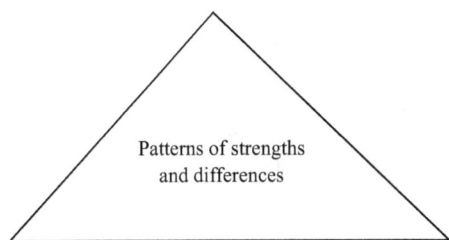

Source: © Marilyn J. Monteiro, PhD.

Now we are ready to start discussing the individual's pattern of strengths and differences in the first of the three areas: Language and Communication. We begin that conversation by writing the words above the first point on the triangle. Remember that we are revealing the individual's story first—all three parts—before we introduce the name or label of autism/autistic.

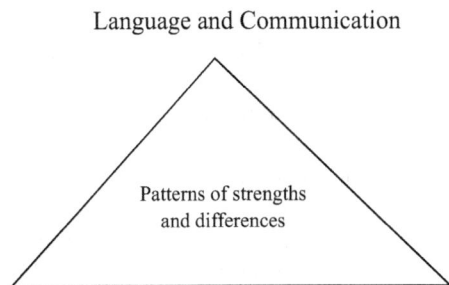

Language and Communication

Patterns of strengths
and differences

Source: © Marilyn J. Monteiro, PhD.

Strengths for Language and Communication include the degree to which the individual has developed the use of spoken language and the way in which they understand and use communication if they are not yet using spoken language. If the individual has developed spoken language, this strength is important to note. For example, descriptive ways to highlight this strength include noting a well-developed vocabulary, the application of language thinking skills, and a strong level of verbal fluency. Also important to note for verbally fluent individuals is the strength of organizing, retrieving, and using their developed language when they are in a regulated state. This helps others understand that accessing language and communicating become more challenging when the person is in a state of stress or distress and dysregulation.

For individuals who are not yet using spoken language, a relative strength to notice and describe is their ability to communicate using vocalizations, proximity, and management of another person's orientation toward the object that is the focus of the communication or request. Oftentimes emerging verbal language includes self-initiated labeling and vocalizing with intent to express protest or enjoyment. Another observation to describe is when the person shows an emerging understanding of spoken language when language is paired with visual contextual cues (showing while telling).

Differences in the area of Language and Communication include describing the conditions under which the individual *initiates* communication with others. The pattern to highlight is noting when the individual's initiation of communication is primarily guided either to communicate needs or to share areas of preferred interest. This gives us an opportunity to describe the way in which the brain organizes, retrieves, and uses language best when the individual self-initiates and by definition has a context for using language. We can then contrast the ease of using self-initiated language with the hard work involved in organizing, retrieving, and using language when the individual is responding to incoming communication demands from others and has to consider the context of that incoming language.

A second important area of difference to describe is how the individual participates in *shared communication exchanges*. Here we want to describe how it is challenging for the individual to organize, retrieve, and use language while simultaneously using, interpreting, and responding to communication input from their conversational partner. This includes both verbal (for example: changes in intonation and inflection, use of nonliteral language) and nonspeaking shared exchange communication (for example: eye gaze, gestures, body orientation). Describing the person's differences with simultaneous communication processing during shared exchanges allows us to highlight that it is hard work for the brain to manage incoming language and communication information in a fluid exchange. By definition, if this process is hard work for the brain, we can help others understand that the person experiences fatigue as a result of participating in shared communication exchanges. This can be characterized as the person showing a relatively low threshold for managing incoming communication demands.

A third area of difference we want to describe are the conditions under which the individual *extends* communication. Here we want to help others understand the contrast between the individual's ability to access and use language when they initiate the conversation and have a context for that conversation, and when the overture for engaging in a conversation originates with a conversational partner. Extension is a natural process when the individual initiates the conversation, but it is harder work for their brain to flexibly shift their thinking in a fluid way to extend communication on topics initiated by others.

This brings us to the fourth area of difference to call attention to, which is the degree to which the individual is able to *flexibly shift* from their thoughts to follow and participate in the conversational topics introduced by their conversational partner. Again, we describe the hard work for the brain to take in and respond to language and communication input from a conversational partner. Additional patterns of differences in the area of Language and Communication are discussed in the sample cases in Part I.

As we reveal the patterns of strengths and differences in this first area of the triangle, we are building the narrative of the autistic brain style for the individual. We contrast ways in which the brain organizes, retrieves, and uses language and communication with the aspects of communication that are harder work for the brain. When we pair these descriptors with personalized examples of what the individual says and does, we create a powerful and individualized way to understand that individual's complex language and communication experience.

Let's move on to the second area of the triangle, Social Relationships and Emotional Responses, and lay out the strengths-based descriptive highlights of strengths and differences. We begin by adding the category to our Descriptive Triangle.

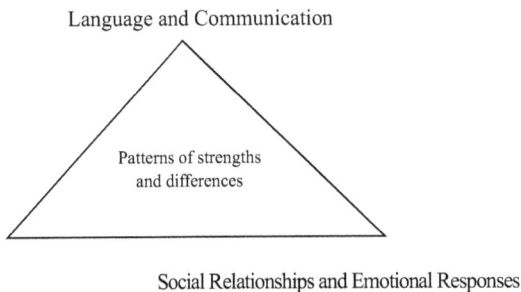

Language and Communication

Patterns of strengths
and differences

Social Relationships and Emotional Responses

Source: © Marilyn J. Monteiro, PhD.

Starting with strengths in the area of Social Relationships and Emotional Responses gives us an opportunity to describe the nature and demeanor of the individual in respectful terms. The goal is to describe the individual's qualities when they are not in a state of stress or distress. Adjectives such as gentle-natured, affable, energetic, loving, kind, respectful, creative, dedicated, passionate, responsible, determined, and curious are ones that are often used by parents to describe their children when asked to do so as part of their child's autism evaluation. Adults seeking a diagnosis often use adjectives such as sensitive, compassionate, funny, gentle, focused, kind, and empathic to capture their essential qualities. As we highlight social and emotional areas of strength in this positive, inclusive way, we can also describe the individual's capacity to connect with others and acknowledge their lived experience of their range and depth of emotions.

Social Relationships patterns of differences that often accompany the autism brain style include the notable gap between the individual's interest in and need for social connections and their ability either to successfully navigate social relationships or to find compatible social pathways. It is also constructive to describe the pattern of the individual's highly developed topic-focused narrative and contrast that pattern with the more challenging area of developing social narratives about self and others.

In the area of differences in Emotional Responses, it is helpful to describe the individual's relatively low threshold for managing incoming demands and the effect this low threshold has on their experiences of stress and distress in daily life. Incoming demands can be described as communication, social, and sensory information that requires the individual to adjust to the input in a flexible way. How do we acknowledge the signs that the individual's threshold for managing input has been breached? In addition to describing the lived experience of increased feelings of stress and distress, we can characterize the triggering of stress and distress by describing the destabilizing effect experienced when the individual's brain switches from thinking or regulated mode to reactive or dysregulated mode in response to incoming stressors.

Describing these social and emotional patterns of strengths and differences reveals the second of the three parts of this complex Brain Style Profile. We depict the individual's way of being in the world when we describe their positive qualities and acknowledge the stressful impact of constantly managing input.

As with Language and Communication, when we pair these descriptors with personalized examples, we create a powerful and individualized way to understand that individual's complex social and emotional experience in the world. Additional patterns of differences in the area of Social Relationships and Emotional Responses are discussed in the sample cases in Part I.

Let's move on to the third and final area of the triangle, Sensory Use and Interests. We begin by adding the category to our Descriptive Triangle.

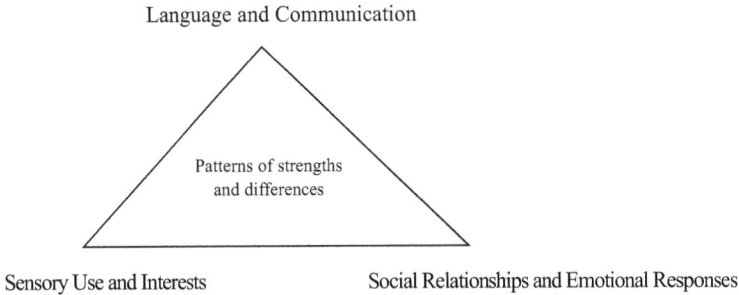

Language and Communication

Patterns of strengths and differences

Sensory Use and Interests   Social Relationships and Emotional Responses

Source: © Marilyn J. Monteiro, PhD.

Notice that we begin by renaming this part of the diagnostic criteria. Instead of using the DSM-5 deficit-based labeling language of "restrictive, repetitive patterns of behavior, interests or activities," we refer to this part of the diagnostic profile as Sensory Use and Interests. This creates the descriptive space to outline the strengths and differences that define the individual's patterns of behavior, interests, and activities and to characterize those patterns using an adaptive and functional frame of reference. Instead of referring to repetitive or restrictive patterns, we can rename the process in a way that explains what is actually happening when a person repeats interests or behaviors. We can describe how the person *creates and maintains predictable routines* that provide a pathway for them to explore the world using their preferred thinking skills (visual, three-dimensional, categorical, and so on).

We begin by describing the *form* of the individual's areas of preferred interests, activities, and behavior patterns. Individuals who enjoy building and making things can be described as visual, three-dimensional, tactile, strategic, and creative thinkers. Other adjectives describing thinking styles that apply across many areas of interest include describing the individual, for example, as a creative, categorical, scientific, critical, analytic, or pragmatic thinker. By carefully attending to the form of the person's interests and activities, we can provide compelling connections with the ways in which they engage parts of their brain and thinking skills. We can also note when the interests are in sync with the person's age and ability level.

Once we describe the form of the interests and link it to thinking styles, we can connect the form of the activities with their *function*. This allows us to illuminate the three main functions of creating and maintaining predictable routines for the autistic brain. The creation and maintenance of predictable routines serves the function of providing the person with a recurring space where they experience their brain and body being organized and regulated. When the person engages in self-directed routines, they not only feel organized and regulated but they are also able to block out incoming sources of stress, as defined by the demands inherent in managing language, social, and sensory input and in shifting from their agenda to follow the agenda of another person.

Another area of strength to describe relates to the person's sensory preferences. When we lay out the sensory preferences without labeling them as deficits, we begin to help the individual identify the detailed environmental components involved in providing them with sensory regulation. A person who identifies the sensory preference of being in a quiet, darkened room while covered in a comforter, seated in a preferred chair while listening to music wearing headphones provides the important narrative about the setting in which the person's brain restores itself. The central narrative for this person's sensory preferences is the need to spend time in a reduced stimulation environment, blocking out incoming sources of stress while engaging in a familiar, self-selected routine.

Moving on to differences in the area of Sensory Use and Interests, we can identify and describe the individual's sensory sensitivities. This includes describing the sensory aspects of the input and whether the input is expected or unexpected. Sensory sensitivities are consistently associated with the individual experiencing stress, distress, or dysregulation of their system. We can also highlight the pattern of challenges in the area of brain flexibility and flexible thinking by defining that process as hard work for the brain to flexibly shift from a self-determined agenda to follow the agenda of others. This leads to an understanding of the connection between the breeching of the person's sensory input threshold and their destabilizing experience of becoming dysregulated, feeling powerless to reset their regulation level.

We can also connect the person's use of recurrent body movements and mannerisms with the concept of regulation and of managing incoming sources of stress. We rename the labels "stereotyped and repetitive motor movements" to *recurrent or distinctive body movements and mannerisms*. This structures the description to focus on illustrating the form of the recurrent body movements and mannerisms and connecting the form to their function. Additional patterns of differences in the area of Sensory Use and Interests are discussed in the sample cases in Part I.

When we summarize recognizable patterns of behavior in all three of the key areas describing the autism brain style, we establish a context for understanding what we mean by the diagnostic label.

Autism/Autistic Brain Style Profile

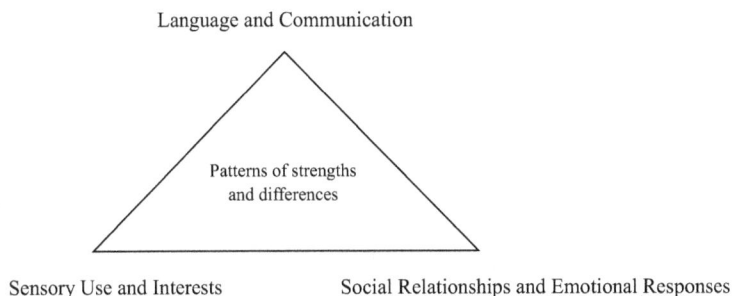

Language and Communication

Patterns of strengths
and differences

Sensory Use and Interests   Social Relationships and Emotional Responses

Source: © Marilyn J. Monteiro, PhD.

How do we reconcile this descriptive language framework with the diagnostic criteria? We are renaming deficits as differences, as the autism brain style is a different or divergent way of organizing in and experiencing the world. For example, instead of labeling a person as having "deficits in social-emotional reciprocity," we change the narrative to describe the lived experience: hard work for the brain to organize, retrieve, and use language while simultaneously interpreting and responding to communication input from a conversational partner.

Let's take the two main sections of the DSM-5 criteria, sections A and B, and provide a descriptive reframe.

DSM-5 Diagnostic Criteria for 299.00 Autism Spectrum Disorder

A. Persistent deficits in social communication and social interaction across multiple contexts, as manifested by the following, currently or by history:

Descriptive reframe:
The person demonstrates patterns of differences in their social communication and social interaction across multiple contexts, currently or by history.

1. Deficits in social-emotional reciprocity, ranging, for example, from abnormal social approach and failure of normal back-and-forth conversation; to reduced sharing of interests, emotions, or affect; to failure to initiate or respond to social interactions.

Descriptive reframe:
Differences in the way the person's brain manages shared exchanges are present, resulting in observable differences in the individual's ability to initiate and extend conversational shared exchanges in an expected pattern of behavior; the person displays differences in the quality and quantity of sharing interests and expressing emotions.

2. Deficits in nonverbal communicative behaviors used for social inter-action, ranging, for example, from poorly integrated verbal and non-verbal communication; to abnormalities in eye contact and body language or deficits in understanding and use of gestures; to a total lack of facial expressions and nonverbal communication.

Descriptive reframe:
Hard work for the brain to organize, retrieve and use language, and simultaneously manage the use of and response to verbal and nonspeaking communication cues, including simultaneously using language and eye gaze, facial expressions, and gestures, and interpreting and responding to those features when used by their conversational partner.

3. Deficits in developing, maintaining, and understanding relationships, ranging, for example, from difficulties adjusting behavior to suit various social contexts; to difficulties in sharing imaginative play or in making friends; to absence of interest in peers.

Descriptive reframe:
Differences include a notable gap between the individual's interest in and need for social connections and their ability either to suc-cessfully navigate social relationships or to find compatible social pathways. The individual shows a pattern of their highly developed topic-focused narrative, contrasted with the more challenging area of developing social narratives about self and others.

B. Restricted, repetitive patterns of behavior, interests, or activities, as manifested by at least two of the following, currently or by history

Descriptive reframe:
The person creates and maintains predictable routines involving areas of preferred interests, preferred activities, and behavior patterns that serve the function of helping the person gain a sense of organization and pre-dictability, regulation of their system, and an opportunity to retreat from the incoming sources of stress and distress inherent in managing inter-personal and environmental demands.

1. Stereotyped or repetitive motor movements, use of objects, or speech (e.g., simple motor stereotypes, lining up toys or flipping objects, echolalia, idiosyncratic phrases).

Descriptive reframe:
The person creates and maintains predictable routines with recurrent, distinctive body movements and mannerisms, and/or use of objects that serve the function of organizing the brain, regulating the system, and blocking out incoming sources of stress as defined by language, social, and sensory demands.

2. Insistence on sameness, inflexible adherence to routines, or ritualized patterns of verbal or nonverbal behavior (e.g., extreme distress at small changes, difficulties with transitions, rigid thinking patterns, greeting rituals, need to take same route or eat same food every day).

Descriptive reframe:
The person creates and maintains predictable routines to organize their behavior and regulate their system, and as a result it can be challenging for them to flexibly shift from their sensory-driven agenda to follow the agenda of others. Managing transitions is a consistent source of stress and distress, and the person faces the daily challenge of managing their relatively low threshold for incoming demands. Demands are defined as the social, communication, sensory, and flexibility requirements inherent in participating in exchanges with others.

3. Highly restricted, fixated interests that are abnormal in intensity or focus (e.g., strong attachment to or preoccupation with unusual objects, excessively circumscribed or perseverative interests).

Descriptive reframe:
The person has a high threshold for engaging in thoughts and actions related to their areas of preferred interest and engaging their brain in the exploration of those interests. Interests may change over time, while the pattern of deep exploration, attention to detail, and engagement with areas of passionate interest is consistently present. The use of objects and routines serves the function of regulating the person's system and is a source of restorative energy.

4. Hyper- or hyporeactivity to sensory input or unusual interest in sensory aspects of the environment (e.g., apparent indifference to pain/temperature, adverse response to specific sounds or textures, excessive smelling or touching of objects, visual fascination with lights or movement).

Descriptive reframe:
Specific sensory preferences and sensitivities define the life experience of the person. The person seeks out their sensory preferences routines to provide a source of organization and regulation for their brain and system and as a needed reprieve from environmental and interpersonal stressors. Specific sensory sensitivities are a constant source of stress and distress, and the person's sensory reactivity to specific sensory input can be unsettling and a source of dysregulation and fatigue.

How would we incorporate the use of strengths-based descriptive language across the three levels that define the DSM-5 Autism Spectrum Disorder criteria? Here is a chart that provides ways to describe the autistic brain style at Level 1 (requires support), Level 2 (requires substantial support), and Level 3 (requires very substantial support).

Applying the Descriptive Triangle Neuro-Affirming Framework to the DSM 5 Autism Spectrum Disorder Levels of Support

	Level 1: Requiring Support Verbally fluent individuals	Level 2: Requiring Substantial Support Individuals with verbal fluency and some unevenness in learning abilities	Level 3: Requiring Very Substantial Support Individuals who communicate primarily using nonspeaking language and who are developing with a range of abilities
DSM 5 Criteria A: Social Communication Descriptive Triangle: Language and Communication	Language skills well developed Usually has developed one or more areas of passionate or preferred interests Language use most organized when the topic or routine is self-initiated, as the person has an established context for the conversational exchange Hard work for the person's brain to simultaneously organize, retrieve and use language while using, interpreting, and responding to verbal and nonspeaking communication in a	The person may be a careful thinker who requires additional time to process incoming language before they are able to organize, retrieve, and use their language to engage in a conversational exchange. As a result, their use of language is often prompt-dependent on others Language skills may be less developed than in individuals at Level 1 and there may be a gap between language skills and the ability to use language in fluid conversational exchanges	Not yet using spoken language Differences are present in the use of and response to nonspeaking communication functions (eye gaze, gestures, body orientation) When use of spoken language is present: Vocabulary is organized around labeling objects with a visual context Use of language is often self-initiated and may include recurrent words and phrases Hard work for the brain to direct communication towards a listener

Often the person has developed one or more areas of passionate interest but has difficulty communicating details with others

May initiate conversation but notable difficulties with extended shared exchanges

Use of recurrent questions, phrases, and topics is commonly seen, as these are social communication overtures that provide a meaningful context for the individual

The simultaneous use of and response to nonspeaking communication during social exchanges is hard work for the person, resulting in fatigue and limiting sustained shared exchanges

Expressive language often more developed than receptive language in everyday situations, as the brain has a context for organizing, retrieving and using spoken language when self-initiated use of spoken language is paired with visual contextual cues

Receptive language most organized when verbal requests are paired with visual contextual cues

shared exchange with a conversational partner

Ability to organize and use language diminishes when responding to others in social situations, and when discussing emotions

Some demonstrated use of nonspeaking communication functions but inconsistent in the ability to interpret and use common cues

May do well in brief or routine conversational interactions but may report internal distress related to managing conversational exchanges

	Level 1: Requiring Support Verbally fluent individuals	Level 2: Requiring Substantial Support Individuals with verbal fluency and some unevenness in learning abilities	Level 3: Requiring Very Substantial Support Individuals who communicate primarily using nonspeaking language and who are developing with a range of abilities
DSM 5 Criteria A: Social Communication Descriptive Triangle: Social Relationships and Emotional Responses	Usually initiates and extends social exchanges and this is most apparent when the there is a clear context for the conversational exchange Children are oftentimes most comfortable with adults or younger children even though a desire for peer relationships is generally present, as adults and younger children provide clearer contextual cues for social exchange routines and are more likely to follow the agenda of the child Peer relationships are often a source of stress and distress and are experienced as confusing	Prompt-dependent on others to structure social exchanges and may be able to initiate and extend as long as structure is present Flexibly participating in play routines with others as a child and in work or social routines as an adult is hard work for the brain and experienced as a source of stress and fatigue May become anxious and agitated during loosely structured language and social interactions Access to language significantly decreases as emotional stress and distress increase	Organizes and regulates their system by creating and maintaining predictable routines with preferred objects, movements, and activities Social overtures and exchanges can be a source of stress and distress as noted by the person moving away from the source of demands Most comfortable with others when sharing sensory interests and when limited spoken language is used Easily stressed and distressed by unexpected changes in routine

When agitated or distressed, responds best when spoken language use is limited and a visual context is provided

Across the life span, the person is most comfortable in routine and established relationships

In work and social settings, adults often find unstructured social exchanges to be a source of stress or distress, a source of fatigue, or unnecessary

May have difficulty regulating emotional states when the person's threshold for managing communication, social, and sensory input has been surpassed, and the brain switches from thinking to reacting mode

The stressors inherent in managing social exchanges often shape the frequency, duration, and types of social exchanges in which the person participates when able to self-determine events

	Level 1: Requiring Support Verbally fluent individuals	Level 2: Requiring Substantial Support Individuals with verbal fluency and some unevenness in learning abilities	Level 3: Requiring Very Substantial Support Individuals who communicate primarily using nonspeaking language and who are developing with a range of abilities
DSM 5 Criteria B: Restrictive Interests and Repetitive Behaviors **Descriptive Triangle: Sensory Use and Interests**	Internal distress is often created by demands for social and emotional engagement Has developed one or more areas of passionate interests that are often age-congruent in content but distinctive in the individual's relatively high threshold for sustaining engagement with the interest or activity "Sensory-driven" quality to the narrative when sharing information with others about preferred topics, as managing the role of a conversational partner in a fluid exchange is hard work for the brain	Displays some drive to establish sensory-driven play or pursuit of interests but can be redirected by others	Tends to organize around the exploration of the sensory aspects of materials and objects and to focus intently on the sensory features of objects

The person has distinctive and recognizable patterns of sensory preferences

Areas of sensory sensitivities such as noises, textures, smells, and changes in routine are a source of stress and distress for the person and often lead to a destabilizing shift from experiencing regulation to dysregulation of their brain and system

Recurrent and distinctive body movements and mannerisms may be subtle but serve the function of organization, regulation and providing a reprieve from external stressors

May only engage in sensory routines at home and not display them when interacting with others, masking sensory differences

During social play as a child and in social situations as an adult, tends to create and follow self-initiated and somewhat inflexible play or conversational routines

Infrequent display of distinctive and recurrent body movements and mannerisms may be noted during times of stress or during solitary pursuit of interests

Often seeks out manipulative materials with visual, tactile, movement or cause and effect features

Creates and maintains recurrent sensory routines as a means to organize and apply thinking skills, to self-to regulate their system, and to block out incoming stressors

Oftentimes engages in recurrent and distinctive body movements and mannerisms that serve the function of organizing and regulating the person's system and blocking out incoming environmental and interpersonal stressors

Displays notable patterns of sensory preferences and sensitivities

Now that we've reviewed the descriptive framework and ways to reframe the way we think and talk about the autism spectrum brain style, we are ready to apply the language to individuals across age and ability levels. We can now explore how to develop Brain Style Profiles that depict the individual's patterns of strengths and differences in the three key areas, starting with young children with varying levels of verbal fluency and moving on to children, adolescents, and adults. In Part I, we'll discuss what the individual Brain Style Profile model is designed to do and how you can apply it to the important work you do assessing and supporting autistic individuals in your clinical practice.

References

Autism Sec. 300.8. (2004). *Individuals with Disabilities Education Act.*

Autism Spectrum Disorder 299.00 (F84.0). (2013).*Diagnostic and Statistical Manual of Mental Disorders* (5th ed.). American Psychiatric Association.

Monteiro, M. J., & Stegall, S. (2018). *Monteiro Interview Guidelines for Diagnosing the Autism Spectrum: A Sensory-Based Approach, Second Edition (MIGDAS-2).* Western Psychological Services; Torrance, California.

Part I

Creating the individual's Brain Style Profile

Why is it helpful to think, talk, and write about the autistic brain style when assessing and supporting individuals in your clinical practice? There are important shifts that happen when you discuss an individual's brain style. The shift in our thinking shapes our language when we discuss the autistic profile with individuals and their families. Our use of descriptive language shapes the context of the conversation. Establishing the context in turn leads to a shift in the emotional experience of absorbing the diagnostic information, which leads to increased flexibility in exploring supports that are the best fit for the individual's needs. Let's discuss three important shifts that occur when we explore an individual's Brain Style Profile.

When you characterize the individual's patterns of strengths and differences as that individual's Brain Style Profile, you are applying language that is *inclusive*. Every person has a brain style, and each individual brain style includes areas of distinctive strengths as well as differences. Each person's brain style includes patterns of thinking and experiencing the world that are sources of energy as well as patterns that are hard work for the brain and sources of stress or distress. When we use the language of brain style patterns of strengths and differences, our narrative path is an inclusive one.

Thinking and talking about an individual's brain style pattern of strengths and differences provides a *context* for understanding and making sense of the individual's complex, singular, and multifaceted lived experience. The specific context embedded in the brain style narrative is the discussion of the individual's neurodevelopmental patterns of strengths and differences that inform that individual's sensory, communication, and social experiences in their daily life. Instead of focusing on the autistic diagnostic label, we describe what the autistic experience is for that individual. When we capture the key elements of the individual's autistic profile of strengths and differences and summarize the profile using strengths-based language, we provide a path for advocacy and self-determination for that neurodivergent individual and their family.

DOI: 10.4324/9781003532576-2

Finally, identifying an individual's patterns of brain style strengths and differences *changes the emotional experience* for individuals and their families. When we focus on describing the individual's Brain Style Profile of strengths and differences, our narrative organizes around exploring that person's experiences in the world while providing an inclusive context. When we move away from labeling language to the descriptive brain style discussion, we support the individual and family in reducing their level of stress and anxiety regarding a diagnostic label. This emotional shift allows individuals to take in information about their brain style patterns in a more receptive and meaningful way. This in turn leads to productive discussions about ways to respect the function of differences, explore the forms of those differences, and create avenues of support that are in sync with the individual and the family system.

The Brain Style Profile model places the emphasis on describing the way in which the individual's brain incorporates patterns of strengths and differences in the areas of Communication, Social Knowledge, and Sensory Use, the three areas in the autism Descriptive Triangle. The conversation around the individual's Brain Style Profile can take place at any point along the diagnostic and counseling support process.

So what does a Brain Style Profile look like? What goes into creating an individual's Brain Style Profile? In this section of the book we'll listen to diagnostic meetings with children, adolescents, and adults and see the Brain Style Profiles that emerge from those conversations. The qualitative diagnostic interview process described in this book is the *Monteiro Interview Guidelines for Diagnosing the Autism Spectrum*, Second Edition (MIGDAS-2) (Monteiro & Stegall, 2018). The MIGDAS-2 is structured around the Descriptive Triangle framework and language, and is a strengths-based interview system that was developed to support neuro-informed autistic assessments across the lifespan from early childhood through adulthood. Woods and Estes (2023) describe the system as a strengths-based way to explore sensory preferences, as the diagnostic interview based on the system creates a setting in which the individual is encouraged to explore sensory materials and topics of interest as the entry point to recognizing the individual's autistic Brain Style Profile of strengths and differences in the three key areas. You will recognize individuals from your clinical experience as you take in the interview conversations and the sample Brain Style Profiles across ages and ability levels, as each profile highlights key patterns of strengths and differences that characterize the autistic lived experience. Because each Brain Style Profile includes distinctive signifiers, or specific personal references to interests, words, and actions, each profile brings the individual's autistic story to life. The Brain Style Profiles provided here can be adapted by you in your clinical practice as you have your autism conversations with the individuals you assess and support.

Although we'll be discussing co-occurring neurodevelopmental brain style differences as you sit in on the sample case conversations, the focus of this book is on developing autistic Brain Style Profiles. When discussing attention, mood, and learning differences, you will be provided with descriptive language to address the co-occurring conditions of Attention Deficit Disorder, Anxiety Disorder, Learning Disorder, and Intellectual Disability. Autism frequently co-occurs with a range of neurological, developmental, and psychiatric differences (Mosner et al., 2019; Hours et al., 2022; Henderson et al., 2023). This book focuses on supporting your ability to recognize and describe the distinctive autism Brain Style Profile as it presents in the complex individuals with whom you have autism conversations in your clinical practice. As you develop the ability to draw out, recognize, and describe the autism spectrum Brain Style Profile across age and ability levels, you will increase your competency and confidence in recognizing when the autistic brain style co-occurs with others forms of neurodivergence.

In Chapter 1, we'll sit in on conversations with Maya and her mother, then with Maxwell and his parents to see how Brain Style Profiles can be generated for young children across levels of verbal fluency. The sample cases are designed to show you how to include three specific elements into your assessment and support process when working with young children. The first element you will read about involves ways to invite, elicit, or draw out the young child's pattern of brain style strengths and differences through the invitation to explore sensory objects, adjusting your use of spoken language, and learning to pay close attention to your role in taking the perspective of the individual child. The second element focuses on developing the ability to look for and identify recurring patterns of behavior; in other words, recognizing autistic behavior patterns of strengths and differences as you engage with young children and their families in your clinical practice. The third element involves applying strengths-based descriptive language to develop the young child's Brain Style Profile. Describing the individualized Brain Style Profile provides an instantly recognizable overview of the child's brain style in the three key areas while setting the narrative to focus on increasing the understanding and appreciation of the young child's worldview and life experience. Let's explore how to reveal the autism story with young children.

References

Henderson, D., Wayland, S., & White, J. (2023). *Is This Autism? A Guide for Clinicians and Everyone Else*. New York: Routledge Taylor & Francis.

Hours, C., Recasens, C., & Baleyte, J. M. (2022). ASD and ADHD comorbidity: what are we talking about? Front Psychiatry. Feb 28;13:837424. http://doi:10.3389/fpsyt.2022.837424.

Monteiro, M., & Stegall, S. (2018). *Monteiro Interview Guidelines for Diagnosing the Autism Spectrum, Second Edition*. Torrance, CA: WPS Publishing.

Mosner, M. G., Kinard, J. L., Shah, J. S., McWeeny, S., Greene, R. K,. Lowery, S. C., Mazefsky, C. A., & Dichter, G. S. (2019). Rates of co-occurring psychiatric disorders in autism spectrum disorder using the mini international neuropsychiatric interview. *J Autism Dev Disord*. Sep;49(9):3819–3832. https://doi:10.1007/s10803-019-04090-1.

Woods, S. E. O., & Estes, A. (2023). Toward a more comprehensive autism assessment: The survey of autistic strengths, skills, and interests. *Front Psychiatry*. Oct 6;14:1264516. doi: 10.3389/fpsyt.2023.1264516. PMID: 37867767; PMCID: PMC10587489.

1 Reveal the story

Young children across levels of verbal fluency – Maya and Maxwell

Describing the young child's autism Brain Style Profile

If you assess and support young children and their families in your clinical practice, you are engaged in the important work of revealing and telling each child's unique developmental and behavioral story. Parents often struggle with uncertainty when they are raising young children who are beginning to show noticeable differences in their development. How do parents navigate the growing sense that something is different with their child's development? This uncertainty may start with noticing differences in their young child's use of language. They may also be observing differences in their child's ability to manage daily changes in expected routines and a notable resistance to participating in family gatherings in a shared way. How do they make sense of these unexpected social and emotional developmental differences? If those differences are present along with differences they are noticing in their child's communication style, what does that mean? They may also be trying to understand why their child shows consistent stress and distress in response to the ways in which everyday things sound, feel, and look. When parents come to you for assessment and support, you can be a source of much-needed reassurance as you help them form the most compelling story to describe their child's unique pattern of developmental strengths and differences. When the story is told in an accessible and recognizable way, you help parents move past uncertainty and into actively developing the best-fit ways for them to connect with and support their child's development. Your guidance helps parents shift away from their growing sense of powerlessness and uncertainty to resiliency and a sense of understanding and capability. The autism spectrum narrative of identifying the child's patterns of strengths and differences provides the context for parents to understand their child's perspective. This leads to an openness toward exploring practical ways to strengthen connections and apply strategies that support the child's and the family's ability to thrive and grow together.

DOI: 10.4324/9781003532576-3

There are two language and communication developmental entry points for parents seeking an autism assessment and support for their young child. The first entry point is when the young child is not yet using spoken language, or is emerging in their use of spoken language but is not yet using that language to participate in shared exchanges with others. The child shows an emerging understanding of spoken language as evidenced by their spontaneous use of labeling language for objects and concepts of interest that have a visual context. The familiar visual context, and especially a visual context that is of high interest to the child, helps the child retrieve their emerging spoken language vocabulary and respond to verbal directives from others. For example, when adults "show" while they "tell" a request to the child, the adult provides a visual context for the spoken language. It can be perplexing for parents to hear their child use spoken language in a self-initiated, object-focused way but at the same time experience their child's consistent differences in their responsiveness to parent overtures to apply that spoken language in a shared context. Along with these differences in the development of spoken language, parents will also note the child's differences in their use of and response to body language or unspoken communication. Unspoken communication includes the use of, for example, eye gaze, gestures, facial expressions, body orientation, mannerisms, and vocal tone changes directed toward a listener or communication partner. Parents will also experience differences in their child's ability to consistently and fluidly respond to these unspoken communication overtures in interactions with their child. This entry point describes autistic young children with limited to emerging verbal fluency.

The second entry point is when the young child has developed an extensive spoken vocabulary and the ability to apply language concepts but uses this vocabulary and understanding in distinctively different ways. The ability to organize, retrieve, and use spoken language is most developed and fluent when the child self-initiates the topic, when the topic is familiar and has a context to support the spoken language use, and oftentimes, when there are visual contextual cues supporting that use of language. This fluent use of spoken language contrasts in a striking way with the hard work for the child's brain that is involved in responding to spoken language overtures from others. Spoken language overtures can be described as incoming language demands. The young child's brain has to work actively to shift flexibly from the way in which their understanding and use of spoken language is organized, to take in the language of others and to work out the context of the incoming spoken language. It is notably hard work for the child's brain to simultaneously use their spoken language along with their body language to communicate and engage with their conversational partner. Responding to their conversational partner's spoken and unspoken communication is also hard work for the child's brain, as demonstrated by the child's limited use of and response to the spoken and unspoken communication overtures provided by their conversational partner. This entry point describes autistic young children who are developing with verbal fluency.

What does the Brain Style Profile look like for a young child who is developing with limited to emerging verbal fluency? Let's sit in on a conversation with Marta, the mother of three-year-old Maya. Marta participated in a conversational interview as part of Maya's autism evaluation process. Using the MIGDAS-2 Parent/Caregiver Questionnaire (Monteiro & Stegall, 2018), Marta was encouraged to tell the nuanced and distinctive story of life with her young daughter. The information from the conversational parent interview provided the foundation for the autism assessment meeting with Maya and her mother. We will also sit in on that meeting, as it leads us to the development of Maya's Brain Style Profile.

The diagnostic conversation with Maya's mother

"There is so much to talk about when it comes to Maya." Marta was eager to start our conversation about her three-year-old daughter. "When her preschool teacher brought up the things she was noticing with Maya, I knew it was time to learn more about what we are dealing with."

"I'm so glad we're able to have this conversation today and I look forward to learning more about Maya. Tell me more about what led you to set up this process and what your main concerns are right now." I invited Maya's mother to start her story with what was on her mind at the present time.

"If Maya could avoid having to deal with everyday demands, the world would be ideal for her. She becomes so upset and frustrated with the small changes that are part of our daily life; following our routines for meals, going places, bath time, sleep...when she has to stop doing what she's focused on, it really upsets her. Lately she's become more intense about it, crying and throwing her body on the ground. I will say that Maya always recognizes the adult in the room and will approach the adult when she needs help with something."

"That's great that she goes to the adult in the room for help when she needs it. Tell me more about how she goes about getting help from the adult after she goes to them."

"Most of the time she just stands there and I have to figure it out. If I talk to her and ask questions, she becomes really frustrated, so I try not to talk too much as I figure out what she is asking me by standing there. Others times she brings me something that she needs help opening or fixing." Marta paused. "I pretty much have to work out what Maya is asking for."

"That's a good thing that she is consistently going to you or other trusted adults for help. And you are working so hard to help her when she asks for it by reading her actions and responding to her requests that she makes in her own way. You've done a great job of noticing that asking her questions is a source of frustration for her and that has led to you giving her some quiet time while you work out what it is she is trying to communicate to you."

"Yes, I'm starting to understand that listening to directions or questions sets Maya off. I'm trying to figure out how to give her directions or help her without setting her off, but it's really hard to manage when it's so hard for Maya to switch gears and go with the flow."

"You are describing her so vividly, Marta. Thank you. When Maya participates in the sensory-based play meeting, we'll learn more about some ways to help you and Maya. At home and at her preschool, it sounds like the daily times when Maya needs to transition from her self-directed routines and interests to flexibly shift her focus and go with the flow are highly stressful for her as well as for you. Is that about right?"

"Completely. She does get stressed by transitions." Marta took in the language and connected transition times to Maya's heightened level of stress as well as her own.

"Well, transitions involve a person's brain being able to flexibly shift their focus to manage incoming demands from others." I connected the concept of transition times and flexibility to the child's reactivity to incoming spoken language demands.

"That definitely describes Maya! She loves to talk in response to her favorite videos when she names things on the screen, but she gets stressed when we talk to her." Marta confirmed that her experience with her daughter centered around differences in Maya's ability to flexibly shift from her focus on her routines to take in, manage, and respond to incoming demands or input from other people.

"You mentioned that you've noticed that Maya gets less stressed when she approaches you for help when you don't talk as much. So you are already understanding that incoming spoken language demands are a source of stress or distress for Maya in everyday life." With this confirmation of Marta's lived experience with her daughter, I invited Marta to talk in detail about Maya's interests and abilities.

"So let's talk about the routines and activities Maya loves and enjoys, because those activities hold the key to understanding what helps her system stay organized and regulated."

I encouraged Marta to begin talking about her thoughts about her daughter when Maya was regulated and not overly stressed. "When Maya is not experiencing the stress and distress she feels when incoming demands are happening to her, tell me a little about what she enjoys doing and how she goes through her day."

Marta visibly relaxed and a shadow of a smile crossed her face. "Maya is such a smart and busy girl! And intense in her focus on the things she loves to do. She is so happy when she can play on her own and explore toys and puzzles on her own. Her favorite thing right now is to find things and nest them. She loves egg-shaped things and places them into containers. She loves to group things into categories. Her favorite show is *Pocoyo*, and she loves to stand close to the screen and jump up and down while she recites the letters and numbers and names of things with the characters. Even when she isn't watching the show, I've noticed that when she uses her words it's always to name things." Marta reflected for a moment. "And she only does this on her terms."

Marta paused and sighed before she continued. "I try to get her to tell me the names of things I know she knows the name of, but she resists me. If I persist in encouraging her to speak, she gets upset."

"So, you're describing Maya's preferred routines as ones that engage her brain in learning and practicing but that provide her with an independent way to do this. It sounds like managing a conversational or play partner and input from others creates a stressed reaction from her."

"Exactly. I hear her using all of these great words and phrases when she is playing on her own, but she won't say them when I try to play with her or ask her to tell me what I know she knows. Her preschool teacher has noticed that Maya is quite aloof from the group, preferring to explore and play on her own." A thoughtful look settled on her face. "It's helped me understand that this is Maya's way of being and not something I'm doing."

"That's a good way to understand Maya, Marta. When you say 'her way of being,' you are really talking about how Maya's brain organizes information and how that affects how she understands the world around her."

Marta's face brightened. "Her teacher told me that to get Maya to join group activities, she gives her one of her favorite egg-shaped maracas to hold. As long as she's holding one of her maraca eggs, Maya will sit and take in what is happening around her. I started to give Maya a special maraca egg that she can associate with when it's time to do something she doesn't necessarily want to do, like change clothes or other basic routines."

"Great idea, Marta! That gives Maya a consistent transition object and creates a routine to help her prepare for incoming demands."

"I hadn't quite thought about it that way, but you are absolutely right… kind of signaling to her that a change is coming up."

"Talk to me about Maya's relationship with you and other family members." I prompted Marta to tell details about her observations about her daughter's social connections within the family and how Maya expresses those connections.

"Maya loves it when we go to the park and I push her on the swing, or when she sits on the merry-go-round. At home, she loves it when I pull her across the floor on a specific blanket." Marta paused before adding an additional important detail. "Maya has started looking at me when we do these movement routines; sometimes just briefly connecting when she's so happy and sometimes to prompt me to do it again. I've started saying 'more' and making the sign for 'more,' and every once in a while Maya signs that she wants more. That's all new."

"That's wonderful, Marta. You've found some great ways to connect with Maya through movement and routines, and now you're adding support for Maya to expand her communication about what she wants."

We went on to talk about Maya's sensory preferences and sensitivities and her early development. We also discussed Maya's reactive behavior routines in greater detail, the specific triggers for her switches from her regulated brain to her distressed brain, and strategies Marta has put into place to create predictable routines for Maya. As our conversation reached its end, I invited Marta to pick three words or qualities that best described her young daughter.

Marta reflected for a brief moment before she replied. "Smart and eager to learn, intensely focused and independent, and so very happy when she isn't stressed over demands."

I told Marta what a pleasure it had been to have her share her experiences and observations about her daughter Maya, and that I was very much looking forward to seeing her again and to meeting Maya in our next scheduled meeting.

Marta nodded and added her thoughts. "Thank you for listening and for asking the questions that helped me get across to you what Maya is like. I feel like you understand our situation and that you are ready to work with Maya. This was so much better than filling out those checklists! They really didn't capture what I needed to tell you."

Over the course of an hour, Marta revealed the lived experience for her and her young child. She felt heard and supported and ready to learn more about Maya during the sensory-based diagnostic interview that was scheduled next.

Let's get to know Maya and watch her brain style story unfold as Maya and her mother participate in the diagnostic session using the MIGDAS-2 process.

The sensory-based diagnostic interview with Maya and her mother

What are the key elements involved in creating a setting that is in sync with young children who are developing with autism spectrum brain style differences? Whether you are formally assessing a child for an initial diagnosis or you are providing supports for a child for whom the diagnosis has already been given, carefully considering how you invite the child into your setting is important. Equally important is having your setting visually communicate an inviting place for the child with objects of interest to explore.

Let's see how the key elements play out when Maya and her mother, Marta, come in for Maya's MIGDAS-2 sensory-based play assessment. Prior to their arrival, I placed a range of cause-and-effect developmental toys at different locations around the room for Maya to explore. Some of the developmental materials were in containers that Maya could engage with by opening the containers and removing the contents. For example, one of the container-based toys was a developmental plastic egg carton which when opened revealed removable eggs divided into top and bottom shells. The eggs contained multiple visual dimensions to explore, including matching the facial expressions on the top shells with the facial expressions on the top of the eggs, and matching shapes on the bottom of each egg shell to fit the shape in the matching insert in the carton. I also placed a gazebo-shaped plastic toy with colored doors and matching colored keys on a key chain in another part of the room. This cause-and-effect developmental toy included colored shapes and animals that when removed from their compartment behind their colored door using the colored key, could be inserted back into their compartment by slotting the shape or animal through the matching color and shape insert. Again, this developmental toy provided multiple visual matching and tactile dimensions to explore.

Other developmental toys and objects placed around the room included sensory stress balls with various textures and tactile properties, sets of magnetitic tiles with safe sized pieces for the young child, and water toys that could be activated by pushing a button to provide kinetic movement with shapes inside the water toy. Picture a water toy with small rings inside and multiple spikes to capture the rings when the button is repeatedly depressed. The pressure created in the water when the button is pushed forces the rings to float and settle, sometimes settling on the spikes. Other developmental toys provided included inset puzzles with hinges and doors to be opened so puzzle pieces could be removed or inserted into the compartment that visually signaled their location, such as a barn for a cow puzzle piece and a cloud in the sky for an airplane piece. Wind-up caterpillars and ladybugs, a push and spin popper toy, a Hoberman mini-sphere that expands and contracts as the child opens and closes it, and a ball that can be pressed together to create a seal with a suction cup that eventually releases so the ball pops back to a spherical ball shape from a flat saucer shape in an unpredictable way provided a range of interesting manipulative materials for Maya to explore by moving around the room. I also had my container where I could access multiple spinning light-up toys, inset puzzles, and several percussion instrument "thunder tubes" to use as noisemakers at some point during our sensory-based play conversation.

As you take in the description of the objects themselves and the placement of the materials in the room, note that the objects communicate to the child that this is a setting where they are invited to explore objects of interest. There is a second key element to include if we are to provide a setting where we communicate to the young child who is not yet speaking that this setting is in sync with their brain style. Take a moment to think about how adults typically respond when meeting a young child. The adult invitation typically focuses on the use of social overtures that emphasize spoken language and amplified unspoken welcoming expressions and gestures. We look at and talk to the child; we place our face at the child's level and smile while talking; all as a way to connect with the child and invite the child to feel comfortable with us.

For the autism assessment or connections process with young children, we actually want to do something quite different from that pattern. Specifically, it is important to focus on what the child is doing and to consider how they experience the world. For young children who are not yet using spoken language, we recognize and respect this way of being in the world by mirroring the child's perspective. We do not talk or use spoken language at the start of our time together. At the same time, we minimize our use of the unspoken social overtures of eye gaze, broad smiling, and entering into the child's facial line of vision. This purposefully reduced spoken and unspoken communication input is a key element, as it provides a welcoming setting for the young autistic child. Consider that for the autistic young child who is not yet using spoken language, they rarely have the experience of adults adapting to them in this key way. The young autistic child often experiences a stress reaction to incoming spoken and unspoken social overtures. By mirroring the child's way of being in the world in our initial interactions, we provide the child with a positive experience that contrasts with their common experience of reactivity in response to adult input.

Developmental toys that provide visual, tactile, movement and cause-and-effect sensory dimensions to start the sensory-based conversation with the young child:

Spinning light-up wands and globes
Sensory stress balls with varying textures
Plastic egg container
Gazebo with colored doors, keys, shapes, and animals
Magnet tiles with safe sized pieces

Water toys with cause-and-effect button
Inset puzzles with hinges, doors, or knobs
Wind-up plastic moving objects (caterpillars, ladybugs, dinosaurs)
Hoberman Mini-Sphere Ball
Ball with suction cups to create a saucer shape and bounce back

So, if you are not speaking to the child or showing unspoken social overtures, how do you provide a social overture and invite the child to engage with you and your setting? Sensory objects provide the additional necessary element to invite the child to feel comfortable and to engage with you. Sensory objects that are offered to the child when the adult is explicitly *not speaking*, while simultaneously explicitly *not emphasizing* unspoken and amplified social invitations to respond in a social communication way provide the invitation for the young autistic brain to engage with us. Let's see what this looks like with Maya as she comes to the assessment setting with her mother.

Marta entered the waiting room holding Maya's right hand. Maya clutched a brightly colored wooden maraca egg in her left hand and held it against her chest. The maraca egg was red with black lines that transformed the egg into a ladybug. Marta and I had discussed the format of limiting spoken and unspoken communication to help Maya make the transition into the assessment playroom, and Marta smiled at me without speaking as she led Maya across the room. As they approached the threshold, I activated the light-up globe spinner I was holding, positioning it toward Maya and at arm's length from me. As the lights and spinning motion captured Maya's attention, she stood still, the ladybug maraca egg continuing its ride nestled in Maya's left hand. Marta let go of her daughter's right hand but continued to stand beside her. All three of us quietly and calmly focused our attention on the routine motion created by the moving lights. Maya took a small step closer to the globe spinner. I moved the spinner a fraction closer to Maya, creating the object-focused social overture for Maya to take the spinner and explore its properties for herself. After attentively examining the visual effects of the toy, Maya carefully reached out and grasped the handle of the spinning, brightly lit ball. I passed it to her as we started our object-focused shared conversation. The three of us continued our quiet sharing of the moment, giving Maya time to explore the visual, tactile, movement, and sound properties of the toy as she held it.

This gave Maya the opportunity to experience a transition into a new environment without the stressors of social communication input she routinely encountered. It gave me the opportunity to experience and appreciate the way in which Maya enters a new setting: holding a familiar object as well as her mother's hand, not speaking or vocalizing, and focusing on the interesting object being offered to her without simultaneously refer-encing the person attached to the object of interest. Maya was organizing around specific elements of objects during this initial meeting. Holding the ladybug maraca egg showed me that she is tactile in the way she engages with materials. The fact that the maraca egg had specific and vivid visual properties, and the way in which Maya became captivated by the visual and movement details of the light-up globe communicated that she was a child for whom visual, tactile, and movement routines were a source of regulation and organization for her brain and system. Her exclusive focus on the object held additional important information about her. By carefully taking in Maya's perspective, I was able to communicate to her with my actions (quiet; calm; focused on objects without placing communication or social demands on her) that this setting was a fit for her way of exploring the world.

To move the conversation forward, I took out a second light-up spinner, stepping over the threshold of the assessment room as I moved the switch on the side of the handle to activate the lights and movement. This second spinner was similar but not identical to the one held by Maya. This spinner had a ping-pong-sized ball sitting at the top of the handle that lit up with a red color when the spinner was activated. In addition, the wand had four drooping fronds with small lights at the end of each frond that lit up in different colors, spinning around the ball to create an effect of a galaxy ring of moving lights. In this way, I provided an object-focused social overture toward Maya to share and expand beyond the initial solo light-up experience. Maya extended her gaze to take in the visual and movement dimensions of the second toy. She followed me into the room as we continued to look at the lights and movement. As she closely observed the galaxy spinner and moved toward it, I offered it to her. Maya was still holding her ladybug maraca egg in one hand, so she hesitated before carefully setting the maraca egg on the table beside her and then reaching out for the galaxy spinner. I handed it to her. Instead of offering her wand to me as she took the galaxy wand, Maya now had both wands. This highlighted her preferred way of exploring materials as independent rather than shared play.

Maya moved away from me and her mother as she continued watching the light patterns. She stood in front of a child-sized table and carefully placed the galaxy wand on the table. This freed up both of her hands and she began exploring the cause-and-effect sequence of pressing the button on the side of the wand to stop and start the light effects. I approached her, picking up the galaxy wand and quickly turning the switch back and forth to create the routine of on/off/on/off. After demonstrating this, still without speaking and without requiring Maya to look at me, I placed the galaxy light back on the table. Maya carefully placed her light-up spinner on the table and picked up the galaxy wand, repeating a systematic exploration of on/off/on/off. Maya was showing us how she is a systematic thinker who enjoys exploring the cause-and-effect aspects of how things work. So now we see that Maya is an independent, systematic thinker who organizes around visual, tactile, movement, and cause-and-effect aspects of materials. She responded to my modeling cause-and-effect use of an object when I provided this demonstration without placing spoken or social exchange demands on her. The pattern for our diagnostic conversation was established: I would provide Maya with a range of developmental materials and objects, model their use, and give her the space to explore them independently in her systematic way. This creation of an object-focused routine is in sync with the young autistic child's lived experience and allows us to explore the individual child's learning style in the absence of spoken language and social demands.

As you recall, developmental toys and materials were set up around the assessment room. After Maya explored the spinners for as long as she needed to, she moved to another set of materials and began her systematic exploration of those materials. Maya was able to show us *how much* and *how long* she absorbed details of materials because she was not directed to stop what she was doing to move on to other things. The experience of sustained exploration of materials on the young child's terms provides essential information not only about the key sensory aspects of materials important to the child but also the child's threshold for sustained sensory input. When Maya was allowed to self-direct her exploration of the sensory materials and when she experienced exploring sensory materials in the absence of communication and social demands or input, I was able to really understand what goes into Maya's experience of organization and regulation in the world. Her mother could also see and experience her daughter's way of being in the world in a clearer way. In this way the compelling story of Maya's Brain Style Profile unfolded during the assessment process. Each time Maya approached a set of objects and started her systematic exploration, I would join her briefly to model various aspects of the objects that Maya had not yet explored. This created a routine in which Maya anticipated and tolerated my presence in her sphere. Maya worked her way through the nesting eggs and the gazebo with the colored keys. When she struggled with the key to one of the doors and dropped the key ring, I picked it up and silently showed her the way the key worked. Maya imitated my actions and successfully opened the colored door to remove the pieces inside the compartment.

What have we been able to learn about Maya so far as we've provided her with this sensory-based environment while paying close attention to minimizing incoming social communication overtures or demands? Maya showed us that she explores her surroundings in an object-focused way. In other words, Maya showed us that she is a systematic thinker who organizes her behavior and regulates her emotional system by creating and maintaining self-initiated, object-focused routines. She showed us that she is emerging in her ability to tolerate and respond to a play partner when that play partner introduces novel aspects of object exploration while minimizing spoken input or social overtures. Additional strengths for Maya that became amplified for her mother and of course also for me to see, included Maya's sustained attention to problem-solving with cause-and-effect materials, her ability to imitate modeled actions, and her interest in exploring a range of developmental materials. Her clear preference was to explore aspects of objects of interest in a self-directed, solitary way. These are all strengths to be noted for Maya's Brain Style Profile.

Maya also showed us a pattern of differences as she explored the sensory toys and was given the opportunity to take the lead in how she explored her surroundings. While exploring the visual, tactile, movement, and cause-and-effect dimensions of objects of interest, Maya showed us that her brain takes a break from engaging in vocalizations, labeling language, and also from the social referencing of others around her. Maya showed us that it is hard work for her brain to simultaneously explore materials of interest and include or reference a social play partner. Each time I entered Maya's space when she was exploring aspects of toys, she communicated her acceptance of my participation through proximity. In other words, she stayed in the shared space instead of moving away. A consistent pattern emerged from this routine, as Maya maintained a close and intense focus on exploring objects. These are some of the differences we will reference in Maya's Brain Style Profile.

I purposefully refrained from using pronounced social play overtures with Maya during the start of the session. This provided her with a low-stress experience, allowing her system to stay organized and regulated. This in turn helps us to see and experience Maya's organizational and regulation routines and the ways in which she manages and responds to people in the absence of demands from others to interact and play in a social exchange way.

Let's see what happens when I take a more active role in modeling sensory-based and object-focused play routines with Maya.

Because Maya arrived with her red ladybug maraca egg, I brought out several red ladybug wind-up toys. I quickly rotated the winder of the first ladybug in a clockwise series of twists, and the ladybug toy glided on its wheels across the table, ending in a flipping motion. While the first ladybug meandered along the tabletop, I wound up another one and also several wind-up caterpillars. Soon the tabletop had a cluster of moving red and green plastic bugs. Maya was delighted by this, as evidenced by her placing her face at an even level with the table to better take in the movement. She engaged in a recurrent and distinctive set of motions triggered by the visual input. These movements included posturing her arms to her sides and tilting her head to one side. She then spoke for the first time, saying: "Ladybug! Ladybug!" I mirrored her exclamatory inflection and shared her excitement by repeating: "Ladybug! Ladybug!" We continued this routine multiple times before Maya darted across the room to retrieve her red ladybug maraca egg. She returned to the table where the now dormant ladybugs and caterpillars were resting. Here was a communication opportunity for Maya to reference me and to request that we restart the enjoyable sensory routine. Maya held her ladybug maraca close to her chest while maintaining her gaze on the objects on the table. I remained quiet and companionably to her side. After a moment, Maya took a small side step toward me, continuing her intensely focused attention toward the motionless toys. This was her way of initiating the request for me to restart the object-focused play routine; it was both a communication *strength* (initiating the request through proximity) and a *difference* (not yet directing her physical proximity request toward her play partner through the use of eye gaze, gestures, or through shifting her body orientation from the objects of interest toward her conversational partner). I responded to her subtle communication overture by winding up the ladybugs and caterpillars, much to Maya's delight. Twice, Maya's delight extended to include her brief use of eye gaze to connect with me before returning to her exclusive focus on the moving objects. Each time I returned her gaze and mirrored her level of joy, Maya withdrew from the shared exchange. Just as her mother described Maya's connections with her during movement routines at home and at the park, Maya showed us for her, the organizing experience of repeated sensory movement input led to her brain's ability to expand from sensory-focused play to briefly reference her play partner—another lovely emerging strength to highlight in her Brain Style Profile.

To experience Maya's threshold for this sensory input routine, I continued to wind up the toys for as long as Maya communicated that she wanted the activity to continue. This is important to experience because it showed us how intensely important sensory-based routines were for her in terms of providing organization and regulation for her system. When we introduce pleasant object-focused sensory routines that are in sync with the child's demonstrated sensory-seeking routines at the start of our sessions, it provides us with an opportunity to create novel sensory routines that contain key aspects sought out by that child's system. When we create, and when we allow the young child to create and maintain their preferred sensory routines for the length of time they seek, we gain a sense and appreciation of the gap between their brain's need for specific types of input and how much of this need for specific input gets met in everyday life. Through this process, the autistic pattern of brain style differences is something we not only see and recognize but we also experience with the child. We literally experience their worldview.

Maya showed me that she was satisfied with the wind-up toy routine by inhaling and exhaling deeply when the routine of winding down the toys happened for about the twentieth time. I held out a plastic bag and dropped one of the caterpillars into it. I held the bag toward Maya without speaking or gesturing further. I handed her a ladybug. She stood very still before reaching out for the ladybug and dropping it into the bag. In this way, I communicated this next routine, and Maya carefully and consistently picked each plastic bug off of the table and placed it into the bag. I waited until she was looking at the bag before I moved the plastic tab at the top of the bag that slid across to close it. After moving the piece, I held the bag closer to Maya. She stood very still before reaching out to complete the movement of the tab to close the bag.

Now that we've experienced Maya's specific and unique sensory entry point to the world, let's see what happens when demands are placed on her in a more typical pattern. In Maya's case, I accomplished this shift from her agenda to my agenda through the transition activity of the routine I created for her with the wind-up toys and then placing the toys into the bag. She was able not only to allow me to be in the same space with her while she explored materials of interest to her but also to create routines with her. I picked up the farm scene inset puzzle with hinged doors leading to puzzle pieces and opened all of the doors. I removed each puzzle piece and placed them in a plastic bag. I approached Maya and placed the puzzle in front of her on the same table where we had played with the wind-up toys. I opened the top of the bag and oriented it toward Maya. She stood very still before reaching into the bag and plucking out a cow piece. I closed the hinged barn pieces on the puzzle board. Maya quickly opened them, placed the cow piece inside, and closed the doors. For the next piece she selected, I did not close any hinged pieces on the puzzle board. Maya studied the puzzle board while clutching the airplane piece. Then she closed and reopened the cloud piece, placed the airplane piece inside the slot, and closed the cloud. We continued this routine until all of the puzzle pieces were removed from the bag and placed in their correct spot on the puzzle board. In this way, Maya showed us that she had an emerging visual vocabulary associating a range of common objects with their locations. This was another strength for Maya's Brain Style Profile.

Because Maya showed us her visual vocabulary through her object matching, I initiated the use of some visual context labeling language. I held the empty bag toward her and said: "Cow!" using an exclamatory and exaggerated intonation and inflection. I repeated this once and stopped.

Maya stood very still before opening the barn hinged door and removing the cow piece. She dropped it into the bag. Maya's receptive vocabulary extended to every single puzzle piece. Marta, Maya's mother, was visibly moved as she watched her daughter work cooperatively on a task and saw confirmation of her daughter's developing language skills without the triggering of stress, distress, and reactivity that typically happened when demands of this sort were placed on Maya.

You may have noticed that each time a request was made of Maya during the session, from handing her the spinning globe to holding out the plastic bag as a prompt for her to place the puzzle piece in the bag, Maya responded by standing very still before she reached for the object and engaged with the materials. Because the requests by definition were incoming demands for her, they were a source of potential stress and distress. By making the demands of her in a nonspeaking way, we were able to clearly see Maya's pattern of taking time to take in the visual context presented to her before she responds. Without the interfering stressor of incoming language demands, Maya's system stayed regulated and she was able to take in the context of the situation and respond accordingly. When we mirror the young child's nonspeaking communication style in our diagnostic and support work, it helps us identify the key ways in which the child engages with the world. In Maya's case, she organized her behavior best when she was given time to absorb the visual context of the request in the absence of spoken language input.

Although Maya's assessment session included many additional pieces, we have enough information now for our purposes of creating her Brain Style Profile. Let's take a look at what her Brain Style Profile might look like and how we can develop it from the parent and child interview process.

Developing Maya's Brain Style Profile

What are the key benefits of creating a Brain Style Profile for a young child like Maya? When we identify the central elements of the child's autistic pattern of strengths and differences, we simultaneously provide a recognizable and accessible portrayal of that child's way of organizing, regulating, and engaging with the world while framing that representation in strengths-based descriptive language. This is the neuro-informed template for thinking, talking, and writing about the autism spectrum brain style as it applies to individual children.

Maya's Brain Style Profile was created after completing the MIGDAS-2 diagnostic interview process. Information from the Parent/Caregiver Questionnaire, Teacher Questionnaire, and Diagnostic Protocol for Individuals with Limited to No Verbal Fluency were used, along with the *Childhood Autism Rating Scale-Standard Booklet* (Schopler et al., 2010) and the Social Responsiveness Scale Preschool Form (Constantino & Gruber, 2012), two autism-specific behavior rating scales. The MIGDAS-2 Pattern of Observations provided descriptive language consistent with autism in the three key areas for the Descriptive Triangle to help identify Maya's pattern of strengths and differences in the three key areas.

For our purposes, let's refer to the portions of the parent interview with Marta and the diagnostic interview session with Maya you've just read about as we develop her Brain Style Profile. As we discuss the essential elements of Maya's profile, think about how you might discuss each point with Maya's mother. In this way, you will experience a model for how you can incorporate this approach into your clinical work with families of young children. Maya's Language and Communication Brain Style Profile of strengths and differences is depicted in Box 1.1.

Because Maya's emerging spoken and unspoken language skills are divergent from the expected developmental profile of children of her age and ability level, we want to organize her profile of strengths and differences to reflect specific patterns that lead to her ability to access, use, and understand communication (strengths), and where the access to, use of, and understanding of communication is harder work for her (differences). Care is taken to describe how Maya uses and responds to language and under what circumstances. Rather than stating that Maya is *not* using particular language skills, we state that she is *not yet* using that specific language skill.

The key strengths to emphasize for Maya and other young autistic children like Maya, center on four main points. The first point is communicating that the child responds best to spoken language when a visual context is provided, and highlighting that the child has acquired some language concepts as demonstrated when they apply those concepts within visual contextual routines. Here the strength is linked to Maya specifically by highlighting her ability to access her emerging labeling vocabulary when watching a preferred program (*Pocoyo*) and when she manipulates familiar objects. The second point emphasizes the link between the child's ability to access language when provided with a visual context and when *spoken language demands are minimized*. In Maya's case, describing how she showed the ability to consistently respond to prompts and follow the adult's lead when she is given time to take in the visual contextual cues and when the use of spoken requests are minimized, clarifies this for her mother and other caregivers, The third point highlights the child's emerging strengths in initiating communication, describing what that looks like. In Maya's case, proximity to adults, taking objects to adults, and vocal protests contextualize this for the reader. The fourth point focuses on the child's emerging shared exchange communication use. For Maya, highlighting how she is beginning to spontaneously seek out eye gaze to connect with adults during high interest and movement play routines brings this descriptor to life.

Let's contrast Maya's language and communication strengths with her Brain Style Profile of differences. The main idea here is to describe the aspects of communication that are *hard work* for Maya. The fundamental pattern to highlight here is what happens to her access to her developing language when she is managing incoming communication from others instead of engaging in self-initiated communication routines. So we start with noting that it is hard work for Maya to retrieve and use her language *outside of her self-initiated and visually contextualized routines*. We indicate the areas in which Maya is not yet consistently using communication routines, including being consistently responsive to verbal requests and her use of and response to unspoken social communication. Finally, we mention that Maya's strength of communicating through vocal protest includes the difference that she is not yet directing her protest toward a listener or conversational partner.

Box 1.1 Maya's Brain Style Profile

Language and Communication

Strengths

Organizes her emerging spoken and unspoken language use around visual labeling in the following ways:

Language use is most organized when Maya has visual contextual cues; that is to say, she is beginning to more consistently access her developing vocabulary when pairing her language with visual observations

Accesses and uses her emerging labeling vocabulary in a self-initiated way when watching preferred videos (*Pokoyo*) or when manipulating familiar objects

Applies language concepts well when given a visual context and when spoken language demands are minimized (matching puzzle pieces of objects with their location; cow in barn, for example)

Communicates her basic wants and needs through the use of proximity to adults, taking objects to adults, and vocal protests

Responds to spoken language best when paired with visual contextual cues

When given time to take in visual context cues and when the use of spoken requests were minimized, Maya showed the ability to consistently respond to prompts and follow the adult's lead

---

Emerging use of eye gaze and gestures directed toward adults in high-interest situations to make requests (initiated shared eye gaze; maintained proximity during sensory movement play routine with preferred toys)

Differences

Outside of her self-initiated and visually contextualized routines, it is hard work for Maya to retrieve and use her spoken language and to follow spoken prompts from adults

Maya is not yet consistently responsive to verbal requests, prompts, or directions

Maya's reactive routine of removing herself from the source of demands and vocally protesting communicates her low tolerance threshold for managing and responding to incoming spoken language

Maya's use of and understanding of unspoken communication functions (eye gaze, gestures, changes in facial expressions, body orientation) is confined to emerging and occasional use

Communication in the form of vocal protest is not yet directed toward the listener

Boxes 1.2 and 1.3 continues Maya's Brain Style Profile list of descriptors in the remaining two areas of Social Relationships and Emotions, and Sensory Use and Interests.

In the area of Social Relationships and Emotions, we start by recognizing Maya's loving connections with family members and her happy demeanor when she is not in a state of distress. Additional strengths to note are her ability to self-regulate by engaging in familiar, independent routines. These descriptors help the adults in Maya's life recognize her qualities and begin to connect her regulated social and emotional state with providing supports that respect her differences. The theme for Maya's listed social and emotional differences helps her caregivers recognize the need for adjustment to the way in which they understand and manage their social overtures. Understanding Maya's social and emotional autistic differences provides the entry point for adults in her life to engage Maya in social exchanges in ways that are the best fit for her brain style.

In the area of Sensory Use and Interests, we have an opportunity to highlight Maya's learning style along with how she manages stress and dysregulation of her sensory system. The essential dimensions describe Maya as a systematic, visual, tactile, cause-and-effect learner who enjoys creating and maintaining routines with predictable patterns. Also of importance to note is that Maya does best with transitions and requests when visual contextual cues are provided and she is given time to take in the visual prompts. Essential differences in her sensory use focus on describing the hard work it is for her to manage input from others, resulting in her patterns of reactivity and resistance when others make requests of her. Maya's specific patterns of recurrent and distinctive body movements and mannerisms are described in recognizable ways, guiding the adults in her world to understand the regulating function of these movements and mannerisms and how they are linked to her sensory brain differences.

Box 1.2 Maya's Brain Style Profile

Social Relationships and Emotions

Strengths

Connected with and affectionate toward family members and enjoys being in their company

Seeks them out for familiar physical play routines (blanket pull, swings)

Generally happy disposition

Enjoys independent time to explore materials and engage in familiar routines

Beginning to consistently initiate social exchanges with others in the context of familiar routines

Oftentimes removes herself from the source of stress to reset her regulation level rather than directing her agitation toward others

Consistently able to reset her regulation level with movement and solitary cause-and-effect play activities

Differences

Spoken language and social overtures are oftentimes sources of stress and distress for Maya, and she responds by moving away from the source of demands or reacting with agitation and distress

Resists social overtures from others unless they are part of a familiar and established routines

Not yet sustaining social exchanges for multiple exchanges

Has not yet established a vocabulary to identify and express her emotions

---

Box 1.3 Maya's Brain Style Profile

Sensory Use and Interests

Strengths

Organizes her exploration of developmental materials in a systematic way

Learns and retains information well when teaching is paired with visual contextual cues

Attends to visual details and is a visual learner

Learns through visual and tactile exploration of cause-and-effect relationships with manipulative materials

Self-regulates by engaging in self-directed activities with preferred materials

Enjoys creating and maintaining play routines that create predictable patterns

Does best with transitions and requests when given time to take in the visual contextual cues and when spoken language is paired with visual prompts

Differences

Transition times are often a source of stress, and result in Maya's inflexibility in response to prompts to engage in routines

Reactive to incoming language, social, work, and sensory demands

Resistant to input from others, but developing the ability to follow structured teaching routines

Engages in some recurrent and distinctive body movements and mannerisms, including close inspection of visual details, holding preferred objects close to her body, hand and arm posturing, and moving away from the source of social and language demands

---

Taken as a whole, Maya's Brain Style Profile reveals her autism story. Within that story, the descriptive language guides the adults in Maya's life toward an understanding of her as a complex young child who does best when she knows what is expected of her and has time to focus on her areas of interest. In other words, Maya does best when she is provided with visual contextual cues paired with minimal spoken language, and when her specific sensory regulation routines are understood and integrated into her daily life in a purposeful and systematic way. This understanding of how Maya experiences communication, social, and sensory input from others, and how she organizes and regulates through her specific sensory-based routines lays the foundation for the conversations with her mother and service providers about the specific types of supports that will be the best fit for Maya's brain style. We'll connect Maya's Brain Style Profile with her recommended supports in Part 2 of this book.

For now, let's focus on how Maya's Brain Style Profile descriptors not only fit her as an individual child but how they also describe the pattern of fundamental strengths and differences in development for many young autistic children who are developing with limited to emerging verbal fluency. Imagine yourself using this basic profile of strengths and differences and customizing it to fit the autistic child for whom you are providing an autism evaluation or clinical supports as you work with that child's parents, caregivers, and service providers.

Imagine yourself using this strengths-based framework to reveal the story for the young children in your clinical practice. See yourself applying this sensory-based approach and descriptive language to help close the disparity gap for autism assessments for Black Indigenous People of Color, as these families often experience increased delays in access to a diagnosis for their children, misdiagnosis, and a delay in access to support services (Aylward et al., 2021).

Maxwell's verbally fluent Brain Style Profile

How does this profile differ when describing young children with highly developed verbal skills? When the child is developing strong language skills, the entry point for parents seeking a diagnostic evaluation for their young child shifts from communication concerns to emotional regulation concerns. They are trying to make sense out of why their talkative, quick-to-learn child becomes so rigid about small changes in familiar routines, and why their child switches so abruptly and unexpectedly from a carefree to a highly agitated state. Once their child switches to a state of emotional reactivity, the experience of navigating through the episode until the child is able to emerge on the other side can be harrowing and exhausting. Autism may not be the first possible diagnosis that comes to mind for either the parents or the diagnostic clinician they approach for guidance. Isn't it likely to have something to do with oppositional or defiant problems? Maybe attention and focusing issues? Maybe extreme mood swings? After all, this highly verbal child pleasantly starts conversations, looks at adults, uses gestures, and seems so social with adults. Surely there are no social communication concerns pointing to an autistic brain style. Or are there actually some clear social communication differences when we look at the child's communication patterns outside of short exchanges and routine situations?

Why is it important to identify the sensory-based autistic brain style in young highly verbal children who are struggling with emotional reactivity and who push back when everyday demands are placed on them? The lens we use to understand the child's experience makes a fundamental difference in how we respond to that child's patterns of challenging behavior. When a child pushes back on requests and demands for their time and energy, and uses words like: "I don't want to!", our first inclination is to understand this behavior using a social intention framework. The child looks at us, tells us they do not *want* to do the requested action, so they must be communicating a social intention. That means we will use a social set of verbal reasoning explanations to point out our expectations. We verbally tell the young child what will happen if they do what we ask, and what will happen if they do not do what we ask of them. We rely on the social communication entry point of talking, reasoning, and using our emotional connection. We expect that this process will help the child develop the ability to internalize and use talking, reasoning, and connections to make different and better choices moving forward. When this social intention framework does not work, frustrations grow along with a sense of powerlessness on both the part of the adult and the child.

When we introduce instead the possibility that the seemingly social response to our everyday requests may be sensory based, we can begin to see patterns of behavior that make sense and lead us to a different course of action. When the child tells us they do not want to do something and they look at us, instead of focusing on the words and orientation toward the listener, let's expand our search for understanding to look for patterns. Does the child's reaction seem familiar? In other words, is there a predictable sameness to the way in which the child reacts to requests or demands? Perhaps we can begin to see a reactive behavior routine in place. A reactive behavior routine can be described as a pattern of words and actions the young child engages in when their threshold for managing incoming demands has been breached. When the child tells us that they don't want to do something, is it possible they are experiencing and trying to tell us: "TOO MUCH!!!", as in too much input, too many demands, too much stress, and so on? The young autistic child who is developing with excellent language and thinking skills often experiences this reactivity to input, resulting in abrupt shifts in their emotional state and behavior from upbeat to distressed. This experience is not only upsetting for the adults in the child's life but also for the child. They live in a world where their sense of well-being can be destabilized at any given moment.

The autistic sensory-entry point framework for reactive behavior routines leads to a different approach to understanding and managing these routines. When we understand the triggering power of input and incoming demands for the young child's autistic brain, it leads us to adjust the ways in which we make demands as well as pay attention to the volume of demands the child has had to manage at any given time. It leads us to the paradoxical understanding that even though the young child talks a great deal, when we look a little more closely, we see that the child fatigues quickly with incoming language and social exchange demands. As we look a little more closely, we notice the pattern of starting conversations with others, getting a response, and then exiting the exchange, only to start the routine of initiation once again. Initiation of conversation, especially conversation that focuses on showing and telling about objects and topics of interest, is energizing for the young autistic verbally fluent child. They have a context for organizing, retrieving, and using their extensively developed language skills. This changes completely when we look at how the child responds to incoming language demands from their conversational partner. Responding to incoming social communication from others in extended and flexible exchanges is hard work for the young child's brain and can lead to a breach in their regulation threshold, so they suddenly shift from their energetic, sociable state to their destabilizing reactive state.

This framework guides adults to pay attention to the types and volume of input the child is managing throughout the day. This includes the way in which the adult approaches the child when making requests so their approach is a better fit for the way in which the child manages input. For example, instead of relying on the social communication assumption that the child will respond without effort to a verbal request or comment made from across the room, the parent recognizes that for their child to successfully shift focus from their activity or thoughts to prepare to take in the incoming request, they do best with proximity and a transition routine prior to delivering the verbal request. The verbally fluent child will also benefit from being given a context for that request, either verbally or visually, and from clear and concise verbal input. In other words, instead of assuming the child will adapt and internalize flexibility, the adult recognizes the child's need for the adult to scaffold requests to support a successful outcome. When the adult scaffolds requests in this way, using proximity, context, and clear language, what are they doing that is a good fit for the sensory-based autistic brain style? They are creating and repeating a predictable transition routine.

Let's see how this plays out with Maxwell, a four-year-old boy who is developing with highly capable spoken language and thinking abilities. Instead of sitting in on Maxwell's parent interview and his diagnostic assessment meeting, let's read excerpts from his summary report that describe him, his interests, and his behavior patterns. These sample narrative passages show you how the parent interview and results of the MIGDAS-2 sensory-based interview can be summarized in a written form using the three essential parts of the Descriptive Triangle's visual framework.

For Maxwell's MIGDAS-2 parent interview summary, we will focus on what his mother shared about her main concerns, including emotional regulation patterns and patterns of sensory sensitivities. We will also read his mother's recounting of Maxwell's relationships with family members and peers, activities he enjoys, and end with three qualities to describe Maxwell and goals for the autism evaluation process.

Parent interview

Maxwell's mother participated the MIGDAS-2 Parent/Caregiver Questionnaire interview process as part of this consultation evaluation process.

When asked to discuss her main concerns regarding Maxwell, his mother noted that her most pressing concern regarding Maxwell was his daily struggles in managing his reactivity to incoming demands, with limited ability to regulate his emotions. Examples given by his mother include Maxwell's reactive response of yelling or screaming in an agitated way in response to simple directives ("Please pick up your toys"; "Your TV time is over and it's time to turn it off."). She noted that Maxwell used to hit and kick, but at the time of this consultation evaluation, his reactive behavior routines typically involved verbal protest. His mother noted that she and her husband have been consistent in using the routine of taking Maxwell to his room to reset his regulation level. However, she added that the need for this intervention occurs multiple times a day and is taxing on everyone in the family, including Maxwell. She reflected that although Maxwell struggles to recognize and manage his emotional reactivity, he is beginning to express his awareness, as he makes statements such as: "I need Mommy to help me calm down," "It was a rough morning. I was so sad and mad." She added that while Maxwell is able to express his emotions after the fact, he struggles to express his understanding of the triggers for his reactivity or to apply regulation strategies the next time he becomes stressed. Once he resets his regulation level, his mother noted that Maxwell regains his positive demeanor, making statements such as: "It turned out to be a good day, though."

Additional areas of concern expressed by Maxwell's mother included her son's sensitivity to loud noises and to smells he experiences as unpleasant. She recalled that anytime someone in the family drops something unexpectedly and it makes a loud noise, Maxwell reacts with a startled scream, covering his ears and crying at times. She also recalled a similar response on Maxwell's part in response to automatic flushing toilets. At home, she noted that Maxwell is sensitive to anyone raising their voice volume, and experiences this as yelling. She noted that Maxwell often yells and does not seems to recognize his own loud voice volume. Additional sound sensitivities noted by his mother included Maxwell's fearful reaction to hair dryers, lawn mowers, blenders, and leaf blowers. Additional sensory sensitivities identified by his mother include sensitivity to food smells and textures. She noted that Maxwell complains about the smell of yogurt and asks her to stop eating it or feeding it to his younger brother, and can become reactive, yelling and crying when the yogurt is not immediately removed from the table. In the area of textures and clothing, his mother stated that Maxwell would prefer to wear pajamas all day, and resists dressing himself on a daily basis. His mother discussed Maxwell's continued dependency when it comes to getting dressed each day. Although he is physically capable, his mother noted that Maxwell constantly asks for help and becomes distressed and agitated for extended periods of time when prompted to do each step on his own. Examples provided by his mother included Maxwell's routine exhortation of: "I don't know what to do!" She reflected that it seems as though Maxwell needs her to tell him step-by-step what to do even though the steps are part of his daily routine.

When asked to describe his relationships with family members, his mother stated that Maxwell lives with his parents and his younger brother, age 36 months at the time of this consultation evaluation. His mother noted that Maxwell has strong loving connections with all of them, and seeks out and enjoys time with both of his parents. With his father, his mother noted that Maxwell seeks out roughhouse play, computer game time, and more recently, sharing his bedtime routine. She noted that Maxwell enjoys a range of activities with her as well. His mother noted that she has been working on increasing her consistent follow-through while reducing her use of verbal reminders. Within the family, his mother reflected that Maxwell seeks out his parents to cuddle and hug and enjoys sharing affection often but on his own terms. She stated that Maxwell is very loving with his younger brother and loves making him laugh and talking about him to others. However, she added that as Maxwell's younger brother has become more mobile and independent, Maxwell has become increasingly likely to grab on to him, push him, and knock him down. She also noted that Maxwell tries to control his brother's access to toys and will hold his brother against his will. This has led to his mother redirecting Maxwell throughout the day, and to Maxwell's increase in assertions that he wants to play alone without his brother's interference.

When asked to describe the activities Maxwell enjoys, his mother noted that Maxwell enjoys his daily hour of screen time watching Dinosaur Train. *She added that he loves playing with Legos and dinosaur Lego character sets. His mother stated that Maxwell enjoys taking his*

Lego mini figures and other objects to recreate aspects of the Dinosaur Train *program, Additional activities enjoyed by Maxwell mentioned by his mother include building with blocks and magna tiles, and swinging on the outdoor saucer swing. She reported additional activities enjoyed by Maxwell, including reading nonfiction books about dinosaurs, the weather, and how things work.*

His mother added that although Maxwell is capable of playing on his own, his preference is to have a familiar person nearby to play alongside him while he describes what he is doing and directs their actions. His mother has noticed when she takes Maxwell to the park that Maxwell watches the other children, but prefers playing alone alongside his mother. She recalled that when she has prompted Maxwell to join others in play, Maxwell struggles to join in and reports that others do not want to play with him, often remaining on the periphery when others invite him to join them in their play. His mother reported that she has worked to provide play opportunities with peers so Maxwell can develop friendships and she provides structured activities for play dates. She noted that Maxwell struggles with anxiety in response to playing games that have a clear winner and loser, and asks if an activity with a friend is going to be cooperative or competitive play. She noted that he is beginning to tell himself soothing statements such as: "It's not a competition; it's okay to take my time," when playing with a friend. His mother noted that Maxwell experiences anxiety in anticipation of entering into new situations or when he is trying anything for the first time.

When asked to pick words or qualities that best describe Maxwell, his mother stated that Maxwell is loving, curious, and cautious. His father noted that Maxwell is playful, stubborn, and cautious. She stated that she hoped this consultation evaluation process would help her gain insight into what goes on in Maxwell's head when he behaves in certain ways. In gaining a better understanding of his emotional responses, his mother would like to find ways to teach Maxwell to express himself in more socially acceptable ways, and to adjust her parenting style to incorporate tools that are meaningful and impactful for her son.

This summary excerpt shows how the parent's narrative unfolds to reveal the story of their child and their lived experience as a family. The autism story also reveals itself, as you take the parent interview content and place it into the narrative summary report. Strengths and differences in the three key areas are illustrated by recounting specific details provided by the parent. When the parent of a young child reads your report, they will instantly recognize their experience. At the same time, the way in which you lay out their story provides the parents with a compelling way to look at and understand the scope of strengths and differences in their child's development, laying the foundation for working together to develop supports for the child and the family.

Now that we've read Maxwell's excerpted parent interview story, let's read his MIGDAS-2 diagnostic interview narrative as it appears in his narrative summary report. The information is organized into the three essential parts of the Descriptive Triangle: Language and Communication, Social Relationships and Emotions, and Sensory Use and Interests. Each section starts with a contextual sentence that highlights the child's distinctive pattern of strengths and differences. The child's strengths are then described, illustrated by memorable words and actions that bring the individual profile into focus for the reader. This is followed by a description of the child's differences, similarly personalized. At the end of each part of the Descriptive Triangle, the reader is provided with a summary contextual sentence that communicates: you've just read about this child's distinctive pattern of strengths and differences in this area of development, and what you've just read describes the autistic brain style.

Before reading the three sections of the Descriptive Triangle narrative for Maxwell, we begin with a paragraph to set the context for the reader. You can adapt this to fit the individual young child for whom you are providing your MIGDAS-2 evaluation and narrative report.

As part of this evaluation consultation process, Maxwell participated in a sensory-based interview session with this psychologist. The MIGDAS-2 Diagnostic Interview Protocol for Children and Adolescents with Verbal Fluency was followed, and Maxwell was encouraged to structure the time at the start of the session using manipulative materials and topics of his preferred interests (dinosaurs, building with magnet puzzles). As an additional part of the sensory-based interview process, Maxwell was asked to participate in shared social communication exchanges, respond to prompts to discuss social and emotional topics, and to take part in physical play. His parents participated in the interview session, along with his younger brother. This provided an opportunity to observe Maxwell's interactions with familiar people, and to assess the proportion of time Maxwell organized his behavior around object-focused routines and contrast this with his engagement in shared social play. Throughout the session, information was gathered regarding Maxwell's brain style in the three key areas of Language and Communication, Social Relationships and Emotions, and Sensory Use and Interests. During the course of this diagnostic interview session, Maxwell displayed a range of behaviors, resulting in an individualized overview of his current brain style pattern of strengths and differences.

A description of Maxwell's behavioral profile, broken down into the areas of Language and Communication, Social Relationships and Emotional Responses, and Sensory Use and Interests is detailed below.

Now that we've set the context for Maxwell's narrative for his behavioral profile of strengths and differences, let's begin with his Language and Communication summary.

Language and Communication

In the area of Language and Communication, Maxwell displayed areas of strength as well as some notable and distinctive differences. Strengths for Maxwell included his well-developed language skills and vocabulary. Maxwell displayed a well-developed understanding of language, and readily applied it when he was engaged in the routine of showing and telling details about his preferred objects (magnetic pieces that formed various balls; dinosaur cards and figures). He was highly verbal, engaging in a continual narrative related to his exploration of the sensory-based materials. During the diagnostic interview session, Maxwell's language was most organized when he was asking questions and making declarative statements about the properties of the materials he was manipulating, or sharing information about his knowledge and areas of interest (Dinosaur Train; *how things work). Maxwell displayed an established routine of starting the conversation as an extension of his visual and tactile exploration of objects. His initiation routine included holding up and showing materials to his conversational partner while describing aspects of the materials, glancing at his conversational partner, and orienting his body toward them as well. Throughout the session, Maxwell initiated conversation multiple times with this psychologist as well as with both of his parents. For example, when Maxwell explored a set of cards depicting different dinosaurs, each time he approached a different card, he would hold up the card in the direction of this psychologist and exclaim: "Look!" as he proceeded to label relevant details about the dinosaur depicted on the card (name, type, and so on) before attentively placing the card into a linear grouping.*

Differences in Maxwell's language and communication usage were also noted. Maxwell spoke in a distinctive style, including the use of an elevated voice volume and an exclamatory inflection that remained constant throughout the session. On the few occasions when Maxwell became overly stressed, his exclamations included shouts and cries. Differences were also noted for Maxwell in the areas of sharing conversational exchanges in a back-and-forth extended way after he initiated an exchange by showing and telling information of interest to him. In other words, Maxwell's pattern of initiating communication with adults was well established, while his ability to take in and respond to the spoken and unspoken communication overtures from his conversational partner were notably challenging for him. When this psychologist consistently responded to Maxwell's overtures to look and listen by matching his enthusiasm level and adding a comment, Maxwell continued his commentary without responding to or building on the shared exchange. Maxwell had difficulty interrupting his routine of showing and telling to respond to or share an exchange regarding the incoming information. His routine included approaching an adult while holding an object of interest, showing and telling information, and then moving away from the adult to continue exploring materials of interest. Throughout the session, it is important to note that when Maxwell explored materials, he approached each of the adults but not his brother to show and tell information. When his brother approached Maxwell to hold up an object or to reach for an object Maxwell was holding, Maxwell moved around his brother to continue his routine with the adult.

When this psychologist made the social statement: "I have a favorite dinosaur," Maxwell stopped talking, stiffened his body, made an involuntary facial grimace, and stood in a static position. When given time to respond to the declaration and ask about the favorite card, Maxwell struggled to access his language to ask the social question. To support Maxwell so he could experience success with this social communication overture, this psychologist asked Maxwell if he wanted to ask her, "What is your favorite dinosaur?" or for her to tell him what dinosaur she favored. He then visibly relaxed before he repeated: "What is your favorite dinosaur?" After this psychologist showed her "favorite" card and told him the name, Maxwell resumed his routine of picking up another dinosaur card, naming it, and placing it in the line of cards he had created. In response to incoming questions and comments, Maxwell's use of language notably decreased, while his recurrent behaviors, such as close visual inspection of objects and engagement of descriptive verbal routines increased.

This pattern of taking in information from his conversational partner but responding either after a delay or not responding, was seen throughout the interview session. Although Maxwell frequently used exclamatory comments when exploring the materials, his use of the corresponding social communication features of eye gaze, orienting toward his conversational partner, and responding to comments made by his conversational partner in an integrated and consistent way that is expected at his age and ability level was not yet established. In other words, although Maxwell verbally started the conversation, he had difficulty engaging in shared exchanges, flexibly shifting to topics brought up by *this psychologist, and extending his comments after Maxwell had made his original statement. By contrast, his younger brother's engagement with materials included the notable shared exchange element of responsiveness to his conversational partner's input, extending the exchanges by responding to comments and actions, and using a range of facial expressions, gestures, eye gaze, and changes in vocal tone. As observers in the session, this provided his parents with an opportunity to take in the differing patterns of behavior and ways of using language and communication that are part of their son Maxwell's development.*

It is important to note that Maxwell displayed a low threshold for incoming language and conversational demands, as evidenced by his routine of staying in the general area of the room adjacent to this psychologist when conversational demands were limited and objects of interest were used to engage Maxwell in object-focused play, and withdrawing from the conversational exchange when shared, extended, and flexible communication was required. Maxwell frequently struggled to use his language to ask questions of his conversational partner, and to provide social information about himself and his life. As part of the hard work noted for Maxwell when he was responding to communication input and conversational overtures from others, he not only struggled to access his spoken language but also displayed a notable increase in his level of distress and emotional reactivity. His contrasting pattern of fluid access to language paired with his emotional regulation when object-focused and self-initiated and his struggles to organize, retrieve, and use his language and to manage his level of emotional regulation when social language requests were made of him was consistent throughout the session. His parents noted this contrast and confirmed that they see this across settings for their son.

Maxwell's pattern of differences in the use of language and communication is oftentimes seen in young verbal children developing with autism spectrum brain style differences.

This narrative summary of Maxwell's Language and Communication profile of strengths and differences highlights four crucial features seen in verbally fluent young autistic children. The first feature highlights Maxwell's distinctive and unvarying way of speaking, with a focus on volume and intonation. The second feature involves making sense out of the child's strengths in using spoken and unspoken communication with adults. The child routinely starts conversations with adults, glances their way, approaches them, and shows them objects, a clear area of strength. If we stop there we will miss the child's communication differences. The differences become apparent when we look at what the child does with incoming communication information from their conversational partner. Here the autistic pattern unfolds as we experience the child's struggles with responding to and managing input from their conversational partner in a fluid exchange. The third feature is the contrast between object-focused initiation of language and communication and the child's response to overtures to broaden the conversation to social and emotional topics. Here the child shows us a dramatic decrease in their access to their impressive vocabulary and fluid language skills, paired with an observable increase in their emotional level of experiencing stress or distress. The fourth feature we see in Maxwell's narrative is the contrast between his seeking out adult conversational partners while avoiding communication exchanges with his brother.

From this narrative, we can generate Maxwell's Language and Communication Brain Style Profile, shown in Box 1.4.

Box 1.4 Maxwell's Brain Style Profile

Language and Communication

Strengths

Has well-developed language skills and verbal fluency and is expanding those skills daily

Uses his language in a fluent way, as evidenced by his use of verbal description of details related to his areas of interest and exploration (dinosaurs; creating and building with a range of materials)

Highly verbal and enjoys narrating his play routines

Initiates conversations with adults and briefly responsive to social communication overtures from others when he is emotionally regulated and when his conversational partner follows his lead

Shows strong emerging skills in his use of unspoken communication features (eye gaze, gestures, body orientation) when initiating spoken communication with adults around his areas of interest

Communicates his wants and needs effectively unless in a reactive state

Does best responding to his conversational partner when given time to take in the information and when he is provided with scaffolding or support from the adult to formulate his response

Consistently seeks out adults to initiate his object-focused conversations

---

Differences

Speaks in a distinctive style, including a consistently elevated voice volume and use of an exclamatory inflection

Language use is primarily self-initiated, object-focused, and focused on initiating conversations with others without the corresponding shared exchange and back-and-forth reciprocity

Hard work for Maxwell to respond to his conversational partner using spoken and unspoken social communication

Displays differences in following social conversational cues in terms of following conversational prompts, participating in shared conversational exchanges with multiple exchanges, and flexibly shifting from his preferred topics to topics introduced by others

Low tolerance threshold for high-load incoming language demands, as noted by Maxwell's struggle to access his spoken language and to manage his emotional regulation level

Use of and understanding of unspoken communication functions is limited

Can be unresponsive or reactive at times to verbal directions and social communication verbal overtures depending on his threshold for input at the time

The second portion of Maxwell's autism profile, Social Relationships and Emotions, includes his narrative summary of strengths and differences and his Brain Style Profile for that area. We'll look at his narrative summary first, provided below.

Social Relationships and Emotions

In the area of Social Relationships and Emotions, Maxwell presented with areas of strengths well as some pronounced areas of difference. Strengths for Maxwell include his outgoing, enthusiastic, and friendly demeanor, along with his genuine pleasure when others share in his play and follow his lead. He showed genuine enjoyment when others responded to his object-focused social overtures. Although Maxwell became dysregulated at times when he had to manage incoming language, social, and sensory demands, he responded well to the routine of alternating language and play demands with times for Maxwell to direct the conversation and play routines. Maxwell was enthusiastic in his exploration of materials of interest. He has established loving and strong bonds with his parents and younger brother, and responded in a positive and engaged way with this psychologist as she mirrored his object-focused play and conversational style. He was alert, engaged, and responsive throughout the session, and was responsive to this psychologist's prompts to show materials and to engage with a range of materials. He readily engaged in a game of catch with his father.

Differences for Maxwell in the area of Social Relationships and Emotions include the current observed gap between his desire for social connections with others and his ability to interpret and use the social behaviors necessary to establish and maintain shared social exchanges. During this diagnostic process, Maxwell consistently became mildly dysregulated and had challenges with retrieving and using his language in response to social and social play overtures. Maxwell's ability to respond to social play overtures, to extend social play with a partner, and to flexibly shift from his object-focused play agenda to follow the social play agenda of his play partner were notably different.

During the evaluation session, Maxwell was observed to have difficulty using eye gaze, gestures, and changes in his facial expressions in a fluid way as part of a social conversational exchange with this psychologist as well as with his mother, father, and younger brother. Maxwell's ability to regulate his behavior and participate in a shared exchange in an age-congruent way were highly challenging for him. In other words, the gap between Maxwell's desire for social connections with others and his ability to use and interpret social cues was significant. In the absence of a repertoire of age-appropriate social skills, Maxwell engaged in a high level of self-initiated behavior routines, including creating and maintaining routines with preferred objects, focusing on systematically examining visual details of preferred objects, and creating a verbal narrative focused on the properties of the objects as he explored them. Maxwell rarely visually referenced others to engage them in shared social exchanges throughout this session. Maxwell consistently retreated from the social overtures to engage in shared play by either reestablishing his self-initiated object-focused routines or retreating from the exchange and playing independently.

Maxwell became notably dysregulated at times with incoming language and play demands. During the session, the prompts to talk about himself, wishes, family members, and to respond to this psychologist's social communication overtures resulted in a pattern of Maxwell's redirecting back to his established routine of showing and telling, moving away the source of demands, and the need for extensive pauses before responding. Although he has well-developed language skills, Maxwell had some difficulty sharing information about himself, social relationships, or emotions. When Maxwell was asked to look at a card depicting a feeling (happy), he responded by taking the card and placing it on the floor next to the dinosaur he had been building out of magna tiles. Maxwell resumed his routine of building and describing the shapes and the building process before responding to a prompt to look at the card and tell a time he felt happy. With support, Maxwell was able to respond to the prompt to tell what types of things make him feel happy by stating: "When I get to play." He spoke in a voice like a younger child with a sing-song intonation during these responses, and even with prompting, it was challenging for Maxwell to extend his comments. This was in marked contrast to his fluid and extended use of language when he was engaged in object-focused play and was initiating the conversation. Each time a feeling card was introduced, Maxwell redirected the conversation by holding up and describing what he was doing with a magna tile before he generated a feeling response. Maxwell responded well to the routine established by this psychologist of alternating requests to respond to feelings cards, generate three wishes, and talk about social activities (work for him) with a retreat from these incoming demands and a reestablishment of Maxwell's object-focused, self-initiated routines (break for him).

Maxwell showed an initial resistance to having a play partner introduce novel play elements but an ability to incorporate those elements after having time to process and consider this unexpected input. For example, after Maxwell created his routine of holding up dinosaur cards, naming them, and placing them into a continuous grouping, this psychologist provided a pouch that when opened contained an assortment of small dinosaur figures. Maxwell opened the pouch and created a routine where he held up each dinosaur, named it, and placed it in a line with the others. When this psychologist took one of the figures and placed it on top of the corresponding dinosaur card, Maxwell quickly and carefully moved the figure back to its place in the figure line up. After a few minutes of resuming his established play routine, Maxwell able to process the novel play overture, and then he began to match each dinosaur figure with the corresponding card, creating a novel play routine. This pattern was repeated when this psychologist created a variation in the routine by starting groupings of carnivores and herbivores. Each time a variation was introduced, Maxwell was initially unable to shift from his routine to respond to this psychologist's introduction of variations in the play routine. He undid her play overture and resumed his established routine. After taking time to process each novel play overture, Maxwell consistently transformed these into self-initiated routines. As he stayed focused on his previously established routine of showing and telling, and throughout his exploration of materials, it was notably difficult for Maxwell to shift his attention away from objects to people.

During the portion of the session when Maxwell was encouraged to explore his surroundings with his mother, father, and younger brother, Maxwell selected solitary exploration activities unless he was prompted to engage in a shared activity, like a game of catch with his father. While playing catch, Maxwell became notably dysregulated as he participated in the play exchange with his father. Mildly dysregulated behaviors included Maxwell laughing in a loud and forced way, throwing the ball with excessive force and without waiting to check for readiness with his catch partner, and jumping and spinning his body.

Throughout the session, his brother made repeated social overtures to engage in shared play with the materials, Maxwell was unresponsive to his brother's overtures, moving around him and asking his mother to move his brother out of the way. However, on several occasions Maxwell initiated interactions with his brother by handing his brother an object and making statements like: "You can take this and go over there!" On two occasions when his brother persisted in inviting Maxwell to engage in shared play, Maxwell clenched his fists and loudly cried out. Maxwell was able to reset his regulation level when his brother was redirected to a separate activity.

Maxwell's pattern of social and emotional strengths and differences is characteristic of young verbal children developing with autism spectrum brain style differences.

This narrative summary of Maxwell's Social Relationships and Emotions profile of strengths and differences starts with a few key words that capture Maxwell's exuberant personality and connect the reader with his outgoing way of connecting in the world. His genuine enjoyment of sharing his world with others is also featured, along with his loving connections with family members. Maxwell's ability to respond to the specific support of alternating the source of demands when he begins to experience stress is also mentioned as a strength for him. Differences for Maxwell are laid out with specific brief narratives that show what each descriptive quality looks like for him. As with the previous section of Maxwell's Descriptive Triangle profile, the sum of Maxwell's narrative describes his singular presentation of the autistic young child's pattern of strengths and differences in the area of Social Relationships and Emotions. The final sentence in this section of his narrative tells the reader that Maxwell's described pattern of strengths and differences is characteristic of young verbal children who are developing with autism spectrum brain style differences.

Box 1.5 takes this summary report narrative of his Social Relationships and Emotions profile and condenses it into his Brain Style Profile.

Box 1.5 Maxwell's Brain Style Profile

Social Relationships and Emotions

Strengths

Has a consistently outgoing, friendly, animated, and spirited demeanor paired with a genuine desire to share his world with others unless his threshold for managing social demands has been surpassed and his emotional reactivity has been triggered

Enjoys it when others follow his lead and respond to his social overtures, and prefers playing in the vicinity of preferred adults

Connects well with family members and peers, especially when engaging in a shared activity within his areas of interest

Differences

Initiates but has difficulty sustaining social exchanges for more than one or two exchanges

Hard work for Maxwell to respond to a play partner on the partner's terms and to include others in shared play exchanges

Inflexible at times when working or playing with others

Sustained shared enjoyment, flexibility, and extension in social interactions is limited

High-load language and social demands are a source of agitation for Maxwell, and he responds by becoming progressively dysregulated, increasing his recurrent, withdrawal, or reactive behaviors (moving away from the source of demands, talking over others, speaking in an exaggerated voice, clenching his fists and shouting, jumping up and down)

Limited but emerging vocabulary to express emotions

Limited but emerging vocabulary to describe himself, his interests, and his life experiences

Fatigues quickly in response to incoming language, social, sensory, and work demands, resulting in increasing levels of emotional dysregulation

Once his system becomes dysregulated, Maxwell is dependent on adults to provide the redirection and structure that allow him to regroup and reset his brain

The third and final portion of Maxwell's autism profile, Sensory Use and Interests, includes his narrative summary of strengths and differences and his Brain Style Profile for that area. We'll look at his narrative summary first, provided below.

Sensory Use and Interests

In the area of Sensory Use and Interests, Maxwell displayed a distinctive pattern of strengths and differences. Strengths for Maxwell include his range of age-appropriate interests (learning information about dinosaurs, building with various materials, outdoor play, learning how things work). He displayed creativity while exploring the materials during this diagnostic interview session, as well as by report from his parents. Maxwell is a visual, three-dimensional, systematic, categorical thinker who seeks out and maintains routines that involve pairing his labeling language with objects and visual input, and engaging in goal-directed routines. He has well-developed language skills, and enjoys using his language to describe visual and cause-and-effect properties of objects. Maxwell pays exceptional attention to visual details, and is highly skilled in building with materials such as Legos and noticing categorical details related to his areas of interest (dinosaurs, building with magnets and tiles). His language was most organized when he had a visual context to scaffold his use of object-focused descriptive speech. Maxwell sought out and followed predictable routines and thrived on being able to anticipate and follow routines. Once he had a predictable visual context, he was not only able to access his language skills but he was also able to take in information and expand his creative use of materials. Maxwell genuinely and clearly enjoyed sharing his passionate interests with this psychologist.

Differences for Maxwell in the area of Sensory Use and Interests included his focus on objects and routines without the corresponding social shared attention dimension. He repeated his self-directed routines multiple times during the session. The proportion of time Maxwell spent focused on objects far exceeded the amount of time he spontaneously shifted his focus and eye gaze to engage in social exchanges with others. Maxwell showed differences in his brain flexibility through his pattern of an initial resistance to having a play partner introduce novel play elements. Each time a variation was introduced by this psychologist, Maxwell was initially unable to flexibly shift from his routine to respond to the introduction of variations in the play routine. He engaged in a routine of undoing her play overture and resuming his established routine. However, after taking time to process each novel play overture, Maxwell

*consistently transformed these into self-initiated routines. As the intro-
duction of novel play elements became a routine during Maxwell's dinosaur play, his ability to integrate new patterns increased in a notable way.
For example, when this psychologist began asking Maxwell the binary
question: "Carnivore or herbivore?" Maxwell created a variation in his
routine of lining up the cards and corresponding dinosaur figures by
creating groupings of carnivores and herbivore with the figures and their
corresponding cards.*

*Maxwell's independent play routines helped highlight the ways in
which his access to his language skills varied across activities. When
he was selecting preferred materials, like the dinosaur cards, Maxwell
paired his exploration of those materials with a continual verbal narrative
describing his recurrent and systematic routines. Each time an activity
required Maxwell's brain to take in new information, including playing
catch with a partner, this pattern changed. While mastering a new task
(building with the magnets for the first time) or managing physical
movement and social routines (playing the game of catch), his access to
and use of his language skills notably stopped. With the added dimension of managing incoming verbal and social overtures from a conversational or play partner, Maxwell showed a pattern of stress and distress.
The behavior patterns of moving away from the source of demands and
positioning his brother away from preferred materials communicated
that his brain was shifting from regulated to dysregulated. His recurrent movements increased, as did his increase in focus on inflexible use
of verbal and play routines. Throughout the session, Maxwell engaged
in some distinctive and recurrent body movements and mannerisms,
including facial grimacing, categorizing objects by lining them up or
naming their properties, close visual inspection of objects, moving
away from the source of demands, body tensing and clenching his fists,
jumping up and down, and vocalizing his distress by shouting or crying
out. Maxwell sought out these movements and routines as a means of
self-regulation to manage his anxiety or reactivity in response to social,
language, and play demands placed on him. By report, Maxwell has
pronounced and long-standing sensory sensitivities in the areas of smell,
touch, taste, and sounds.*

*During the diagnostic interview session, Maxwell's sound sensitivity
was noted when this psychologist shook a "thunder tube" percussion
instrument, a cardboard tube with a drum skin and metal coil that made
a rumbling sound when shaken. Maxwell responded with a startled
look and his hands reflexively shot up toward his ears. He shouted: "So
loud!" Noting his sensitivity to incoming sounds, this psychologist
immediately dampened the sound and handed the tube to Maxwell.*

Maxwell reached out and gingerly grasped it with one hand, holding the metal coil with his other hand. After he closely inspected it and self-directed a question about "How does this work?" Maxwell proceeded to shake the tube repeatedly and vigorously, stopping several times to comment on and describe what was happening: "The sound bounces and comes out!" This psychologist brought out a second thunder tube and matched Maxwell's pattern of shaking, listening, stopping, examining, and repeating this pattern. As she joined him, Maxwell displayed some involuntary body movements and mannerisms in response to the auditory input. These included body tensing, facial grimacing, hand posturing, close visual inspection, and holding the tube close to his ear. He continued this routine for multiple rounds before he reached his capacity for this specific input and placed the tube on the floor beside him. It is important to note that although Maxwell showed a pronounced sensitivity to the unexpected sound made by the tube, when he was in charge of producing the sound, he sustained a routine of creating and responding to the sounds created by both tubes for an extended period of time. Just as he stayed focused on his previously established routine of showing and telling, while Maxwell took in the sensory experience of the thunder tubes, it was notably difficult for Maxwell to shift his attention away from objects to include or reference people. In general, throughout the sessions and by parent report, Maxwell displayed some notable differences in being able to flexibly shift from his object-focused agenda to take in information and follow the agenda of others.

Maxwell's profile of strengths and differences in the area of Sensory Use and Interests shows a pattern of differences commonly seen in verbally fluent children with autism spectrum brain style differences.

This narrative summary of Maxwell's Sensory Use and Interests profile of strengths and differences starts with linking his interests and exploration of materials with ways to describe his thinking or learning style and how they relate to his sensory preferences. His interests are listed and his creative nature is acknowledged. The relationships between his way of exploring materials and his access to and use of spoken language is also highlighted as a strength. Differences for Maxwell include noting his object-focused play, his recurrent and distinctive body movements and mannerisms, and his sensory sensitivities. Finally, Maxwell's pattern of differences in his ability to shift flexibly from his agenda to take in information and follow the agenda of others is pointed out and exemplified.

Box 1.6 takes this summary report narrative of his Sensory Use and Interests profile and formats it into his Brain Style Profile.

Box 1.6 Maxwell's Brain Style Profile

Sensory Use and Interests

Strengths

Has developed a range of age-appropriate interests (learning how things work and information about dinosaurs, building with various materials, outdoor play)

Well-developed visual, three-dimensional, systematic, and categorical thinking skills

Systematic in his routines of building structures, categorizing and labeling the properties of objects, setting up play routines

Pays close attention to visual details and learns through tactile exploration of cause-and-effect relationships with manipulative materials

With a predictable visual context, Maxwell is able to access his language skills, take in information, and expand his creative use of materials

Seeks out and regulates best with self-initiated, structured, predictable, object-focused routines

Seeks out movement and manipulating objects as routines to self-regulate and manage environmental demands

Responsive to visual input and information

Organizes best when he establishes an object-focused routine

Genuinely and clearly enjoys sharing his passionate areas of interest with others

Differences

Sensory-seeking routines include specific interests

Setting up and maintaining his self-initiated object-focused routines provides energy for Maxwell and is a source of emotional regulation

Sensory sensitivities are pronounced in the areas of sound, smell, touch, taste, and changes in his established routines

Transitions from his agenda to the agenda of others often a source of stress and can lead to reactivity and dysregulation

Reactive at times to transitions, and sensory, language, and social demands

Challenging for Maxwell to flexibly shift from his agenda to the agenda of others, and this challenge increases when he is in a state of stress or distress

Fatigues quickly with social communication demands and input

Challenging at times for Maxwell to self-regulate, resulting in the need for adult redirection to a reduced stimulation setting to reset his regulation level

Engages in distinctive and recurrent body movements and mannerisms, including body tensing, clenching his fists, facial grimacing when stressed, close visual inspection of objects, self-directed narration of his actions and properties of materials when engaged in sensory-based play, moving away from the source of demands, self-directed vocalizations when dysregulated, and loss of access to his words when distressed

The final summary sentence for this section of a narrative report referencing the use of the MIGDAS-2 diagnostic system highlights the qualitative Pattern of Observations conclusion:

On the MIGDAS-2 overall Pattern of Observations, Maxwell displayed a pattern of behavior consistent with autism spectrum brain style differences.

After reading Maxwell's narrative summary in the three key areas, you may find yourself recognizing patterns you've seen in young children with whom you've worked in your clinical practice. The descriptive language used in his narrative report provides a sample of how you can write about the young autistic children you assess and support who have highly developed language skills paired with emotional reactivity.

Maxwell's written narrative tells his singular autism story in a layered way. Each part of the autism spectrum Descriptive Triangle reveals patterns of behavior. As the patterns of strengths and differences are described and specific examples are provided, his autism story is told in a strengths-based individualized way. The confusing contrast between Maxwell's extensive use of language and his reactivity in response to incoming language begins to make sense to his parents. They can absorb the diagnostic profile with a solid understanding of what autism means in relation to their child. They can describe his way of being in the world to themselves and others, as the narrative descriptions in the summary report are designed to represent the perspective of the child. Now that the diagnosis is provided in a way that can be understood and revisited in the written report and Brain Style

Profile summary pages, his parents can move into the next chapter in their family story: crafting the supports that are the best fit for their son's needs as he prepares to make the transition from early childhood to school-aged life. We'll connect Maxwell's autism spectrum brain style profile and story with his recommended supports in Part 2 of this book.

Co-occurring conditions and differential diagnosis considerations in young children

Before we leave the early childhood autistic world and move on to exploring what Brain Style Profiles look like in children and adolescents, let's take a few moments to talk about co-occurring conditions and differential diagnosis considerations in young children. Just as it is important to think, talk, and write about the young child's autistic brain style and diagnosis in strengths-based language, it is equally important to be able to do so regarding other neurodevelopmental conditions that can occur along with or instead of autism. Assessing developmental differences in young children can be challenging, as there is a range for children as they meet their expected developmental milestones. That being said, within that range there is an expected scope and sequence of language, learning, physical, social, and emotional development.

The most common experience for clinicians working with young autistic children is to see children who have multiple areas of developmental differences that come together to form that child's lived experience. A way to think and talk about this is to understand that young children often present with *complex developmental and behavioral profiles*.

So what are we saying when we refer to a young child's complex developmental and behavioral profile? We are acknowledging that there are multiple dimensions we need to identify to tell the most compelling story about the particular child. Getting the complex story right for young children informs the way the adults in the child's world understand and support them. In the absence of the most compelling story to make sense out of the individual child's complex set of developmental differences, we leave parents adrift and uncertain about what path to take to best support their child's interconnected patterns of divergence from the expected course of early childhood development.

Young children who are referred for an autism assessment often initially present as showing neurodevelopmental differences in one or more areas of their development. When the term *developmental delays* is applied, we are talking about notable differences in the young child's development in one or more of the following areas: speech and language, cognitive, sensory and motor, and social and emotional abilities (Mody & Beliveau, 2013; Shan et al., 2022; Miller et al., 2024). The young child may have a medical condition, including specific genetic differences or seizures. They may have a history of premature birth or a birth trauma. Other general differences are often present as well, including divergences in development in the areas of toileting, eating, and sleeping patterns (Adams et al., 2011). Mood differences can also be present, in the form of anxiety or reactivity to environmental demands. Early trauma may also be a part of the young child's life experience.

When we have a way of understanding the specific autistic patterns of behavior and development and pair that understanding with clear ways to describe other forms of developmental differences, we are better equipped to do the important work of partnering with parents and caregivers to reveal the young child's complex and multifaceted story. Let's take each of the components that fall under the umbrella of neurodevelopmental delays—referring to them as aspects of neurodevelopmental *differences* rather than calling them delays—and explore how they fit with autistic developmental differences. We'll discuss key dimensions to look for that will help us recognize co-occurrences with autism as well as when the young child's developmental differences may not overlap with the autistic brain style.

We'll start with speech and language development, as this is a common entry point for most young children receiving a referral for an autism assessment. The key differential factor here is looking closely at specific differences in the child's speech and language development and use. Are the child's speech and language differences best described as developing in the expected sequence but at a slower pace or rate, or are they developing with distinctively different qualities than expected? In other words, we look for a co-occurrence of a specific speech and language neurodevelopmental difference along with autism when we can identify and tell the story of the child's divergent use of spoken and unspoken language features along with the child's use of speech and language developing at a slower than expected progression. We look for a differential diagnosis of speech and language developmental differences when the child is developing language with the expected sequence but at a slower than expected pace, and is doing so in the absence of the essential language and communication differences that define the autism spectrum communication profile.

What elements do we need to consider when a young child is developing with cognitive, learning, or general developmental differences? As with speech and language development, general developmental differences can be described as the child developing skills in an expected sequence but acquiring and maintaining skills at a slower than expected rate. In other words, the child requires extensive and repeated practice to acquire and maintain developmental skills. This is contrasted with the autistic general developmental differences, which can be described as uneven patterns of development, including one or more areas of ability that approach or exceed the child's age. Co-occurrence for these two types of neurodevelopmental differences captures the story that the young child is learning both at a slower than expected rate and is learning in a way that differs from the expected trajectory. Here we also need to consider the autistic sensory entry point to help us with differential diagnosis considerations. The young child who is developing on the expected course but at a slower pace organizes around the social communication entry point. The young child's brain seeks out connections with significant others in ways that are familiar and conventional. This of course contrasts with the young autistic child who may also be learning or developing with general delays, but expected social connections are a notable source of stress and distress rather than comfort. The young autistic child organizes and regulates their system by creating and maintaining sensory routines.

An additional area of early development to consider is the child's sensory and motor skills development. Here we are looking at how the child is developing the use of their body and how they are integrating sensory input. Differences in the development and use of motor coordination and control are the key aspects of sensorimotor development. The young autistic child shows us distinctive differences in their sensory development with their pattern of pronounced sensory sensitivities and preferences. These sensory differences can affect motor development in uneven patterns. For example, the child may have exceptional gross motor skills and engages in running, climbing, and jumping with ease but struggles with fine motor skills. Conversely, the child may struggle with large motor movements but engages in fine motor recurrent routines. The child's sensory sensitivities to sounds, visual details, taste and smells, movement, and so on may affect their ability to integrate that sensory input into motor development activities. This is contrasted with sensory and motor delays, or differences in the rate at which the young child acquires and maintains developmental skills in these areas in the expected course. Recurrent movements and mannerisms that are part of the young child's pattern of creating and maintaining predictable routes for system regulation, when paired with the specific social communication divergent patterns descriptive of the sensory and object-focused autistic brain style, guide us to the differential diagnosis between autism and specific sensorimotor developmental differences. It also helps us describe the co-occurrence profile when both the autistic brain style of development and specific sensorimotor developmental differences are part of the child's story.

This brings us to the area of social and emotional development. As clinicians we are well aware that many factors affect a young child's social and emotional development. When we are looking at whether the child is developing with autism spectrum differences, we are looking for the distinctive pattern of the child's sensory entry point as a means to organize and regulate their system paired with the notable hard work for the child's brain to use and respond to social and emotional overtures. When a young child is seen in an environment that is a match for that child's needs, we begin to see an amplification of the young child's entry point into the world. We can explore by observation and direct experience the difference between a child for whom social and emotional referencing is the means to orient to their surroundings, and the child for whom sensory routines and preferences are the salient factors. Young children who show some emerging patterns of expected social and emotional responses but who also show us the recognizable pattern of social and emotional differences we describe as the autistic brain style, tell us their autism story of social and emotional strengths and differences.

Attention and impulsivity neurodevelopmental differences are also frequently recognized in young children age four years and older (Zablotsky et al., 2020; Hours et al., 2022; Leitner, 2024). For young children who are developing with both the autistic brain style and attention and impulsivity differences, the two overlapping conditions begin to come into focus as the young child prepares to make the transition from early childhood to school age. The child begins to show clearer patterns of neurodivergence from the expected course of development when contrasted with their peers. How do we distinguish attention and focusing patterns of neurodivergence from autistic patterns? How do we determine whether the most compelling story for a particular child includes one or the other or both? With young children who have attention, focusing, and impulsivity differences, these patterns are readily observable to the clinician in the assessment or support clinical setting. The child initially orients to their environment by touching and exploring all of the sources of novel input. This routine precedes broadening their focus to include referencing and participating in exchanges with the adult. When the child is organizing in the world with both attention, focus, and impulsivity differences along with autism spectrum brain style differences, the child then begins to select the materials that provide opportunities to create and maintain a predictable routine. As they settle into creating and maintaining their object-focused, self-initiated routines, their differences in their ability to simultaneously participate in shared social exchanges become markedly apparent.

We will revisit co-occurring and differential diagnosis considerations when we discuss children, adolescents, and adults in the next two chapters. For now, let's explore what the autism spectrum brain style looks like in children and adolescents.

References

Adams, J. B., Audhya, T., McDonough-Means, S., Rubin, R. A., Quig, D., Geis, E., Gehn, E., Loresto, M., Mitchell, J., Atwood, S., Barnhouse, S., & Lee, W. (2011). Nutritional and metabolic status of children with autism vs. neurotypical children, and the association with autism severity. *Nutr Metab (Lond)*. Jun 8;8(1):34. doi: 10.1186/1743-7075-8-34. PMID: 21651783; PMCID: PMC3135510.

Aylward, B. S., Gal-Szabo, D. E., & Taraman, S. (2021). Racial, ethnic, and sociodemographic disparities in diagnosis of children with autism spectrum disorder. *J Dev Behav Pediatr*. Oct-Nov 01;42(8):682–689. doi: 10.1097/DBP.0000000000000996. PMID: 34510108; PMCID: PMC8500365.

Burns, J., Phung, R., McNeill, S., Hanlon-Dearman, A., & Ricci, M. F. (2023). Comorbidities affecting children with autism spectrum disorder: A retrospective chart review. *Children (Basel)*. Aug 19;10(8):1414. doi: 10.3390/children10081414. PMID: 37628413; PMCID: PMC10453739.

Constantino, J. N., & Gruber, C. P. (2012). *Social Responsiveness Scale, Second Edition (SRS-2)*. Torrance, CA: Western Psychological Services.

Hours, C., Recasens, C., & Baleyte, J. (2022). ASD and ADHD comorbidity: What are we talking about? *Front Psychiatry*. Feb 27;13. https://doi.org/10.3389/fpsyt.2022.837424

Khachadourian, V., Mahjani, B., Sandin, S., Kolevzon, A., Buxbaum, J.D., Reichenberg, A, & Janeka, M. (2023). Comorbidities in autism spectrum disorder and their etiologies. *Transl Psychiatry*. 13:71. https://doi.org/10.1038/s41398-023-02374-w

Leitner, Y. (2014). The co-occurrence of autism and attention deficit hyperactivity disorder in children – what do we know? *Front Hum Neurosci*. Apr 29;8:268. doi: 10.3389/fnhum.2014.00268. PMID: 24808851; PMCID: PMC4010758.

Miller, H. L., Licari, M. K., Bhat, A., Aziz-Zadeh, L. S., Van Damme, T., Fears, N. E., Cermak, S. A., & Tamplain, P. M. (2024). Motor problems in autism: Co-occurrence or feature? *Dev Med Child Neurol*. Jan;66(1):16–22. doi: 10.1111/dmcn.15674. PMID: 37332143; PMCID: PMC10725993.

Mody, M., & Belliveau, J. W. (2013). Speech and language impairments in autism: Insights from behavior and neuroimaging. *N Am J Med Sci (Boston)*. 5(3):157–161. doi: 10.7156/v5i3p157. PMID: 24349628; PMCID: PMC3862077.

Monteiro, M., & Stegall, S. (2018). *Monteiro Interview Guidelines for Diagnosing the Autism Spectrum, Second Edition*. Torrance, CA: WPS Publishing.

Schopler, E., Van Bourgondien, M. E., Wellman, G. J., & Love, S. R. (2010). *Childhood Autism Rating Scale – 2nd Edition*. Los Angeles: Western Psychological Services

Shan, L., Feng, J. Y., Wang, T. T., Xu, Z. D., & Jia, F. Y. (2022). Prevalence and developmental profiles of autism spectrum disorders in children with global developmental delay. *Front Psychiatry*. Jan 18;12:794238. doi: 10.3389/fpsyt.2021.794238. PMID: 35115968; PMCID: PMC8803654.

Zablotsky, B., Bramlett, M. D., & Blumberg, S. J. (2020). The co-occurrence of autism spectrum disorder in children with ADHD. *J Atten Disord*. Jan;24(1):94–103.

2 Reveal the story

Children and adolescents – Malik and Marisa

If your clinical work includes assessing and supporting neurodivergent children and adolescents, you already have a sense of the impressively broad range of stories and experiences this age group represents. For each individual child or adolescent, how do we sort through their complex network of history, behavior patterns, interpersonal relationships, and intrapersonal experiences? How do we uncover their most compelling story, including their autistic story, to support that young person's strengths-based narrative? We start by remembering that verbally fluent children for whom the autistic brain style is a diagnostic question, almost always have a different area of neurodivergence identified before autism is addressed. By definition, they are developing and living with complex behavioral profiles. Their parents, caregivers, and school staff are dealing with challenging and puzzling behaviors. Everyone involved has an implicit sense that there is an essential factor they are missing; a clear understanding of the child or adolescent has not yet fallen into place. Without the most compelling story, piecing together the needed supports is difficult.

The main areas of neurodivergence we see occurring in children and adolescents fall into two categories: neurodevelopmental differences and emotional differences. These two categories overlap to form part of the complex behavioral profile for individual children and adolescents for whom we consider adding the autistic story. Neurodevelopmental differences include attention, focusing, and impulsivity profiles; learning differences profiles; and language processing differences profiles, along with other specific areas of developmental differences such as genetic differences profiles. Emotional differences include the experiences of anxiety, depression, disruptive behavior patterns, and complex trauma responses related to adverse experiences.

In this chapter we will focus on identifying the key descriptive patterns that come together to form the autistic triangle of strengths and differences within profiles that include both neurodevelopmental and emotional

DOI: 10.4324/9781003532576-4

differences. This will allow us to see how the autistic brain style story is revealed, surrounded by other parts of the young person's complex and multifaceted behavioral profile and life experience. These examples and the Brain Style Profiles we generate from them will help you recognize and apply these essential autistic features as they pertain to the complex children and adolescents you support in your clinical practice.

Malik's complex behavioral profile

Our first case is Malik, a nine-year-old boy. Prior to exploring his autism profile, Malik's diagnostic journey included identification of the neurodevelopmental differences of ADHD-Combined Type, dysgraphia, and the emotional difference of generalized anxiety. He was being seen by both his pediatrician and a child psychiatrist, and was taking medications to help manage his focusing, impulsivity, and anxiety differences. Although the child psychiatrist had suggested that Malik was showing signs of oppositional and defiant behavioral differences, his parents and pediatrician wanted to include an autism consultation to make sure they were not missing an important perspective to better understand and plan for Malik's complicated behavioral and emotional profile.

Strengths for Malik included his cognitive abilities, measured in the well above average range, and his academic work, which he maintained at or above grade-level expectations. He was creative and applied that creativity to his areas of interest, including his emerging interest in playing the keyboard so he could play themes from his favorites video games. Malik relished his time playing preferred games, including Nintendo games and *Minecraft*, and he also enjoyed writing code to create original game snippets. When Malik focused on his areas of interest, he did so in an intensely concentrated way. His preference was to spend as much time as possible absorbed in his areas of interest without interruption or input from other people. In school, his intense nature and resistance to teacher directives resulted in his teacher describing Malik as sometimes being "willful and defiant." When asked to describe his greatest areas of strength and ability in her classroom, his teacher stated that Malik was smart and capable. Academically, she noted that during math and science activities, Malik joined the class discussion when he was interested in the topic being discussed.

Notable differences for Malik spanned a wide range. His parents noted that since early childhood he had shown extreme reactivity in response to everyday transitions and that the intensity of his responses had increased over time. The behaviors that made up his reactivity included expressing refusal, yelling, throwing objects, destroying objects and running away. These reactive behaviors were more pronounced at home. In the school setting, his teacher observed that Malik oftentimes seemed oblivious to events around him and could be defiant and resistant when given directions to shift his focus to the task at hand. She stated that he did not often initiate asking for help or clarification of assignments and tended to rush through his work. His teacher noted Malik's areas of academic challenge to be reading analysis, especially when he was required to relate to the feelings and emotions of the characters. In addition, his teacher stated that Malik had received an occupational therapy consultation to provide strategies for his handwriting differences. Socially, his teacher observed that Malik's perception regarding what was going on around him oftentimes seemed to be off or missing the main point. He showed a preference for working independently and resisted group assignments. When asked to pick three words or qualities that best describe Malik, his teacher noted that Malik was often intense and focused on his interests, displayed a childlike innocence, and was usually independent and introverted when around his classmates.

Both his teacher and parents described his physical movements of walking with a distinctive bobbing and loping gait, and his preference for perching rather than sitting on his chair. Malik's parents noted that Malik was highly sensitive to the way fabric feels on his skin, preferring soft long-sleeved shirts and pants as his daily outfit. He routinely slept in a sleeping bag to avoid contact with bedsheets. Malik showed a preference for wearing headphones to block out incoming sounds, both at home and in the classroom.

His parents noted a pattern of reactivity not only when Malik was required to shift his focus and follow directions but also whenever he perceived a situation to be unclear or uncertain in terms of the sequence of events and outcomes. They also commented on noticing that their son displayed a limited awareness of the impact of his behavior on others and often blamed others for his reactivity. They noted that his reaction of heightened irritability in response to everyday demands has intensified over time. They added that Malik had begun talking about feeling like he is doomed to a life where other people are always stressing him out. His increase in irritability level, combined with his comments about feeling tired and stressed, deepened concerns his parents had regarding their son's self-esteem and well-being. Three words or qualities chosen by his parents to describe their son included: creative, self-focused, and smart.

To gain a sense of Malik's profile of strengths and differences in the three key areas, let's read a description of his MIGDAS-2 diagnostic conversation.

A diagnostic conversation with Malik

Malik entered the room with his parents, his long thin legs making their entrance first with his distinctive, loping gait. When he looked at the table with partially constructed magnet balls and several Rubik's Cubes on it he abruptly halted and jolted his body into a straight line.

"This looks interesting…" he announced, drawing out the last word as he bolted toward the table. Malik's body collapsed into a perched position in front of the objects, and he rapidly began to assemble each of the magnet balls. He talked himself through the process.

"Okay, this one makes a dodecahedron…oh, and you can reverse it and go from multi to single color…interesting…" Malik's self-directed, rapid, and staccato speaking style was notable as he trailed off at the end of each sentence before speaking up again.

I pulled a chair up beside him and companionably watched and listened without placing demands on him for conversation or interaction. Malik continued his self-directed narration as he assembled each of the five magnet balls, and proceeded to combine the magnets to form novel structures. When he held up one of his creations and waved it wildly over his head, I responded to his social overture.

"Very cool, Malik!"

He responded by saying, "I used the X pieces and the solid ones for this masterpiece, haha…" Even though Malik maintained his perched body orientation and intense visual focus on the creation he was holding, he was clearly inviting me into his play and exploration. We were starting our object-focused conversation.

"Yes, a masterpiece for sure! What about the ball with the Y pieces?"

"Interesting…now that is a tricky one…you have to connect Y pieces with star pieces to make the recurring rhombus pattern…" He demonstrated by holding up individual pieces directly in front of his face as he spoke.

In this way, Malik systematically explored the range of puzzles and fidgets that formed the basis of our conversation. His organizing and regulation pattern of behavior provided an opportunity to comment on Malik's strengths. The shift from object-focused comments to observations about Malik himself and how his brain works was a purposeful one.

I used this opportunity to reflect back to Malik what I was noticing about his brain style. This provided him with an experience in which his perspective was noted and appreciated in a positive way. It also provided an opportunity for Malik to confirm or clarify the descriptive observations.

"Malik, I really admire how creative your brain is! It's great to see how your brain works when you look at things and figure them out."

Malik considered this. "Interesting…"

"I noticed how well you talk yourself through the steps when you build something. You describe what you are doing while you are doing it. Just now, for example, I saw how your brain really understands how shapes work together and how to name them too. Impressive."

Malik remained with his back toward me as he manipulated magnet pieces. His quiet demeanor communicated that he was listening, so I continued.

"So, Malik, I have a question for you. I am noticing something about how your brain works and want to make sure I'm getting this right." I paused. "Ready for my question?"

Malik nodded without changing his body orientation.

"It looks like when you work on something, you get really focused. Does that describe how you work?"

Malik nodded again.

"So I'm guessing when your brain has to shift from focusing on your excellent building skills to listen to someone else asking you to do something, that is it *hard work for your brain*." I emphasized the last phrase.

"Yes!" Malik exclaimed in response. He lightly patted the top of his head four times. He paused for a moment and added: "They don't get it!"

"Thank you for helping me understand how it works for you, Malik. This is really important. Knowing how it works for you will help you and your parents find a better way to switch back and forth from focusing on the things your brain loves to do and doing the things your parents need you to do."

I added a final statement before directing Malik back to the regulating routine of exploring materials. "Thank you for talking about this with me, Malik. I'm guessing that's enough talk for now. Is that about right?"

"Bingo!" Malik asserted in a forceful exclamation.

With that confirmation, Malik was able to successfully experience the demands of a substantive conversation and make the transition to an object-focused, calming routine while staying regulated. The introduction of a routine of alternating engaging play with substantive conversation helped Malik experience regulation throughout the meeting, a contrast from his more common experience of exiting substantive conversations in an agitated and dysregulated state.

We could see and experience with Malik the sources for his regulated system (object-focused, self-directed routines) and the sources that trigger his stress level and system dysregulation (participating in shared exchange conversations about personal topics).

Pay Attention and Comment on Patterns

Through this process with children, we can observe and comment on each child's pattern of brain style strengths and differences. Pay attention to whether the child finds it better to explore materials while simultaneously narrating the details, or whether their style is to explore without engaging their language brain.

We can ask the child clarification questions after we notice patterns. For example, we can notice and then ask:

I notice that when you figure out how things work, your brain gets quiet instead of talking. Is that about right?

When you are figuring out how things work, I'm wondering if it works better for you if others are quiet around you, or if it's okay for them to keep talking?

When you build with the magnets: Does it activate your brain and give you energy, or is it hard work for your brain and it wears you out?

When you answer questions and talk with people: Does it activate your brain and give you energy, or is it hard work for your brain and it wears you out?

With Malik, it was time to alternate back to object-focused play. I handed him a pouch containing a repeating metal ring that expanded into a spiral when placed on his forearm. This Geoflux three-dimensional kinetic sculpture moved fluidly from arm to arm as Malik instinctively interlocked his fingers and guided the spiral back and forth. As he explored it, Malik stood up and paced the room, all the time commenting on the physical properties as they happened in real time.

He plopped down on the floor, pushed his shoes off, and placed the Geoflux on one leg. As it expanded, he reclined onto his back, raised both of his legs, and managed to get the spiral to flow from one leg to the other.

"Wow, that really is amazing, Malik! I've never seen anyone do that with their legs before. So creative and also so flexible!"

Malik assumed a booming announcer voice, declaring: "And they called him the Amazing Pretzel Boy!"

I met Malik where he was by replying: "Yes, Amazing Pretzel Boy!"

Even though the flow of the meeting had returned to his self-directed object-focused play, Malik was showing that it was hard work and somewhat dysregulating to his system to have participated in the shared exchange about his experience. His change in regulation level as he returned to object-focused play provides us with confirmation that engaging in extended conversational exchanges with others was a source of dysregulation for his system. The introduction of the alternating routine between work (conversational demands) and break (object-focused routines) provided Malik with a way to anticipate when social and emotional conversational topics would be introduced, allowing his brain to participate and engage, as he was able to anticipate the upcoming reprieve to focus of objects and topics of interest to him.

So in this way we were able to observe and experience the subtle but notable trajectory of Malik's regulation level. This shift in conversational focus from self-directed play narration to the discussion of his brain style resulted in the strength for Malik of staying connected in the interactional routine. The notable differences were his increase in the use of emphatic movements, his elevation of his voice volume, and his veering into distinctively exclamatory comments. When we notice these subtle shifts and their connections to our purposeful social overtures, we are able to help the child reset their level and experience a success loop. This experience contrasts with their more typical experience of becoming increasingly dysregulated and reactive to input.

Wordlessly, I handed him the Geoflux pouch. Malik reached out and took it, disentangled the spiral from his legs, and placed it back into the bag. I reached out for it while offering him the exchange to a handheld puzzle, the Cube Bot, that I had kept in reserve. This reprieve from spoken language paired with the organizing action of placing the object into a container visibly reset Malik's regulation level. Handing him the Cube Bot re-established the familiar routine from earlier in our meeting.

"Interesting…" Malik was back.

Sensory-based materials that are a good fit for exploration with children and younger adolescents:

Roger von Oech's magnetic design pieces that create varying patterns
GeoFlux 3D kinetic sculpture
Rainbow puzzle ball, Cube Bot, Rubik's Cubes, and similar tactile handheld puzzles
Sensory stress balls with varying textures
Sensory fidget materials such as Monkey noodles, popper silicone shapes, and spinners
Wind-up plastic moving objects (caterpillars, ladybugs, dinosaurs)
Hoberman Mini-Sphere Ball
Thunder Tube percussion noisemakers

As he continued to manipulate the Cube Bot puzzle, I introduced a preferred topic. This would provide a sample of how Malik managed a conversation that focused on something he had an interest in and a context for discussing with others.

"Malik, your parents told me that you really enjoy playing *Minecraft*." Malik's movements became still as he took this in. "That is so interesting. I have a question for you about *Minecraft*. Let me know when you're ready for my question." Malik continued to maintain a static posture, anticipating my question. After a short pause, I posed my binary question related to his topic of interest. The binary question provided a clear context for Malik to organize his response.

"When you play *Minecraft*, do you prefer creative mode or survival mode?"

Malik briefly considered this. "Technically, there are five player modes. You should be asking me if I prefer playing in creative, survival, adventure, spectator, or hardcore mode."

I replied, mirroring his attention to detail. "Of course. Thank you for pointing that out. However, technically, most players switch between creative and survival mode. So I asked you about your preference between the two most used modes."

"Well, that makes sense. And you are correct. Most people use creative or survival mode. Personally, I toggle back and forth between creative and survival modes." Malik extended this conversation by sharing details about his game play. Each time he added details, I responded by restating something he had said and asking a question that fit into the sequence of his narrative. We discussed his development of theme music for some of his creative mode play and discussed his interest in video games. Malik started many of his detailed narrative statements using the words technically, personally, actually, and realistically.

We then switched to talking about social and emotional topics. Just as Malik told me that he toggles between creative and survival mode when playing his game, I guided him to toggle between answering queries about social and emotional topics and focusing on watching and commenting on his exploration of materials. Each time I asked Malik to switch his focus to take in my questions and directives, I handed Malik his "pause" button. This was a folded piece of paper with two lines on it representing the pause button. The act of exchanging the pause button created a predictable transition routine.

As Malik was asked to discuss social and emotional topics and his system began to experience increasing levels of stress, a new pattern emerged in his use of his body and his language. Malik sprawled out on the floor, rolling back and forth several times as he organized his responses. He engaged in a pattern of responding to several of the cards depicting feelings by using an exaggerated voice and blurting out: "Meep!" I created a T-chart on my notepad and wrote the word "Meep!" on the left-hand side. As I wrote on the notepad, we took a break from talking and handing Malik the next feelings card. With the pause in the incoming language, the room became quiet and Malik was able to notably reduce his level of physical and verbal agitation.

"Malik, I think I just figured something out about your brain. May I tell you what I noticed?"

Malik rolled slightly in my direction.

"When you say 'Meep!' I know you are trying to tell me something."

Malik responded by producing and long, drawn out, question inflection "Meeeeep?" as a way to encourage me to expand on this idea.

"I'm wondering if when you say 'Meep,' if you are really telling me: 'I don't know how to answer your question,' or, 'I don't know how to keep this conversation going.'" As I spoke, I wrote the two ideas on the right-hand side of the paper and held this out for Malik to examine.

Malik seamlessly rolled his body into a perched position as he read the T-chart. He nodded his head vigorously as he tapped the right-hand side of the page.

"So, Malik, maybe your brain has hit a glitch and needs to reset."

Malik instantly affirmed this observation. "The 'Meep' glitch!"

Introducing this reframe for his increasingly dysregulated behavior routine laid the foundation for developing regulation supports for Malik. We'll revisit this and discuss regulation supports for Malik in Chapter 5.

I also used visual supports in the form of writing keywords and concepts for additional social and emotional topics as we discussed them. As I asked Malik to clarify his experience when he reacts to his parents and their request or directions, I drew a vertical line across a page. As I spoke, I wrote the words "overloading my system" on the left side of the line, and the words "make things hard for them" on the right side.

"So when your parents ask you to do something, they need to understand what happens to your brain and body. Is it about what overloads your system…" I held up the paper for Malik to read "overloads my system."

"…or is it about making things hard for them?" I wrote, "make things hard for them" on the left side and held the page up for Malik to read. In this way, I provided Malik with two possible descriptions of his experience to endorse, one with a sensory basis and the other with a social cause.

"System overload! System overload!"

"So that tells us we need to help them figure out ways to ask you to do things without switching your brain from okay to overload."

Malik made a fist of his right hand and raised his thumb in agreement.

Malik's diagnostic interview conversation included other components, but we've read enough to absorb some essential strengths and differences for his Brain Style Profile. Box 2.1 depicts Malik's Language and Communication Brain Style Profile. As you read the descriptions included in Malik's profile, you should be able to recognize the child for whom you've just read his diagnostic interview excerpt. Correspondingly, you should also be able to recognize behavior patterns you've seen with children in your clinical practice. Boxes 2.2 and 2.3 complete Malik's autistic profile.

Reframing Malik's refusal behaviors through the autistic lens

How do we explain Malik's reactive behavior routines of refusal that escalate at home to highly dysregulated episodes? Here is a paragraph to describes his reactivity through an autistic lens.

> *Understanding Malik's reactive and dysregulated behavior through the lens of his autism spectrum brain style differences is important, as his behavioral reactivity is communicating that the demands of the environment are exceeding his capabilities at the time his reactivity is triggered. Malik has a low threshold for managing incoming demands, including routine verbal directives prompting him to flexibly adapt to everyday transitions. Malik has established a routine of responding to demands and to the anticipation of unfamiliar events in a reactive way. His reactive behavior routines include expressing refusal, yelling, throwing objects, destroying objects, and running away. Many of these reactive behavior routines are not yet occurring in the school setting. In the school setting, Malik's reactive behavior routines include refusal, avoidance of engagement with expected routines and interactions with his peers, and avoidance of initiating requests for assistance or clarification. Malik's autism spectrum brain style differences affect his ability to take in and respond adaptively to situations in which his reactivity and agitation are triggered. He has not yet developed the ability to self-monitor and reset his regulation level, or to discuss and problem-solve about alternative, positive ways to manage his reactivity and agitation. As Malik continues to mature and move through upper elementary and middle school, the demands to follow teacher and parent directives and the social rules with peers become increasingly more complex and challenging to navigate. He will greatly benefit from specific positive supports that are a fit for his sensory, social, and communication brain style differences.*

In this descriptive passage, we are explaining not only the sensory aspects of Malik's reactive behavior routines, but we are also helping the adults in his world understand why his reactivity is more pronounced in one setting versus the other. When we describe differences in the child's behavior across settings by stating that the demands of the environment are not yet consistently exceeding the child's capabilities in a given setting, we help dispel the social intentionality narrative that the child could manage consistently across settings if they wanted to or tried harder. You may find this description a compelling narrative you can apply when discussing individual autistic children in your clinical practice who struggle with refusal behaviors.

Describing Malik's complex diagnostic profile

Now let's see how we could describe his complex diagnostic profile to include his autistic differences. We will also link his autism diagnosis to the medical diagnostic criteria and describe Malik's autism diagnosis using the DSM-5 criteria and language.

Malik presented a complex developmental and behavioral profile. He has been identified as a child with attention and focusing differences, handwriting differences, and generalized anxiety in response to everyday circumstances. In addition, he has a long history of reactive behaviors in response to incoming demands. Although Malik is highly verbal, his ability to use his language for social communication purposes shows significant differences. He has a notably low threshold for managing incoming language demands, resulting in his deeply embedded routines of resisting directions and reacting with dysregulated behavior routines. Malik also presented with a distinctive and significant array of sensory sensitivities that affect his ability to navigate through daily demands.

In addition to his previously diagnosed Attention Deficit/ Hyperactivity Disorder (ADHD), generalized anxiety responses (Generalized Anxiety Disorder), and his documented handwriting differences (dysgraphia), Malik displayed a profile of behaviors consistent with a diagnosis of Autism Spectrum Disorder (Level 1 for Social Communication; Level 1 for Restricted, Repetitive Behaviors) 299.00, F84.0, without intellectual impairment, without language impairment, and with other known medical conditions (ADHD and Generalized Anxiety Disorder). Although Malik did not present with language delays, he displayed significant challenges in his ability to recognize and apply social language or language pragmatics skills in everyday social exchanges.

In the area of social communication, without supports in place, Malik displays challenges in social communication that cause noticeable impairments. He struggles in his ability to participate in shared conversational exchanges with others. His tolerance for incoming language demands is notably lower than his drive to initiate communication related to his preferred areas of interest. Malik often becomes agitated, stressed, and reactive when communication demands are placed on him, as evidenced by his behavioral responses of avoidance and refusal. Malik struggles to communicate when he becomes reactive to environmental demands, and responds by withdrawing from the source of demands or escalating to reactive behavior routines (yelling, screaming, throwing objects, threatening to run away). His ability to participate in fluid, back-and-forth conversational exchanges is limited, and interferes with his ability to make and sustain peer friendships commensurate with his age and ability level.

In the area of restricted, repetitive behaviors, Malik's inflexibility of behavior, reactivity to incoming demands, and his sensory sensitivities appear frequently enough to be obvious to the casual observer and interfere at times with his functioning in a variety of contexts. Malik experiences distress or difficulty managing his need for predictability, for controlling social interactions with others, and for regulating his agitation and anxiety levels.

You may recognize this profile in children you evaluate and support, as Malik's parents, teachers, and physicians did when they read his narrative profile described in this way. Leading with the assertion that Malik *presented a complex developmental and behavioral profile* provides the reader with a context to understand that multiple factors are in play. We follow that by describing his previously diagnosed conditions and then add the diagnosis of autism. When we identify our autism diagnosis for Malik, we do so by providing the DSM-5 diagnostic label and terminology. We follow this with descriptions of Malik's autistic profile broken down into the social communication and restricted, repetitive behaviors categories from the diagnostic criteria. When we provide descriptions of Malik's behavioral profile and contextualize that information through the autistic lens, we provide the adults in his world with a way to understand him that is in sync with his lived experience. His Brain Style Profile, provided in Boxes 2.1, 2.2, and 2.3, summarizes Malik's distinctive but clearly autistic pattern of brain style strengths and differences in his use of language and communication, his understanding of and engagement in the areas of social relationships and emotional responses, and his singular pattern of sensory use and interests.

We will revisit Malik and connect his Brain Style Profile to specific areas of positive behavior support in Part II.

Box 2.1 Malik's Brain Style Profile

Language and Communication

Strengths

Well-developed language skills

Uses his extensive vocabulary to precisely describe properties of objects (dodecahedron; rhomboid shapes))

Fluidly accesses his language when he has a context for the conversation (manipulating objects and describing their properties; discussing areas of preferred interest such as *Minecraft* and other games)

Initiates conversations by commenting on objects and his activities

Extends communication well when in charge of the conversation and discussing a preferred topic

Processes spoken information quickly when listening to his conversational partner

Differences

Hard work for Malik to integrate his use of and response to shared communication exchanges with a conversational partner, as evidenced by his body orientation away from the person and toward objects of interest, the high proportion of time with eye gaze directed at objects instead of visually referencing the person with whom he is speaking, and the infrequent use of shared exchange use of comments or queries to extend a conversational exchange

Depends on his conversational partner to find a way to join the conversation, as Malik is not yet directing his comments toward the listener

Low threshold for managing incoming language demands, demonstrated by Malik's challenges in extending conversations outside of his preferred areas of interest, and his elevated voice volume and increase in repetitive words and behaviors in response to input from his conversational partner

Flexibly shifting his focus to take in input from his conversational partner in a fluent way is challenging for him

Frequently corrects statements made by others as part of his precise use of language

Avoids conversational interactions that require sustained, back-and-forth exchanges

Uses routines with starter words to organize his language in conversation (interesting, technically, actually)

Speaks in a distinctive style that ranges from measured pacing when describing properties of objects and his actions to exaggerated repeating of words and phrases at an elevated volume when emotionally dysregulated

---

Box 2.2 Malik's Brain Style Profile

Social Relationships and Emotions

Strengths

Connected with family members and has established unique and positive relationships with each one

Happy when he knows what is expected of him and he has time to focus on his areas of interest

Genuinely enjoys it when others share in his passionate interests

Can identify and describe basic feelings and their link to situations

Enjoys it when others follow his lead and respond to his social overtures

Regulates by retreating from social situations and engaging in solitary routines and activities

Thoughtful and responsive to hearing descriptions of his lived experiences related to emotional reactivity and his struggles with managing incoming demands

Differences

Low need to seek out and sustain social exchanges with others

Sustained ability to integrate his use of shared enjoyment, flexibility, and extension into social interactions is limited

High-load language and social demands are a source of anxiety for Malik

Limited but emerging vocabulary to express emotions

Limited but emerging vocabulary to describe himself, his interests, and his life experiences

Beginning to develop a negative self-narrative related to his communication, social, emotional, and sensory sensitivity differences

Experiences a stress response to incoming language, social, transition, and work demands

Dysregulated reactive behavior routines include expressing refusal, yelling, throwing objects, destroying objects, and running away from the source of demands

Once he becomes dysregulated, it is challenging for Malik to regroup and reset his system

---

Box 2.3 Malik's Brain Style Profile

Sensory Use and Interests

Strengths

Well-developed skills in the areas of visual-spatial thinking; systematic in his routines of electronic games, mastering speed puzzles like Rubik's Cube, reading for facts and information

Has developed age-appropriate interests (playing various modes of game play, for example *Minecraft* where he applies his creative and strategic visual thinking skills, playing the keyboard, creating theme music for videos, beginner game coding, reading and retaining science and other facts-based information)

Learns quickly through tactile exploration of cause-and-effect relationships with manipulative materials

Seeks out visually-based tactile exploration of materials as routines to self-regulate and manage environmental demands

Organizes best when he establishes a routine and has low load verbal and sensory input

Differences

High threshold or need for solitary routines to organize and regulate his system and to block out incoming sources of stress (language, social, and non-preferred tasks demands)

Struggles with flexibility when required to shift from his agenda to the agenda of others

Transitions from his agenda to the agenda of others is oftentimes a source of anxiety, agitation, stress, and distress

Challenging for Malik to self-regulate when the demands of the environment exceed his capabilities, resulting in frequent behavior episodes of dysregulation (heightened anxiety and agitation as evidenced by his reactive behavior and escape and avoidance behavior routines)

Once he becomes dysregulated, it is challenging for Malik to regroup and reset his brain, and he loses his access to his words to express himself or calm himself down

Has some distinctive and recurrent body movements and mannerisms, including withdrawal from the source of demands, close visual inspection of objects, perching, pacing, assuming exaggerated gestures, voice intonation, and voice volume when agitated, repeating words and phrases

Marisa's adolescent autistic profile

For now, let's turn our attention to what the complex autistic profile might look like in an adolescent girl. We'll do that through meeting Marisa, a 15-year-old at the time she received her autism diagnosis. Marisa was a highly capable adolescent who had a history of debilitating anxiety in response to everyday stressors. She experienced significant worries, gastrointestinal upsets, panic attacks, and crying outbursts on a routine basis. However, in the school setting she was able to internalize her level of distress, masking the extent to which her emotional state was affecting her development. The toll of this internalization over time resulted in a profound level of fatigue, an overpowering sense of ineffectiveness in being able to crack the code to overcome her cycle of feeling out of sync with the world around her, and a withdrawal from her participation in all but the essential and required school and social activities. Marisa had begun seeing a therapist who specialized in treating anxiety disorders. After several meetings in which the therapist noted the differences in Marisa's responses during their conversations as contrasted with her other adolescent clients, her therapist suggested a referral for an autism evaluation. Specifically, her therapist recounted that Marisa's reluctance to engage in a dialogue regarding her emotional experiences was at a standstill that needed to be understood and addressed to move the therapy process forward in a meaningful way. Her parents reported not only patterns of emotional regulation challenges for their daughter but also sensory sensitivities to foods, crowds, transitions, and participation in social events. They identified several well-established areas of interest and a pattern of preferring her independent pursuit of those interests over participating in peer social activities.

What was the narrative Marisa, her parents, and her therapist were bringing to their exploration of Marisa's possible autism spectrum brain style differences? Amid all of her identified complexities, something essential was missing. They were looking for a way to make sense out of Marisa's distress and misery within her clear competencies and abilities. What were they missing? What was really going on here?

In the absence of a context to understand her unique and singular set of strengths and differences, Marisa was creating a negative story about herself and internalizing that worldview. Surely something was wrong with her. Her lived experience as an adolescent was defined by an endless cycle of fatigue, a sense of dread, relentless anxiety, and steeling herself for the next wave of panic that might overtake her system at any time. To the outside world she appeared to be an intelligent and capable student and classmate, and the gap between her internal and external experiences was not immediately visible or apparent to others. Her exhaustion was directly related to the effort it was taking her to perform externally as a competent adolescent while feeling internally like she was on the edge of collapse or catastrophe. For Marisa, interacting with others was a stressful performance for which she felt ill-prepared. Responding to the demands of routine daily life felt out of sync to her. Where could she just be herself? There was never enough time to focus on the routines that provided her with comfort and restored her energy level. As an adolescent, Marisa was uncertain about how to make sense out of the routines she enjoyed and needed that were not part of the experience of her peers. As the gap intensified, so did her efforts to conceal her interests and needs, along with her level of distress in her everyday life. Like many autistic adolescent girls, Marisa was adept at applying her concealment efforts. The depth of her anguish was only apparent within the family, and even then, Marisa relied on isolation to manage her emotional state. She did not have a context to understand or talk about her increasing levels of stress and distress.

To reveal the autistic story with highly verbally fluent and capable adolescent girls, the coping tool of concealment needs to be recognized, respected, acknowledged, and directly appreciated. How does one go about creating a diagnostic conversation that communicates to the neurodivergent adolescent that you are providing a safe space to reveal and explore the individual's lived experience? Marisa had seen many doctors and participated in therapy with an anxiety expert. She followed the lead of the adults trying to help her. However, she was dependent on them to understand her and to crack the code. Marisa's expertise in creating expected verbal and behavioral response routines in her interactions with others, paired with her expertise in concealing or masking her internal experiences resulted in the well-intentioned adults in her life missing this absolutely essential part of her story. Without a context for her complex story to be recognized and told, Marisa's level of distress was increasing over time in an unsustainable way. She was at risk for developing add-itional self-harm co-occurring behavior routines.

Creating a safe setting for Marisa to reveal her lived experience meant providing her with a diagnostic conversation that was in sync with her aut-istic way of organizing and regulating in the world. To create a place where concealment was unnecessary and she could experience being her true self with another person who understood and accepted her, the requisite starting point was to invite her to share information about her passionate interests. Mirroring her pacing and style of speaking was another essential part of creating a safe and supported exchange. At the same time, pro-viding Marisa with sensory fidget objects to explore that were appropriate for her age and developmental level communicated that the conversational setting prioritized Marisa's well-being. The MIGDAS-2 diagnostic interview protocol (Monteiro & Stegall, 2018) was followed to help Marisa show and tell her lived experience in the three key diagnostic areas.

Marisa's diagnostic conversation

Because Marisa was an avid artist, she was invited to bring one of her sketchbooks into the meeting with her. In this way, even before she arrived, she had a context for the start of the conversation. Marisa arrived with her sketchbook under her arm. She was dressed in leggings and an oversized shirt that was buttoned to the top. Her short hair was shaved on the left side and cut at an angle that stopped just short of covering her right eye. The cotton cord woven bracelet on her left wrist showed signs of well-worn and frequently twisted hanging ends. Marisa's parents had shared that their daughter had a long-standing interest in Japanese anime and manga series, and enjoyed drawing characters in the manga style. This information provided the social overture entry point for our conversation.

We exchanged greetings and Marisa seamlessly completed this routine. She settled in her chosen chair with her sketchbook in her lap without additional conversational prompts from me or input from her. I followed Marisa's gaze as she took in the sensory fidgets on the table beside her. I mentioned that the sensory stress balls have a range of distinctive textures, depending on her preferences. She studied them for a moment before selecting the deep pressure input color changing ball that was a primary shade of green on the outside and vivid yellow when squeezed. Continuing our companionable focus on the object, Marisa was able to take in that the pacing of the meeting would be organized to fit her style. I told her I had learned from her parents about her interest in manga and anime. I added that manga and anime were fascinating and that there were some amazing artists and writers who create series for all ages and types of people. I noted that I was very interested in the wide variety of subgenres within this art form. This provided further context for Marisa, as I explicitly noted an interest in her area of interest. I asked her if there was a manga genre she was especially interested in.

Marisa responded with alertness and engagement, "Oh, yes. The mahō shōjo or magical girl genre has had my interest for a long time. Princess Night, Cutie Honey…great art and stories." Marisa put down the sensory stress ball so she could use her thumb and forefinger to systematically twist the strands of her cord bracelet as she spoke. "I just finished the *Puella Magi Madoka Magica* series for the third time, so good!"

I asked Marisa to tell me the aspects of the storyline that drew her to reading the series multiple times and we went from there. Themes that were suggestive of her interior life showed themselves in her narrative about the series, including feeling like an outsider, the transformative power of discovering gifts and talents, and battling unseen dangers.

With my mirrored and genuine interest expressed through comments and questions, Marisa quickly warmed to her beloved topic. Her communication style unfolded, showing her ability to carefully take in the comments of her conversational partner, respond, and share information. She used eye gaze when speaking and to a lesser extent, when listening. When listening, Marisa showed a pattern of tilting her head to her right side while looking at and manipulating the well-used strands of her wrist cord bracelet.

"Do you also draw in the manga style yourself?" I asked, as a continuation of the conversation focusing on Marisa's areas of interest, skills, and talents. She opened her sketchbook and began sharing her highly detailed and creative manga character art. This included representations of some of the girl hero characters she loved but also original characters she created who had specific magical powers and attributes. Marisa initiated and extended her use of language with this energizing and familiar context.

As I continued to follow the MIGDAS-2 diagnostic interview protocol, Marisa was then invited to recount her sensory preferences and sensitivities. She kept on systematically kneading the strands of her bracelet throughout the conversation. Unlike her previous therapeutic conversations that focused on identifying and exploring her areas of stress and distress, the conversation focused on encouraging Marisa to describe what her preferences were first. In this way, the conversation provided a natural context to reflect to Marisa the form of her sensory preferences and link those forms to their regulating function for her system. Many of her sensory sensitivities could be readily implied by her stated preferences, so Marisa could have the experience of telling the narrative of what works for her instead of the more familiar narrative of what bothers her. For example, instead of starting with questions about the sensory aspects of the school environment that bothered her or were sources of stress for her system, we started with identifying settings in which she experienced regulation of her system and restoration of her energy level. Through this lens, Marisa told her story in her own words, identifying the importance of quiet solitary time when she could engage in activities that were meaningful and pleasurable for her while gaining a respite from social communication and sensory demands. This emphasis on sensory experiences that provide respite and restorative energy helps the adolescent shift from the perspective of internalizing that something is wrong with them to understanding that the demands of their environment are oftentimes out of sync with their experience and needs.

Paying attention to the actions of the adolescent during the diagnostic interview conversation opens up opportunities to discuss sensory regulation routines. Marisa's twisting the strands on her bracelet provided an opportunity to explore the organizing and regulating effects this tactile routine had on her system, along with how she had naturally discovered a way to meet this need in a portable and unassuming way. In this conversational way, Marisa went on to describe her food preferences, sleeping routines, clothing preferences, and key aspects of her environment that she preferred over others. Marisa was encouraged to reveal her story but to tell it in a new, strengths-based way.

This sequence of conversational topics provided Marisa with a positive and regulating experience before the more challenging topics of social and emotional challenges were introduced. For Marisa, as is the case with neurodivergent, complex adolescents, it is important for us diagnostically to share the regulated experience with the young person prior to exploring the more stressful and distressing elements of their complex behavioral and emotional profile. Marisa was able to talk about her experiences navigating the daily group and individual interactions with her peers during the school day. She described how much effort it took her to come across as being a part of conversations when internally she was experiencing panicked feelings and genuine confusion about how what she was saying might come across to others. She disclosed that she experienced anguished hours each day replaying conversations without feeling relief that she was any closer to figuring things out for the next round of social conversations.

The preceding conversation between us, around Marisa's treasured interests, provided the opportunity at this point in the conversation to help Marisa reframe her social and emotional distress. We could talk about the context in which her brain and system experience restorative energy, access to her language, and emotional regulation, and contrast that with the context in which the demands are harder work for her brain to decode, process, and respond to in a fluid and confident way. Marisa's response to this contextualization was an instant recognition of the description of her experience. Marisa was able to directly experience the contrast between her fluid initiating and sharing of a preferred topic-focused conversation, and the harder work and increased response time she required to respond to social and emotional topics introduced by her conversational partner.

Because we started with the invitation to share Marisa's areas of interest, and the availability of sensory fidgets gave her options to engage in self-soothing routines during the conversation, Marisa was able to have an experience with another person where she could be her genuine self as she talked about her interests and showed her creative artwork. This shared experience regarding her interests, paired with a setting in which regulation with fidgets is framed as an adaptive routine accomplished two important goals. The first was to provide Marisa with a positive experience when she shared information about herself and her worldview. Because the interview conversation started with her interests instead of her distress, Marisa was able to experience her comfort level and ease with navigating this type of shared exchange with an actively engaged conversational partner mirroring her perspective. This provided me with a window into Marisa's way of organizing and regulating her system and how she communicated when she is not in a state of stress or distress.

The second was to establish an entry point to introduce the concept of brain style patterns of strengths and differences and to make observations for Marisa to confirm or clarify. Noticing and commenting on the obvious strengths in Marisa's communication skills could then be linked to queries about the degree of effort required by her to participate in conversations. Does the inside experience match her outside behavior? What was the process of engaging in a conversational exchange like for her privately? Marisa, as happens with many autistic adolescent girls, expressed relief that she could discuss the disparities between her external behavior routines and her internal experiences. Which was harder work for her brain and more taxing: sharing information about her interests or following a more conventional social agenda set by others? Marisa was able to disclose her interior experience precisely because she had a conversational partner who observed, experienced, and reflected on her brain style strengths and differences. This could then be contrasted with Marisa's need for supports to extend her participation in conversations about her social and emotional experiences and perspective.

Before we look at Marisa's Brain Style Profile, let's read the narrative summary of her strengths and differences in the three key areas from her MIGDAS-2 diagnostic interview.

Marisa's MIGDAS-2 Descriptive Triangle Summary

Language and Communication

Marisa's Language and Communication profile showed a pattern of strengths as well as some distinctive differences. Strengths for Marisa include her highly developed vocabulary, her well-developed higher-order thinking skills, and her rapid processing of verbal information related to discussing her familiar and preferred areas of interest (describing details related to her range of current interests, including describing aspects of the Japanese manga series she reads and the characters she has developed and draws). Marisa's use of language was most fluent and detailed in her conversational skills when the conversation involved one of her areas of interest. Marisa was consistently thoughtful in response to questions and comments posed by this psychologist, and was able to share her thoughts and experiences, most notably when this psychologist provided distinctive choices of preferred responses instead of asking open-ended questions. Marisa also has highly developed creative thinking skills, as evidenced from her extensive exploration of creative writing, drawing, and music, and her enthusiasm when discussing these areas of interest with this psychologist.

Differences for Marisa in the area of Language and Communication included her distinctive and unvarying way of speaking. Marisa consistently used a serious, deliberately paced cadence, often placing her hands together and bouncing her leg up and down rapidly as she collected her thoughts and took in information from her conversational partner. Marisa spoke about her topics of interest when invited to do so by this psychologist, and her narrative was focused on describing details related to those topics. At times, Marisa had difficulty integrating the use of nonverbal communication functions, including eye gaze and gestures into the conversational exchange in a fluid way.

When the conversational topics were introduced by this psychologist and fell into the category of invitations to discuss social and emotional information and insights, it was more challenging for Marisa to organize her thoughts and provide detailed information. Marisa became notably more prompt-dependent to keep the conversation going than when she was sharing facts and details about one of her beloved areas of thinking and interest. It is important to note that processing incoming social language required additional time for Marisa, and she often replied after a notable wait time. Marisa did best with verbal queries when this psychologist provided a context for the question or comment. Marisa endorsed the observation by this psychologist that participating in extended social conversational exchanges outside of the scope of her areas of preferred interest were harder work for her and less preferred than having conversations that had the expected context of a topic of interest to her. Marisa did best when given binary choices to express her preferences than when she was invited to formulate and express her preferences without that type of conversational scaffolding. Marisa noted when asked, that she finds it stressful in conversations when she is not given the wait time she needs to organize her response before her conversational partner begins talking again. Marisa's ability to describe details related to stories she told about topics for which she had an interest and context (Japanese stories in manga form; drawings she has created) far exceeded her ability to discuss social and emotional topics.

Marisa's pattern of strengths and differences in the area of Language and Communication is commonly seen in highly verbal adolescents with autism spectrum brain style differences.

Social relationships and emotional responses

In the area of social relationships and emotional responses, Marisa displayed a pattern of notable strengths as well as some distinctive differences. Marisa has established strong emotional connections to family members and several peers with whom she shares school experiences in the areas of art and creative writing. She is an appealing, engaging, adolescent girl who, when comfortable with the people and the setting, is able to respond to structured conversational scaffolding and show genuine enjoyment in sharing her interests with others.

Differences for Marisa in the area of social relationships and emotions include her differences in being able to flexibly include a conversational partner in a back-and-forth, fluid shared exchange. As her conversational partner places demands on her, it becomes increasingly more stressful for Marisa to participate in the conversational exchange. Both by report and direct observation, Marisa manages incoming social communication stressors by retreating from the conversation. This takes the form of quietly waiting for her conversational partner to continue. Once Marisa exits a conversation, it is challenging for her to reset her regulation level and re-enter the exchange. During the diagnostic interview conversation, when this psychologist introduced topics inviting Marisa to describe her emotional life, insights into herself, and how she manages stressors, Marisa became visibly stressed, as noted by her increase in moving one leg rapidly up and down, manipulating fidget items in her hands, and quietly reflecting on her response for an extended period of time before making a brief statement. Marisa confirmed that she found it quite helpful to be given extended time in the conversation before a response was required. When this psychologist asked if she could rephrase an observation and did so in a binary choice way, Marisa was able to reengage in the conversational exchange. In social conversations that include social topics, Marisa is currently prompt-dependent on her conversational partner to scaffold and guide the course of the conversation. Marisa quickly fatigues with social input unless it is organized around a shared, preferred activity. She requires time with reduced social communication input to restore her energy level and sustain her focus on less structured interactions. It is important for Marisa to have time to herself to regroup and restore her energy level, and she does best when she can balance regrouping times with times that place high social interaction and work demands on her. Emotionally, Marisa is showing some emerging awareness of the limitations currently in place in her ability to recognize, describe, and express her emotional state. It is important to note that Marisa shows a pattern of internalizing the degree to which social communication demands and emotional reactions distress her. This masking of her stress level, paired with her intelligent and gentle-natured demeanor, makes it challenging at times for others to recognize how hard Marisa is working to manage her stressors in everyday situations. This pattern of masking is oftentimes seen in verbally fluent, highly intelligent adolescents with autism spectrum brain style differences.

Marisa displayed a pattern of strengths and differences in the area of social relationships and emotional responses that is oftentimes seen in adolescent girls with autism spectrum brain style differences.

Sensory Use and Interests

Marisa displayed a pattern of strengths and differences in the area of Sensory Use and Interests. Strengths for Marisa include her highly developed verbal thinking as well as her visual, three-dimensional, systematic, and strategic thinking skills that are readily evident in the way she describes and enacts her interests in drawing, reading, music, and creative writing. She plays close attention to visual details in her artwork and story interests. Marisa engages in solitary activities to regroup and reset her energy level. These activities provide Marisa with calming sensory input and help her manage and regulate when she goes into daily situations that place social, work, and sensory demands on her.

Differences for Marisa include her drive to pursue her areas of preferred interest at a level of depth, and in a solitary way that separates her from engaging in social time with others. It is important to note that for Marisa, pursuing her solitary areas of passionate interest is a source of brain energy, alertness, and engagement. It also serves the function for her of blocking out outside stressors, providing her with a reprieve from the exhausting work of navigating through daily demands. This directly contrasts with the energy drain and stress she experiences when engaging in other life activities, including interacting with others. Managing the relative unpredictability of incoming demands (social, communication, sensory) is stressful for Marisa, and she is just beginning to develop a systematic set of strategies to recognize this pattern and manage it with positive results. As Marisa's stress level and anxiety go up in response to demands, her brain flexibility and ability to recognize and change negative thinking routines goes down. She engages in reactive behavior routines and thinking loops at times, including retreating from the source of demands and telling herself negative global outcomes that increase her level of distress. Throughout the diagnostic interview, Marisa engaged in some sensory-driven body movements and mannerisms, including the use of fidget objects to create systematic tactile input routines while listening to a conversational partner and organizing her responses.

Marisa displayed a pattern of strengths and differences in the area of Sensory Use and Interests that is oftentimes seen in adolescents with autism spectrum brain style differences.

On the MIGDAS-2 Pattern of Observations, Marisa displayed a pattern of responses that were consistent with autism spectrum differences in the three areas of Language and Communication, Social Relationships and Emotional Responses, and Sensory Use and Interests.

Marisa's autism spectrum Brain Style Profile of strengths and differences in each of the three key areas is outlined in Boxes 2.4, 2.5, and 2.6. Each area of her profile describes essential aspects of the autistic brain style in verbally fluent adolescents, allowing you to recognize the pattern in adolescents whom you assess and support in your clinical practice. Marisa's profile includes signifiers that allow the reader to instantly bring her to mind. For Marisa, the signifiers include naming her interests in manga series and drawing, describing the link between her anxiety and her differences in processing incoming information from a conversational partner, and illustrating her distinctive recurrent body movements and mannerisms.

Box 2.4 Marisa's Brain Style Profile

Language and Communication

Strengths

High level of verbally fluency and high level of higher-order concep-
tual thinking
Has developed an excellent vocabulary
Is in the process of developing a repertoire of fluid conversational skills

Enjoys and frequently initiates conversations about her areas of interests, including manga book series, drawing and artwork, creative writing, and other topics

Does best in conversational exchanges when she is given time to formulate her responses and when her conversational partner provides her with a context (offering choices versus open-ended questions)

During brief conversations, Marisa uses and responds to shared exchange communication features, including eye gaze, body orientation, head nods, and gestures

Differences

Speaks with a somewhat deliberate and deliberately paced style

Processing incoming language is hard work for her brain, and she requires additional time to formulate her response to incoming queries and comments when there is not a clear and predictable conversational context and when her anxiety level is triggered

In extended conversations Marisa's ability to use and respond to shared exchange communication features becomes more challenging as she has to expend more energy taking in and processing spoken and unspoken information from her conversational partner

Struggles with listening to her conversational partner and incorporating the perspective of her conversational partner into a fluid back-and-forth flexible exchange

Frequently revisits conversations with her peers after they occur in an effort to decode and understand nuances

---

Box 2.5 Marisa's Brain Style Profile

Social Relationships and Emotions

Strengths

Somewhat serious, thoughtful, and friendly demeanor

Has a genuine desire to connect with others

Has loving and connected relationships with her family

Genuinely enjoys sharing her time and interests with others as long as she also has extensive time to explore those interests alone

Is beginning to develop one or two genuine friendships around a shared interest in manga and art

Has a sense of humor

Showed awareness of the struggles she is experiencing in managing her emotions

Motivated to expand her emotional coping skills repertoire

Differences

Low threshold for incoming social demands outside of those that have a shared interest context

Emerging but limited repertoire of coping strategies to manage her anxiety and reactivity to uncertainty and unexpected outcomes

Emotionally reactive behavior routines include heightened anxiety or agitation as evidenced by withdrawal and shutting down in conversations, repetitive and inflexible thinking, uncertainty about how to interpret conversational nuances and details, and attributing negative qualities to conversational outcomes

Has not yet developed a nuanced vocabulary to identify, express, describe, understand, and manage her emotional states

---

Box 2.6 Marisa's Brain Style Profile

Sensory Use and Interests

Strengths

Enthusiastic and engaged learner who has passionate interests and pursues those interests diligently (art, reading, creative writing)

Learns and retains facts exceptionally well and excels at schoolwork

Loves to learn and engage in creative projects

Attends to visual details and retains information well when encoded visually and when there is an established visual context

Has developed a range of age-appropriate interests and genuinely enjoys engaging in those activities, gaining skills as she goes

Systematic thinker who enjoys learning facts and information as well as applying skills in creative projects through her independent pursuit of her interests

Differences

Relatively low threshold for incoming demands (social conversations, open-ended conversational overtures) requiring systematic, planned, and extended brain reset breaks

Internalizes and masks stressors related to incoming demands

Relies on routines with body movements and a retreat from speech to manage the stress inherent in social conversations

Has a well-established routine of isolated activities (drawing, writing, researching areas of interest)

When her reactivity, agitation, or anxiety is triggered, Marisa loses her ability to express herself clearly, engaging in a routine of shutting down her critical thinking abilities and making assumptions about negative outcomes or reactions from others

Recurrent body movements and mannerisms include twisting a bracelet cord while tilting her head to one side, raising and lowering her shoulders, rapidly bouncing one leg up and down, and twisting a strand of hair below her right ear

Defining therapeutic mirroring in the autistic diagnostic conversation

Let's take a few moments to discuss the therapeutic aspects of mirroring the child or adolescent with whom we are engaged in a diagnostic or support conversation. As clinicians, when we enter into the interaction with a neurodivergent individual with the mindful intention of respectfully taking their perspective, we do so by aligning ourselves to be in sync with the way in which that individual communicates their way of being in the world. Using the Descriptive Triangle framework, we can carefully notice how the child or adolescent enters our setting and meet the individual there. Our diligent invitations to explore objects with interesting sensory properties and interesting topics communicates that the exchange is a fit for the individual's social communication style and their sensory use and interests preferences. This is contrasted with their more common experience of being expected to follow the adult's social communication and task demand agendas.

Mirroring provides the entry point that allows us to actively recognize, understand, and share that individual's life experience. By definition, clinicians are diagnostically and therapeutically focused on observing patterns. The process of mirroring adds another nuanced and layered path to connecting with and appreciating the individual's singular way of organizing and regulating in the world. It helps us enter into the dynamic and interactive exchange with the child or adolescent in a shared way. We are guided not only to pay attention to patterns in a systematic way but also to genuinely appreciate and share the function of those patterns. When we mirror the individual child or adolescent, we gain a richly layered understanding and appreciation of the individual's worldview. We also provide that child or adolescent with the exceptional experience of acceptance and shared enjoyment.

How does mirroring contrast with the process of masking or camouflaging? When we mirror, we are engaging in the act of taking the perspective of the child or adolescent. We attentively absorb their style and reflect that back to them as we share their approach and response to us and their surroundings. This creates connections, as we are adapting to the child or adolescent and noting the dimensions involved in truly sharing that individual's worldview. The degree to which the child or adolescent depends on us to adapt and sync up with their style gives us a profoundly valuable understanding of their patterns of strengths and differences and the ways in which they organize and regulate when managing exchanges with people and the world around them. When the child or adolescent experiences this shared connection, a bond of trust is established with the clinician. The bond of trust is based on their experience of the clinician as a person who understands, accepts, and appreciates them. When the clinician then makes observations about the individual's brain style and their strengths and differences, the way in which the clinician describes that individual's experiences visibly resonates with them. As in Malik's case, when he gave me the "thumbs up" sign in response to describing his reactivity as having a fundamentally sensory foundation as contrasted with social intent. As in Marisa's case, when she was able to have the shared experience with a trusted adult who was able to notice and describe the contrast between her ready access to language when discussing her beloved manga and the hard work it was for her to manage conversation around social and emotional topics.

Masking or camouflaging is a process that involves hard work for the child's or adolescent's brain. The individual expends energy in social interactions as they watch and listen to what others say and do and try to respond in real time while experiencing increasing levels of stress and distress. The integral feature of this lived experience is the oftentimes tremendous disparity between the individual's external behavior and their internal experience. As clinicians, when we are able to mirror and appreciate the child's or adolescent's worldview, we provide opportunities to explore masking as it relates to each child's lived experience. It allows us to contextualize masking or camouflaging in strengths-based terms as an adaptive response to stressful social demands. Understanding masking as an adaptive coping tool that comes with a high cost to the adolescent's well-being leads to an appreciation of their lived experience contrast between internal experiences and external patterns of behavior. This in turn provides a pathway for that individual to find relief from the stress and distress created by masking routines through the development of positive support strategies they self-determine to be a fit for their singular and complex brain style.

Co-occurring conditions and differential diagnosis considerations in children and adolescents

Before we move on to discuss the autism brain style of strengths and differences in adults, let's talk about a few key considerations regarding co-occurring conditions and differential diagnosis in children and adolescents. Although it is beyond the scope of this book to provide an in-depth review of conditions beyond the autistic brain style, we will discuss ways to navigate through the diagnostic question of co-occurring conditions to some extent.

Rubenstein et al. (2018) reviewed patterns of co-occurring medical conditions and autism, providing four distinctive groupings for the types of conditions that commonly co-occur with the autistic brain style pattern of strengths and differences: 1) developmental (differences and/or delays in the areas of attention, language, learning, and developmental skills); 2) psychiatric conditions (mood, behavior, and thinking differences); 3) neurological conditions (seizures, epilepsy, hearing or vision loss, cerebral palsy, Tourette's syndrome); 4) genetic differences that are possible causative conditions (tuberous sclerosis, Down syndrome, Fragile X syndrome).

As clinicians working with autistic individuals and their families, it is important to recognize that autism almost always co-occurs with additional differences. Familiarity with the range of different developmental, psychiatric, neurological, and genetic conditions that are often a part of the individual's complex developmental and behavioral profile is essential. At the same time, developing a compelling way to describe the autistic brain style is a fundamental skill set that allows us to recognize autism as it coexists with other forms of neurodivergence. We want to be able to describe all of the neurodivergent pieces to reveal each person's complex story. For our purposes, we will focus on ways to describe developmental and psychiatric conditions as they co-occur or differentiate from the autistic brain style.

What are the current rates of conditions that co-occur with autism? ADHD occurs with autism at a rate of between 50% and 70% of the time (Hours et al., 2022), while psychiatric conditions, including mood and behavioral challenges, co-occur with autism with a 95% co-occurrence rate (Mosner et al., 2019). Autistic children also experience the specific adverse experience of childhood of bullying at a three to four times higher rate than the general childhood population. At the same time, they are not shown to be overrepresented in the government child social services population in terms of referral for child maltreatment (Hoover & Kaufman, 2018). Learning differences, specifically the mastery of developmental milestones at a slower than expected rate, co-occur with the autistic brain style at a currently reported rate of 37% with one in 36 children identified as autistic (Etyemez et al., 2022; Maenner et al., 2023). As we become better able to recognize and describe the behavior patterns associated with the range of possible co-occurring conditions that are often present along with the autistic brain style, we improve our ability to reveal and tell each child's lived experience story with all of its complexities and nuances.

Now let's describe how ADHD and the autistic brain style differ and overlap.

The ADHD brain style differences can be depicted in a Descriptive Triangle distinctive from the autistic triangle of strengths and differences by identifying the key features of attention, focus, and activity. We can identify the child's ADHD patterns of strengths and differences in the way in which they organize their attention and learning, how they manage the executive functioning brain features of organization and planning, and how they manage their activity level and sensory input. Conceptualizing the ADHD brain style in this way can be a helpful way to organize the way in which we reveal the story of this distinctive developmental pattern of strengths and differences. The Descriptive Triangle for ADHD brain style differences is depicted in Figure 2.1.

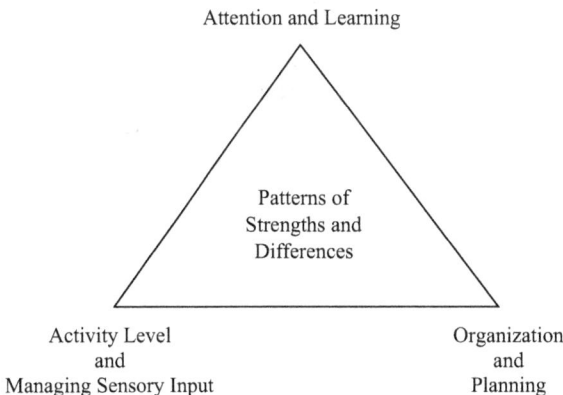

Figure 2.1 The ADHD Descriptive Triangle.

After you have a framework to discuss the ADHD brain style in contrast with the autistic brain style, the challenge becomes finding ways to recognize and describe how the two brain styles overlap in many of the children and adolescents for whom you are providing assessment and support services. What are some descriptive ways to recognize and talk about the ADHD behavioral profile and to contrast this with the autistic behavioral profile?

Both brain style differences affect how the child organizes and focuses when engaging with their surroundings. One way to think and talk about how the two neurodevelopmental brain styles differ in terms of how the person's focus is affected, is to look at the *locus* of focus. The ADHD brain organizes and orients to the environment by seeking out novel input. This is paired with challenges in screening out or prioritizing incoming information or input. The ADHD brain searches for the next source of input. Once novel input is absorbed, the brain asks: What's next? The key here is novel input, and the routine is seeking out novel input. Let's contrast this with the autistic brain's pattern of organizing and orienting to the environment. The autistic brain scans the environment for objects that fit into the person's internal autism-driven agenda for self-regulation purposes. The brain asks: What is available here that will help me create and maintain a predictable routine which will feel good and block out stress? The key here is finding things in the environment to create and maintain a predictable routine. We can think of this as the sensory agenda for the ADHD and autistic brain styles.

What about the social drive agendas for each of the different brain styles? Both styles include children who initiate social exchanges with others. The ADHD brain that does not co-occur with the autistic brain includes a pattern of shared exchanges that takes in and responds to the conversational or play partner. Reciprocity and extension are present, as the brain is able to simultaneously process incoming social and language overtures, and use social and language overtures in a fluid way. The autistic brain relies on initiating in the same or in a similar way each time (creating and maintaining a routine) while showing it is hard work for their brain to simultaneously use and respond to social overtures from their conversational or play partner.

There are two important considerations in looking for the distinctions between the ADHD and the autistic brain style in the area of social drive agendas. The first is to understand that the differences become apparent in the absence of familiar prompts or routines provided by the adult. When we purposefully limit our use of routines, we are able to observe how the child fills in the existing space. The ADHD child invites us to join them in their exploration of their surroundings and checks in on and acknowledges our responses. The autistic child shows us how challenging it is for them to engage in shared exchanges, extend topics or play initiated by their partner, and shift flexibly from their agenda to follow the agenda of others. The second consideration becomes a priority when we are meeting children who have the combined brain styles of ADHD and autism. The ADHD sensory routines are immediately apparent, as the child seeks out novel input as a way to orient to their surroundings. But wait for it. As the time together extends and the autistic brain fatigues with social communication demands, the distinctive patterns of creating and maintaining routines to block out incoming sources of stress, and the hard work of sharing exchanges become more pronounced and recognizable.

Autism Spectrum Disorder and/or Attention Deficit Hyperactivity Disorder?

Sensory Locus of Focus

Autism:
Scans the environment for objects to create and maintain predictable routines that fit in the child's internal autism-driven agenda for self-regulation purposes

ADHD:
Orients to the environment by seeking out novel input
Challenging for the child to prioritize or screen out information

Social Drive

Autism:
The child initiates social overtures in the same or similar way each time (creating and maintaining a routine) while showing it is hard work for their brain to simultaneously use and respond to social overtures from their conversational or play partner

ADHD:
The child fluidly engages in shared social exchanges that include reciprocity and extension, as the brain is able to simultaneously

process incoming social and language overtures while using their own social and language overtures

Co-occurring Patterns of Behavior

Both brain styles include children who have a social drive and initiate social interactions with others

Children with combined brain styles initially engage with their surroundings showing the ADHD sensory pattern outlined above before the autistic pattern of creating and maintaining predictable routines becomes apparent

As the autistic brain fatigues in response to social communication demands, the autistic drive to establish and maintain routines takes precedence, while shifting flexibly from the child's sensory routine and agenda to follow the agenda of their conversational and play partner becomes increasingly more challenging

How do intellectual and learning brain style differences and the autistic brain style differ and overlap?

Intellectual and learning brain style differences include the range from global delays in acquiring developmental and adaptive skills and abilities to specific learning differences. The Descriptive Triangle depicted below identifies three key features of learning and cognitive differences in development: the degree to which modes of learning require adjustment to match the child's learning level; the specific patterns of differences that are present in the way the child processes information and experiences fatigue in response to cognitive input; and the degree to which the child displays patterns of differences in the way in which they retain and recall learned information. When we assess and support autistic children who are also developing with the neurodivergence of cognitive brain style differences, it is helpful for us to be able to describe how the two sets of differences affect the child's worldview. When we are making a differential diagnosis between cognitive and adaptive differences either with or without the addition of the autistic brain style, there are three key differences to note. Figure 2.2 shows the Descriptive Triangle for intellectual and learning differences, contextualizing the three key features.

Modes of Learning Adjusted to Learning Level

Patterns of

Strengths and

Differences

Retention
and
Recall of Information

Processing Information
and
Fatigue Level

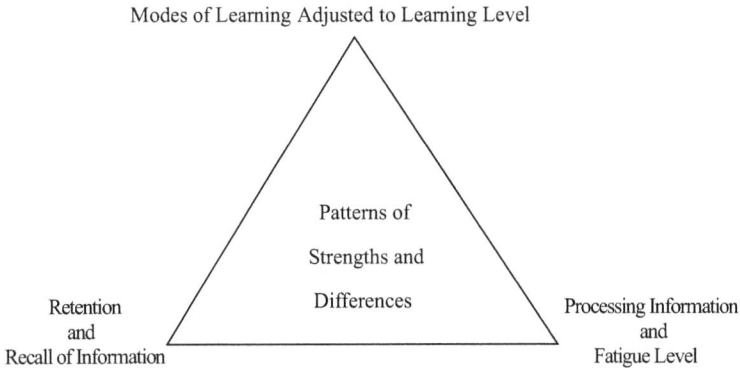

Figure 2.2 The Intellectual and Learning Differences Descriptive Triangle.

The first key difference is the pattern of delays in development. When we identify that a child is learning with developmental delays, the child is acquiring skills and knowledge at a slower than expected rate but in an expected sequence of development. We can describe the child as a person who is learning at a rate that requires adjusting the teaching approach to fit their learning level. We anticipate pacing the instruction to allow the child to process and retain the information being taught. We will know that the child will acquire information best when we consider the fatigue level the child experiences when their brain is required to take in, apply, and retain information. The key elements here are the pacing of acquiring skills paired with learning skills in the expected developmental sequence. Along with this learning profile, the child will show us their innate drive to explore the world through social connections. In other words, the child's social development is like that of a younger child: developing at a slower pace than expected but progressing in a developmentally expected way. The child will also show us patterns of sensory exploration of materials and their surroundings. Their sensory patterns of behavior differ from the autistic brain style patterns of sensory use and interests in that sensory exploration is directly linked to the child's level of development.

Now that we've described the learning pattern for children who require additional time and repeated practice to acquire their developmental sequence of skills and abilities, let's add the autistic brain style dimension to that child's learning profile. The child with a dual diagnosis shows us that they are not only learning and retaining skills and information at a slower than expected rate, but they also often show us a pronounced uneven pattern of development. One or more skill areas may be at or above the child's age level, while other skills are developing at a much younger age level. In the area of social development, the dual diagnosis child organizes their world around creating and maintaining predictable routines with objects of interest and/or with their recurrent body movements and mannerisms. The child's object-focused world includes distinctive sensory preferences and sensitivities. In contrast, children who are developing with specific learning disabilities without the autistic brain style will show us a recognizable and expected social level of engagement, the development of their personal social narrative, and a pattern of expected responses to sensory aspects of their environment.

That brings us to the overlap and differentiation between the autistic brain style and conditions that fall under the category of psychiatric, mood, or behavioral differences.

For children and adolescents who have acquired language and are developing with skills and abilities at or above the expected level for their age, there are some key considerations for us as clinicians in identifying autism as a fundamental diagnostic piece alongside psychiatric, mood, or behavioral conditions. Mazefsky et al. (2012), reported that in a study of verbally fluent adolescents receiving their initial autism diagnosis, 77% had at least one prior psychiatric diagnosis and 60% had two or more previously given psychiatric diagnoses. The key to differentiating between the overlapping symptoms and to revealing the most compelling and comprehensive story is to understand the autism framework and apply it in your diagnostic and therapeutic work with the children and adolescents you support in your clinical practice. Understanding how sensory and social communication differences affect the mood and emotional landscape for the child or adolescent tells a fundamentally different narrative than labeling that individual as anxious or depressed. When we describe the child or adolescent so others can understand what lies behind their struggles, we provide a foundation to develop meaningful supports for that individual and their family.

Applying the descriptive language framework to trauma and autism can be helpful as well. The formation of trauma responses originates in external circumstances or experiences. The adverse childhood experiences profoundly affect the emotional well-being of the child. The child's social and emotional development are disrupted in serious and deep ways, resulting in behavior patterns that can overlap with those observed in autistic children. In contrast, the formation of autistic responses originates in the internal experiences of how the child's brain and system are developing, and the gap between what they need and what their environment requires of them. This in itself is a form of trauma. How do we determine whether the child is experiencing the external genesis (trauma), internal genesis (autistic brain style), or both? We discover the subtleties for each child or adolescent as we apply the tools of systematically inviting the child to share their worldview with us and see where that takes us together.

A common dilemma for clinicians new to assessing and supporting autistic children and adolescents is to struggle with the distinction between the autistic brain style and trauma, or complex trauma history and experiences, including attachment challenges (McKenzie & Dallos, 2017). Many of the behaviors present in a similar pattern, including limited use of eye gaze, and what Hoover et al. (2018) described as "frozen watchfulness." When you provide a child who has experienced significant trauma with the sensory-based autistic entry point during your diagnostic or treatment exchanges with the child, you are by definition creating a safe environment, essential for children and adolescents who have experienced complex trauma. What follows in the absence of the autistic brain style is a social and emotional entry point that you will both recognize and experience with that child or adolescent. This entry point allows you to better observe and experience the autistic behavioral profile and either make a co-occurring condition diagnosis or differential diagnosis that you can feel confident about because you have described that child and their lived experience.

There are so many more things we could discuss about co-occurring conditions, but now you should have an starting point to explore your autism conversations with the children and adolescents in your practice so that you can better identify their complex developmental and behavioral profiles and reveal their lived experience stories.

Let's turn our attention to how to think, talk, and write about the autistic brain style in adults in Chapter 3.

References

Etyemez, S., Esler, A., Kini, A., Tsai, P-C., DiRienzo, M., Maenner, M., & Lee, L-C. (2022). The role of intellectual disability with autism spectrum disorder and the documented co-occurring conditions: A population-based study. *Autism Res*. Dec;15(12):2399–2408.

Hoover, D. W., & Kaufman, J. (2019). Adverse childhood experiences in children with autism spectrum disorder. *Curr Opin Psychiatry*. Mar;31(2):128–132. PMID: 29206686; PMCID: PMC6082373.

Maenner, M. J., Warren. Z., Williams A. R., et al. (2023). Prevalence and characteristics of autism spectrum disorder among children aged 8 years — Autism and Developmental Disabilities Monitoring Network, 11 Sites, United States, 2020. *MMWR Surveill Summ*. 72(No. SS-2):1–14. doi: http://dx.doi.org/10.15585/mmwr.ss7202a1.

Mazefsky, C. A., Oswald, D. P., Day, T. N., Eack, S. M., Minshew, N. J., Lainhart, J. E. (2012). ASD, a psychiatric disorder, or both? Psychiatric diagnoses in adolescents with high-functioning ASD. *J Clin Child Adolesc Psychol.* 41(4):516–23. PMID: 22642847; PMCID: PMC3601822.

McKenzie, R., & Dallos, R. (2017). Autism and attachment difficulties: Overlap of symptoms, implications and innovative solutions. *Clinical Child Psychology and Psychiatry, 22*(4), 632–648.

Monteiro, M., & Stegall, S. (2018). *Monteiro Interview Guidelines for Diagnosing the Autism Spectrum, Second Edition.* Torrance, CA: WPS Publishing.

Mosner, M. G., Kinard, J. L., Shah, J. S., McWeeny, S., Greene, R. K., Lowery, S. C., Mazefsky, C. A., & Dichter, G. S. (2019). Rates of co-occurring psychiatric disorders in autism spectrum disorder using the mini international neuropsychiatric interview. *J Autism Dev Disord.* Sep;49(9):3819–3832. https://doi:10.1007/s10803-019-04090-1. PMID: 31175504; PMCID: PMC6669096.

Rubenstein E., Schieve L., Wiggins L., Rice C., Van Naarden Braun, K., Christensen. D., Durkin, M., Daniels J., & Lee L.C. (2018). Trends in documented co-occurring conditions in children with autism spectrum disorder, 2002–2010. *Res Dev Disabil.* Dec;83:168–178. doi: 10.1016/j.ridd.2018.08.015. PMID: 30227350; PMCID: PMC6741291.Maenne

3 Reveal the story

Adults across the lifespan – Morgan, Miranda, and Matt

In this chapter, we'll explore ways for you to better recognize and reveal the autistic Brain Style Profile of strengths and differences in adults across the lifespan. As clinicians like you routinely integrate the autistic adult brain style diagnostic question into your mental health assessment process, adults seeking clinical support for one or more identified mental health conditions will increasingly encounter having their lived experiences recognized and contextualized in a neuro-affirming framework.

If your clinical practice focuses on supporting adults, you are helping bridge the wide gap between adults seeking autistic assessments and their access to clinicians who are able to provide neuro-informed care. The autistic Brain Style Profile of strengths and differences in verbally fluent adults is often either missed or misdiagnosed (Fusar-Poli et al., 2022; Kentrou et al., 2024). A common experience for adults seeking an autism diagnosis is to have been previously given one or more psychiatric diagnoses, including both personality and mood conditions (Jadav & Bal, 2022). Social anxiety and mental health outcomes are significantly improved through the exploration of a positive autistic identity and access to a community with an understanding of autism spectrum brain style differences (Cooper et al., 2023). The work you do in recognizing the adult autism profile and guiding adults through their diagnostic process profoundly changes lives in terms of improving mental health outcomes.

Consideration of autism as a possible differential diagnosis for adults who seek out mental health supports can lead to a powerful neuro-affirming and life-changing reframe for understanding the years of struggle that often characterize the adult autistic individual's lived experience. Verbally fluent women (McCrossin, 2022) and individuals with an ADHD diagnosis (Lau-Zhu et al., 2019) often come to the formal diagnosis of their autism spectrum brain style well into adulthood instead of during their childhood or adolescent years. Physicians (Bell, 2023; Shaw et al., 2023) as well as clinicians who provide autism assessment and support services in their

DOI: 10.4324/9781003532576-5

clinical practices (Welsh et al., 2022) are included in the population of autistic adults receiving a diagnosis during their adult years.

Although more clinicians are beginning to understand and recognize the intersectionality between the autistic brain style and gender and sexual diversity, the assessment and support needs for this population of adults far exceed the availability of and access to experienced clinicians equipped to provide neuro-informed care. Transgender, nonbinary, and gender-diverse individuals are up to six times more likely to also be autistic (Stokes, 2018; Warrier et al., 2020; Gratton et al., 2023). The vulnerability of this population of adults in terms of mental health needs is significant, and access to supportive and neuro-informed care is greatly needed.

Why do adults seek out their autistic assessment process? Let's explore four likely entry points you'll see in your clinical practice as you provide adult autism assessment and support services. The first of four common entry points for adults seeking an autism assessment is *self-discovery*. Although self-discovery is the entry point for adults across the lifespan, it often happens for young adults as they explore other aspects of their personal identity. Oftentimes, discovering their autistic brain style provides a vital and missing piece in the young adult's understanding of why their narrative includes a lifelong theme of stress and distress in their response to life events and demands that diverges from the experiences of others around them. A common experience for adults across the lifespan who have not yet had their autistic brain style identified is receiving one or more mental health diagnoses. This often leads to the adult's participation in therapies and to taking medications based on those diagnoses without the corresponding relief of positive changes in their level of ongoing intrapersonal and interpersonal patterns of stress and distress. Asking the autism question and going through the diagnostic process with a knowledgeable clinician fundamentally changes the individual's story. The missing dimension of understanding the brain-based reasons behind ongoing struggles and describing the person's singular life experiences through the lens of autistic patterns of brain style strengths and differences shifts the narrative in a neuro-informed and empowering way. The ambiguity and holding pattern of not quite knowing how to understand and tell their most compelling life story is given a genuine sense of closure. This allows the adult to move out of their state of uncertainty and step into their self-determined progression toward creating the quality of life that fits their needs.

The second entry point for adults seeking an autism diagnosis is when they *recognize the profile in themselves when one or more of their children receives a diagnosis*. When one or more children in a family receive an autism brain style diagnosis and the child's patterns of strengths and differences are described by the clinician, the parent may recognize their own story. When you guide a parent through the process of revealing their autistic brain style patterns and when their brain style strengths and differences are described in a way that resonates with their lived experience, a powerful shift occurs that affects that parent on multiple levels. Behavior patterns and emotional states they have grappled with now have a context that makes sense. You can support the adult in reframing their current and lifelong patterns through the autistic and sensory brain style lens of strengths and differences, and link this understanding with ways in which they can support their needs and those of their autistic children within the family. When you uncover the autistic brain style story for adults, it allows you to work with the adult as they self-determine ways to better appreciate and benefit from their unique worldview and life experiences and how to apply that understanding to themselves, their partner or partners, their parenting roles, and their vocational life.

The third entry point you may experience when you offer autistic assessments and supports for adults is somewhat different from the first two we discussed. Adults may come to you for an autism assessment after *a family member recognizes the profile and encourages the adult to pursue an evaluation*. An adult fitting this description would not be as likely to consult with you unless urged to do so by an important person in their intimate circle. However, the fact that they made the appointment and are meeting with you tells the narrative of self-determination for change. Oftentimes the adult's partner or family member encourages the adult to seek the assessment process by framing it as part of a path toward necessary change to either improve or sustain the relationship moving forward. When asked what brought them to the meeting with you, the adult may tell you that it was a partner's idea and that they are exploring the assessment explicitly for their partner's benefit rather than for themselves. This initial resistance to exploring an autism diagnosis provides the starting point for your diagnostic conversation. Encouraging the adult to tell you the compelling story that is their current story to make sense out of their social communication, emotional regulation, and sensory differences allows you to share the adult's perspective. When the adult experiences your openness to hearing their narrative without pressure to apply the autistic label, you will notice a decrease in the adult's safeguarding of the story that led to this exact conversation with you to discuss possible autism spectrum brain style differences. When you then begin to rename their narrative using descriptive language that highlights the form and function of the adult's behavior patterns and pair that with inviting the adult to consistently confirm or clarify your observations without using labeling language (e.g., autism), there is room to explore alternative narratives, including the autistic narrative first recognized by others in the adult's life. Through this systematic person-centered diagnostic interview process (Monteiro & Stegall, 2018), the emerging story is often the story of autism spectrum patterns of brain style strengths and differences. In some cases a different story emerges. In either case, the adult experiences a setting in which their habitual resistance and objections to well-meaning input can be set aside. Their observable self-determination to change aspects of their life can now be paired with an exploration of a different way to understand their own story. This leads to discussions of the possibility of changing things to make them better for the adult as well as for the relationship that initially prompted them to meet with you.

The fourth entry point for an adult autistic assessment occurs when *the clinician recognizes the autistic profile as it emerges during the therapy process.* Adults who seek therapy to address life issues, including the effects of complex trauma and adverse life experiences, mood regulation differences, relationship challenges, and addictions, to name a few, may also be autistic. How does one differentiate whether the autistic brain style should be considered as part of the adult's profile and story? Oftentimes when a clinician begins to notice divergent patterns in their therapeutic conversations that they associate with autistic differences, the clinician then introduces the possibility in the context of the therapeutic dialogue. The clinician may then refer the adult to an autism specialist for assessment. Familiarizing yourself with the neuro-informed framework for recognizing and describing the adult presentation of the autism spectrum brain style of strengths and differences will enhance your ability to support autistic adults in your clinical practice, including formalizing the diagnostic process for adults as part of your ongoing therapeutic support.

Morgan's path to understanding her autism spectrum brain style

So what does the autistic diagnostic process look like in a young adult? Let's explore the diagnostic process with Morgan, a 20-year-old nonbinary person who used the pronouns she/her and they/them. She had gone through the initial transition with her gender identity during adolescence. Morgan's family was supportive of them after traveling a lengthy path of learning about gender identity and expression alongside Morgan. Morgan initiated her autism assessment process after exploring the question about her possible autistic brain style and discussing her observations with her parents and friends. Motivators for Morgan to pursue her evaluation included gaining a better understanding of herself, managing her almost ever-present underlying sense of anxiety, and obtaining tools to help her identify school accommodations as she prepared to start her university program.

Morgan had two long-standing diagnoses prior to pursuing her autism assessment. Both her attention and focusing issues (Attention Deficit/ Hyperactivity Disorder, Primarily Inattentive Type) and her constantly recurring bouts of intense anxiety (Generalized Anxiety Disorder) were treated primarily with medications. Morgan was highly verbally fluent and was considered gifted, applying her skills in the areas of art design, computer graphics, and creative writing.

Keep in mind that although Morgan presented with a complex developmental and behavioral profile that contained many elements, her autistic brain style patterns were the focus of the MIGDAS-2 diagnostic interview conversation.

The MIGDAS-2 adult diagnostic interview protocol (Monteiro & Stegall, 2018) was used as the central part of Morgan's adult autism evaluation process. The MIGDAS-2 adult diagnostic interview protocol supports clinicians in structuring a diagnostic interview conversation in which the adult is encouraged to talk about their areas of preferred interest while the clinician comments on patterns related to the form and function of behavior preferences. Throughout the conversational exchange, information is gathered in the areas of the adult's social communication, emotional regulation, and sensory patterns of preferences and sensitivities, both currently and by history. The systematic qualitative MIGDAS-2 Pattern of Observations is then laid out using the Descriptive Triangle to reveal a pattern that is either consistent with the autistic Brain Style Profile or not.

When asked her preference, Morgan self-determined to complete the diagnostic conversation independently of her parents but requested that they participate in a separate interview to provide their perspective and input. Morgan, her parents, and her long-standing best friend completed an adult autism behavior rating scale, the *Social Responsiveness Scale-Second Edition* (Constantino & Gruber, 2012) in addition to Morgan's participation in the MIGDAS-2 adult diagnostic interview process.

Revealing Morgan's autism story: her MIGDAS-2 diagnostic interview conversation

Morgan, a person with a slight build and voluminous shoulder-length wavy hair, was clearly eager to participate in the diagnostic interview conversation. Throughout the conversation, Morgan engaged in her signature pattern of placing her hands up to her hair as she gathered her thoughts and took in information. At various times during the conversation, Morgan picked up and manipulated an aluminum alloy metal infinity cube (a fidget object that can be folded over and over again, amplifying patterns of finger movements), and a wooden Playable Art ball with a rainbow spectrum of colors (a set of connected, movable smooth wooden balls), creating and maintaining predictable tactile and movement routines.

After Morgan outlined her main concerns at the time as centered on anxiety related to being able to manage the organizational demands of her college program and independent living situation, Morgan reflected on her lifelong pattern of becoming intensely interested in exploring a topic of interest in extensive detail, and then moving on to another area of preferred interest, leading to worries about being able to sustain an interest in a way that results in the high degree of mastery and skills development required in completing a university degree program. She noted that she had a long-term goal of completing her art design degree and working in art design or computer science while pursuing her interest in developing creative projects outside of a work setting.

Morgan was invited to reflect on the activities she enjoyed, including talking about the balance between shared activities and solitary ones. Beloved shared activities included her *Dungeons & Dragons* group. She noted that when she was younger, she enjoyed playing Magic the Gathering and collecting the game cards. Morgan noted that she had developed a solid group of friends who shared overlapping interests. She described how her interest in role-playing games led her to meet others who not only shared her interests but who had also explored their gender and sexual identities. In this way, she described how she had found compatible social pathways for herself. Other interests named by Morgan included drawing and writing creative stories related to her originally developed characters, along with exploring electronic music and other genres. Morgan added that she assiduously avoided activities that involved physicality.

Morgan collected her thoughts as she systematically manipulated the infinity cube. "Technically, I would describe myself as an ambivert. In other words, I have a tight group of close friends and really enjoy being with them, mostly one or two at a time. At the same time, I really need my alone time. That's when I draw, write, and do my deep dives into whatever I'm into at the time."

Morgan's creation of her tactile and movement routines with the fidget objects provided the entry point to notice these routines and to invite her to describe her experience. She reflected that the objects provided a source of reliably soothing her system, and commented that she was already thinking about getting the infinity cube to use for that purpose. We discussed the sensory aspects involved in her creation and maintenance of the routines, noting the tactile and movement elements. Morgan made the independent observation that she usually touches her hair as she talks, a pattern she became more aware of when her friends noted the routine.

"Yes, one of my autistic friends commented on my hair touching and connected it with their signature finger tapping routine...really got me thinking about all of my different habits or idiosyncrasies."

This led us to an exploration of Morgan's sensory preferences and sensitivities. She emphasized the importance to her of having the time and space to explore her brain's need to pay close attention to visual details, and to focus on them for as long as necessary. This led to Morgan's endorsing the organizing and regulating functions provided for her system when she is able to be in charge of when she shifts from her agenda to take in the agenda of others, and is why she uses headphones to manage auditory input, and why she sets boundaries around food and clothing types and textures.

"When food and sound dimensions collide, wow…it takes a lot to make sure I keep my foods separated, and when I have to share a meal, listening to the sound of people while they eat, really, it's too much." Morgan paused. "Actually, three dimensions: visual, tactile and auditory…"

This allowed me to summarize the pattern of sensory preferences Morgan was laying out in her narrative. Each time Morgan described her lived experience in the areas of sensory use and interest, social communication, and emotional regulation, the interview format allowed time for reflection back to Morgan of what had been said. The language of brain style strengths and differences, of organizing her system, of regulating her system, and of blocking out stress could be introduced, and Morgan was then invited to either confirm of clarify whether the descriptions matched her experience.

"So, Morgan, when you describe your sensory preferences, they definitely include low input auditory for unexpected sounds, and time to explore visual details and content before meeting the demands of the agenda of others, is that accurate?"

This identification by Morgan of the sensory "dimensions" that governed her life provided an opportunity to compare and contrast what sensory elements helped her system stay organized and regulated with the elements that triggered her levels of stress and distress, including the spiking of her anxiety and agitation levels. Morgan noted that she rarely becomes angry or agitated, but reflected that the triggers for agitation include reaching her threshold for managing sensory input and demands, not feeling heard or understood, and when she worked on solving a problem but was unable to complete the process. When Morgan reflected that being in large groups was fatiguing for her and resulted in her leaving events after a brief period of time, it provided an opportunity to amplify how her understanding of her sensory needs can help her plan for events that tax her system so that she can go into the group activity with energy and a plan, participate, and then recoup by engaging in a preferred activity in a restorative setting.

Sensory-based materials that are a good fit for exploration with adults:

Lifidia or The Fube Infinity cube
Brass Fingertip Gyro with decompression benefits
Playable ART ball, Rainbow 20
Playable ART Angle
Roger von Oech's magnetic design pieces that create varying
    patterns
Nee Doh deep pressure cubes
Magnetic putty pebbles
Sensory stress balls with varying textures
Sensory fidget materials such as Monkey noodles, popper silicone
    shapes and spinners
Invite adults to share or describe their preferred self-soothing fidgets

In the area of social communication, as the conversation unfolded, Morgan engaged in the pattern of differences that characterize autistic adult exchanges. These included a pattern of interrupting and overriding her conversational partner to continue her narrative. Morgan also showed the pattern of differences in the time she required to shift from her narrative to take in and respond to her conversational partner. As she visibly struggled with simultaneously managing her verbal and unspoken communication features and the incoming communication used by her conversational partner, it became possible to stop the conversation to point out the patterns. Again, when the diagnostic interview focuses on inviting the adult to share and expand on their narrative, the social communication and sensory patterns are revealed, and you have an opportunity to name the observed patterns using descriptive language. As you name the observed patterns, you consistently invite the adult to confirm or clarify whether your description of the observed patterns matches their lived experience.

Because our diagnostic conversation started with the invitation for Morgan to share her story about her interests, strengths, and competencies while exploring interesting tactile fidget objects, when we began to explore her narrative surrounding her long-standing struggles with feeling a sense of dread and anxiety, we were able to explore her experiences around anxiety within a context. We could compare and contrast her experienced levels of anxiety when she was engaged in a conversation with a familiar context with a conversational partner who both listened attentively and followed her lead, and when she was recalling and sharing information about her emotional states. The level of vocabulary available to Morgan around themes with facts and details readily associated with an organized system far exceeded her vocabulary to express nuances regarding fluctuations in her emotional state. We were able to explore those contrasting experiences, and this led to Morgan's ability to remain emotionally regulated during this difficult part of the conversation.

Because she was able to remain in her regulated, thinking brain, Morgan was able to identify the patterns of words and actions she typically experiences when she becomes anxious, stressed, or distressed. This allowed for a reframe of those experiences as patterns, or routines, that were maintained to help her manage when her stress level was triggered. We could also explore and identify the sources of stress for Morgan as being in the possible categories of interpersonal, intrapersonal, or environmental (sensory input). This contextualization of her anxiety placed the conversation into the familiar and helpful category of a conversation with systematic components to be identified, explained, and understood in terms of form and function. Like making a *Dungeons & Dragons* strategic plan, or structuring a creative story, Morgan had the experience of using her well-developed analytical skills to revisit her long-standing and seemingly unsolvable anxiety dilemma.

Toward the end of the diagnostic interview conversation, Morgan was encouraged to identify three qualities to describe herself. She touched her hair as she gathered her thoughts. "Well, four actually, since I've already described myself to you as an ambivert…thoughtful, friendly, and…quietly ambitious."

The adult interview with Morgan's parents provided additional information in the three key areas, including their recollections of Morgan as a child. Their input supported and supplemented the information gathered during the diagnostic interview with Morgan. Her parents added that at home, Morgan continued the pattern from childhood of becoming somewhat reactive when reminded about personal care tasks, or when other demands were made in the process of daily life routines. They noted that Morgan often shut down and withdrew from comments and demands. The three qualities they chose to describe Morgan included gentle-natured, bright, and passionate about pursuing her interests.

How do we summarize the autistic patterns that led to Morgan's autism diagnosis within the context of her other identified learning and emotional differences? Let's read her summary from her diagnostic report.

Summary

Morgan displayed a complex developmental and behavioral profile. Morgan presented as a highly intelligent, articulate, and well-spoken young adult. She has the long-standing diagnoses of Attention Deficit/

Hyperactivity Disorder, Primarily Inattentive Type (DSM-5 314.00; ICD-10 F90.0) and Generalized Anxiety Disorder (DSM-5 200.02; ICD-10 F41.1).

In addition to Morgan's previously identified diagnoses, Morgan displayed a pattern of differences in her development consistent with a diagnosis of Autism Spectrum Disorder, (F84.0; 299.00; ICD-10 F84.5) Level 1 (requires support). The degree to which Morgan's autism spectrum brain style differences are currently affecting her ability to function is considered to be mild, requiring support. It is not uncommon for individuals to have the co-occurring conditions of ADHD and Autism Spectrum Disorder. In Morgan's case, her behavioral profile is most compellingly understood through the identification of both of these conditions, in addition to an understanding of her superior cognitive abilities.

In the area of social communication, without supports in place, Morgan displays challenges in social communication that cause mild but noticeable impairments. It is challenging for Morgan to engage in sustained social communication exchanges that require flexible thinking and taking in the perspective of her conversational partner when the social conversation does not occur within a predictable and shared interest context. She has a well-established coping response of withdrawing from stressful conversations, and struggles at times with her ability to reset her regulation level and communicate her internal level of distress and needs.

In the area of restricted, repetitive behaviors, Morgan's inflexibility of thinking and behavior appears frequently enough to be obvious to the casual observer and interfere at times with her functioning in a variety of contexts. Morgan occasionally experiences distress or difficulty organizing her behavior, sequencing multistep tasks, and regulating her anxiety and distress levels.

Morgan is a young adult who is showing an emerging aware of her differences and is able to advocate for herself. She is in the process of developing the necessary skills to manage her differences and to help others understand how her differences affect her ability to participate in social, work, and other life situations.

Now that you've read Morgan's autism narrative, you may recognize aspects of Morgan's story in the young adults you assess and support in your clinical practice. Morgan's Brain Style Profile is outlined in Boxes 3.1, 3.2, and 3.3. Her pattern of strengths and differences is characteristic of many highly verbally fluent autistic young adults and yet reflects her singular profile. We'll revisit Morgan and link her Brain Style Profile to positive supports in Part II of this book.

Box 3.1 Morgan's Brain Style Profile

Language and Communication

Strengths

High level of verbal fluency and high level of higher-order conceptual thinking
Has developed an excellent vocabulary
Learns and retains facts exceptionally well
Loves to learn and engage in creative projects
Enjoys and frequently initiates conversations about her areas of interests, including role-playing games, arts, and other topics

Differences

Speaks with a somewhat deliberate and fast-paced style
Frequently interrupts or overrides her conversational partner to regain a one-sided narrative
Processing incoming language is hard work for her brain, and she requires additional time to formulate her response to incoming queries and comments when there is not a clear and predictable conversational context, and when her anxiety level is triggered
Nonverbal communication functions not always integrated with verbal communication (eye gaze, gestures, facial expressions)
Is in the process of developing a repertoire of fluid conversational skills
Struggles with listening to conversational partner and incorporating the perspective of her conversational partner into fluid back-and-forth flexible exchanges

Box 3.2 Morgan's Brain Style Profile

Social Relationships and Emotions

Strengths

Enthusiastic, friendly, caring, and outgoing demeanor
Has a genuine desire to connect with others
Has loving and connected relationships with her family

Genuinely enjoys sharing her time and interests with others
Has developed some long-standing genuine friendships and actively
    maintains those relationships through shared interests
Has a sense of humor
Can identify and describe basic feelings and their link to situations

Differences

Displays a consistently low threshold for incoming social demands
    outside of those that have a shared interest context
Limited repertoire of coping strategies to manage her anxiety and
    reactivity to uncertainty and unexpected outcomes
Reactive routines include heightened anxiety or agitation as evidenced
    by withdrawal and shutting down in conversations, repetitive and
    inflexible thinking, reactivity, and escape behavior routines

---

Box 3.3 Morgan's Brain Style Profile

Sensory Use and Interests

Strengths

Enthusiastic and engaged learner who has passionate interests and a
    vision of how to translate those interests into a life path (creative
    pursuits for avocation and art design as a vocation)
Attends to visual details and retains information well when encoded
    visually and when there is an established visual context
Has developed a range of age-appropriate interests and genuinely
    enjoys engaging in those activities, gaining skills as she goes
Systematic thinker who enjoys learning facts and information as well
    as applying skills in creative projects, gaming campaigns, and
    learning through her coursework and independent pursuit of her
    interests

Differences

Relatively low threshold for incoming demands (social conversations,
    multifaceted directions), requiring systematic and planned brain
    reset breaks

Internalizes and masks stressors related to incoming demands

Relies on routines with body movements and speech to manage the stress inherent in social conversations

Pronounced and long-standing sensory sensitivities in her response to ambient sounds, textures, visual details, and the requirement to shift flexibly from her agenda to follow the agenda of others

Has a well-established routine of isolated activities (drawing, writing, researching areas of interest)

When her reactivity, agitation, or anxiety is triggered, Morgan loses her ability to express herself clearly, engaging in a routine of shutting down her critical thinking abilities, having intrusive and negative thoughts, and revisiting previous negative situations

The autistic adult profile identified later in the lifespan

What does the adult autistic profile look like in a high-masking, verbally fluent individual whose internal experiences of stress and distress are not readily apparent in their outward words, actions, and behavior? For adults in professions where they have developed notable competencies, including but not limited to physicians and other health-care professionals, attorneys, architects, researchers, artists, and educators, it is not uncommon for the individual's autism spectrum Brain Style Profile to remain undiagnosed until later in life. From the outside looking in, the world sees the person as competent and perhaps a bit distant or blunt in their delivery of information. Or they are seen as quiet and introverted, or pleasant but somewhat out of step with unspoken and expected social routines.

From the inside looking out, the autistic story is being lived long before it is recognized and contextualized as a brain style. Autistic camouflaging or masking routines include working hard not only to appear to follow social conventions and norms but also to minimize the visible signs of the destabilizing effects of the breaching of the individual's sensory sensitivities threshold. Energy is expended in the masking process when the adult focuses on inhibiting their self-soothing sensory routines that often involve recurrent movements or mannerisms. As a result of this endless hard work for the brain to conceal the individual's authentic lived experience in social situations, the adult often experiences bone-crushing and constant fatigue, a sense of dread, and the need to manage an interior narrative that is negative and filled with doubts about their abilities that may at any moment become revealed to the world. More common in females (Hull et al., 2020), masking almost always leads to an internal state characterized by ongoing feelings of anxiety and depression. This in turn leads to the cognitive and behavioral patterns that are associated with managing the person's chronic state of stress and distress. Even when the undiagnosed adult has a support system in place, they are at risk for any number of persistent mental health conditions when there is a gap between their external behavior and their concealed interior authentic life.

Just as at every earlier stage in the life cycle, when an adult in midlife reaches the point where they ask the autistic brain style question, it is vital that the diagnostic assessment process include an understanding of the form and function of camouflaging or masking routines. Structuring the diagnostic conversation in a way that provides the adult with a safe setting to show their authentic self will make the difference between recognizing the adult's autistic brain style pattern of strengths and differences or adding to that adult's experience of once again not being truly seen, heard, or understood.

Unmasking considerations during the MIGDAS-2 adult diagnostic interview process

The MIGDAS-2 adult interview invites the verbally fluent adult to show their authentic self through two key structures. The first is the way in which the conversational probes are configured and organized. The goal of the diagnostic interview is for the adult to share and describe their lived experience, as defined by telling the narrative of their life story from their perspective or worldview. Instead of focusing on questions that stop at the description of external behavior patterns, the conversation is structured so you explore the adult's experiences. This means spending time listening to and reframing their narratives around their internal and external experiences, and how the two are in sync with or disparate from one another. It also means listening to and reframing the narrative that emerges around the adult's intrapersonal and interpersonal experiences and life patterns.

The second structural piece is the way in which sensory materials and topics are introduced and considered. As with children and adolescents, starting the conversation with the invitation to talk about enjoyed activities and interests sets the tone for the supportive interview. The follow-up questions are also designed to show an understanding of the underlying autistic brain style that may not be immediately apparent. The conversation invites the adult to confirm or clarify the autistic narrative reframes the clinician introduces when the adult discusses the form of their preferred activities and sensory preferences. And finally, the straightforward invitation to explore sensory fidgets that allow the adult to create self-regulation routines provides a setting in which the adult has the experience of being seen, heard, and accepted as their genuine self.

The MIGDAS-2 diagnostic conversation reveals Miranda's autism story

Let's explore the camouflaged midlife autistic narrative through Miranda's story. Miranda participated in her MIGDAS-2 diagnostic interview conversation as part of her adult autism evaluation process. Miranda was a 52-year-old with a degree in library science. She held a long-term position as a secondary school librarian in charge of her school's media center. Her work encompassed both general librarian support for students as well as providing reference and research support for specialized student and faculty projects. She was well loved by her students, and her peers held her in high regard. They particularly admired her unfailing passion and the energy she devoted to supporting students, along with her exceptional organizational skills. In her personal life, Miranda and her husband lived with their two dogs, to whom Miranda affectionately referred as their children. In addition to her love of research and library science, Miranda was an avid listener of music of several genres. She played percussion instruments in a school band during her secondary school years. Miranda sought out her adult autism assessment after struggling for many years with high levels of anxiety. She had received therapy and treatment for her anxiety over the years but continued to experience ongoing internal distress. After noticing that she experienced most of her anxiety related to interactions with other people, she applied her research skills and began exploring information about autism and adults.

During the diagnostic interview conversation, Miranda shared the connections she made when she learned about patterns of behavior associated with the autistic brain style.

Miranda sat with her back perfectly aligned with the back of her chair and with her legs crossed at the ankles. Her fingers lightly and rhythmically brushed the tips of the strands of the Koosh fidget ball she held in her hands. "Teddy and Beatrix would love this," she commented, referring to her beloved small and fluffy dogs as she settled into the conversation. "I love the way this feels too. At home I often have one of my dogs on my lap, and petting their fluffy ears helps me relax and think."

She furrowed her brow slightly as she collected her thoughts. "So, researching autism was like reading about my life. Especially the part about getting stuck on details. I do get stuck on details and a lot of the time they aren't the key details, and when I focus on the details, I can miss the point someone is making." She sighed as she continued to manipulate the stress ball.

"So, you've noticed you miss key details while you tune into other details?"

"When I was younger, I'm pretty sure I was oblivious, but now I most definitely do. At work I constantly ask people to clarify things and I repeat back to them what they've said so I can process the information after they've gone to make sure I got it right. I work hard to get it right in my work. Many of my students make comments to me about how precise I can be. For me, personally, it's exhausting." Her lips moved slightly to form an outlet as she expelled a long, focused breath.

This provided an opportunity to connect with Miranda and communicate that I was in sync with her narrative. "Yes, it takes a lot of energy. You are describing the hard work it is for you to manage input from your conversational partner. But you are also describing that you have figured out a great strategy: asking for clarification. Strategies can become patterns and patterns become routines."

Miranda straightened her already straight posture a bit more as she took this in. Her eyebrows lowered slightly as they pulled together. "Thank you for that. And you're exactly right about the strategy but also about the amount of energy it takes to use it. Absolutely hard work." She paused again, gathering her thoughts. "Then there is what I call 'the aftermath.' That's what happens to me after I have a *social* encounter with anyone." She deliberately distinguished the types of encounters with others that were challenging for her.

"Say more about that."

"So, 'the aftermath.' A lot of time and energy goes into that. I revisit every detail over and over again. I worry about what I said, how I said it, how I looked...what the other person said, how they said it, what they really meant...all with no end point of figuring it out." She expelled a small puff of air.

She added another thought. "It took me awhile to make the connection to social conversations, but eventually I got there. That was when I started noticing there were times when I wasn't getting stressed talking with people and when I didn't have to pay with 'the aftermath.'"

Miranda was prepared to spontaneously highlight the conditions under which conversations were fluid and predictable for her. "That's a very important connection. What was the difference you noticed between conversations where you got stressed and those that were more manageable for you?"

"So, when I'm walking Teddy and Beatrix and people stop to chat, they would never know the stressed side of me. We talk about our dogs and then go on our way. Same thing at the dog park."

I listened attentively and responded to her narrative. I started my sentence with her signature lead-in as I mirrored her way of speaking and her point of view. "So, Miranda, those conversations center on a shared topic that is familiar and of interest to you. You and your conversational partner can literally focus on something visible and tangible: your dogs. There is a clear context for the conversation."

Miranda's head nodded up and down as she rocked her shoulders while she listened intently. "Yes!" She drew a deep breath before continuing. "And that's what it's like with my students. We have a problem to solve, and my job is to guide them to figure it out. No aftermath." She repeated my words as she took in their meaning. " 'A clear context.' I like that. It totally describes it."

Miranda drew in an extended breath and raised her eyebrows as she processed an observation aloud. "So, I just thought of something related to context. I love my schedules and routines and depend on them to keep me going. When they get interrupted, that's when things get shaky. As long as I have my work and home routines, I can keep going. They give me the context I need, don't they? It's when my routines are interrupted that things get bad."

"Miranda, you are making some important connections. One is your observation that conversations that are part of a recognizable topic or object-focused routine work well for you. You talked about loving your schedules and routines. Schedules and routines help your system stay regulated, including topic-focused conversational routines like talking about dogs on your walks and about projects with your students. Those routine conversations contrast with the tremendous toll 'the aftermath' takes on you from having social conversations with other people."

Miranda continued her gentle rocking while she took in my observations. Another burst of air gently escaped through her pursed lips. "It feels good to get that out there. This isn't something I talk about or show to people."

Miranda expressed the experience of unmasking in our conversation, and I appreciated her disclosures. "Thank you so much for talking about what happens to you during conversations with others. It's a lot to keep inside."

Miranda had more to share. "It's been difficult ever since I was a girl and I started noticing that I was always at least one beat off of the rhythm with the girls around me. I learned how to act like I was a really good listener and to stay away from being the center in a group or conversation. I was always terrified of being called out. It always felt—and still feels—like I am making a narrow escape when I get through an encounter. I try to keep it 'short but sweet.' The part people don't see is what happens afterwards." She paused and drew a breath. "So, the really bad part is when I can't stop all of the negative thoughts and self-doubt. That's 'the aftermath' of the conversation. Things can get pretty brutal. My anxiety really spikes, and I get drawn into all of the familiar details about my shortcomings and how I am not really capable and people are going to figure out what a fake I am." She resumed after drawing another deep breath. "I've talked about those thoughts in therapy for years but never really felt like things changed inside. And then I read about autism and masking, and it really struck a chord with me. The disconnect started to make more sense. Maybe this process will help shift things inside."

"I'm so glad you are talking about your experiences, Miranda, and the contrast between what people see and the way you are living on the inside." Miranda exhaled in a steady extended breath as she listened. "Making sense of the reasons behind the gap between how you appear on the outside to others and yet feel so differently on the inside can be quite helpful. You've made the important connection about which type of conversations trigger the gap and which ones do not. That's a meaningful starting point to explore how your brain takes in information and manages the unexpected nuances involved in a social conversation without a clear, shared context."

"Thank you for that. So, when I don't have a clear context, as you say, I can't stay in my comfort zone of my routines."

"Exactly. And when there isn't a way to make sense out of the gap, your brain fills it with the routine of repeating negative thoughts and worries. Developing systems and routines is something you do exceptionally well. As you explore that strength, you can begin to develop alternative routines that calm and reset your system instead of creating more stress." I connected her internal distress patterns to her drive to create and maintain predictable routines.

Miranda gently rocked back and forth as she considered this. "Of course. They are definitely a routine. But not a very pleasant one." She paused as she processed the idea. "So, maybe I can figure out a way to switch out 'the aftermath' with 'the reset.'"

"I love the way you put that, Miranda. 'The reset.'"

Miranda continued to make connections as the reframe for her experiences took hold. "All these years I've worked on making lists of what I should say to myself during 'the aftermath' but nothing took hold. I really didn't see the pattern of creating a routine, just tried to tell myself something positive instead of negative. Understanding that not having a context during social conversations is a fundamental difference for me that most other people don't have to deal with, makes so much sense. They actually have a context, don't they?" She paused again, reflecting on her new thoughts as she listened to her words. "So, the more I understand my differences, the better. This already makes so much sense. I know this process will help me because you've already asked me about my situation in a way that shows me you get it."

"I am very glad to hear that, Miranda. We have a lot more to talk about so you can fully understand your brain style pattern of strengths and differences. Once we have your full story, we can begin to identify and structure some course corrections to make things better."

We went on to talk about Miranda's sensory preferences and sensitivities. Miranda talked about her well-established and definite preferences and sensitivities in the areas of food, clothing, sounds, smells, and sleep patterns. In the area of food preferences, Miranda stated that she planned ahead so she could eat the same foods for breakfast and lunch every day, and she maintained a routine rotation of foods to share with her husband at dinner. Miranda noted that she had a pronounced aversion to eating with anyone outside of her immediate family. In the area of clothing preferences, Miranda stated that she preferred baggy, soft clothing, and did not like clothing that clings to her body, She added that when she found clothing she liked, she bought the item in multiples. Miranda discussed her love of music and the joy she experienced when she selected a preferred piece of music and settled into listening to the intricate patterns of rhythms and notes. Continuing to reflect on auditory input, Miranda asserted that she was routinely bothered by loud or sudden noises, and described herself as having an aversive reaction to a range of ambient sounds. Sounds that Miranda described as frequently creating distress for her included the sound of people eating, coughing, or sniffling; squeaky shoes; and repetitive sounds such as clicking pens, knocking, tapping, buzzing, or drilling. Miranda noted that in addition to her sensitivity to sounds, she experienced a pronounced sensitivity to smells, including the smell of other people, perfumes or floral scents, doctors' offices, or the lingering smell of cooked foods. In the area of sleep patterns, Miranda stated that she often had trouble falling and staying asleep, and experienced constant fatigue during the day.

Miranda stated that going into crowded stores was a stressor for her, and she did most of her shopping online. She added that when she did need to go to a store, her preference was having a list of items to collect and purchase quickly. Miranda noted that when she had to attend group events, she tried to arrive early to find a back corner to position herself. She often took a book with her to block out the input when she felt overwhelmed but it was not yet time to leave the event. Miranda stated that at times she wore earbuds so that others would not approach her and start speaking to her. Each time Miranda stated her preferences and strategies, we connected her narrative to the exploration of context and routines.

When asked to describe how she expressed anger or agitation and what situations triggered those emotional reactions, Miranda noted that triggers for her anger or agitation were when she felt that she was being treated unfairly, and when she felt as though she was not being heard or understood. Miranda added that her husband had commented to her that she seemed to frequently express anger, agitation, and irritation at home in response to routine conversations and daily events. Miranda recalled that presently, and historically as a child living with her siblings, she frequently became agitated when others touched her things, were too loud, and when things were out of their expected place.

We came to the end of our time together with Miranda revealing her nuanced story. I had three final questions for her.

"So, Miranda, if you had to choose three words or qualities to best describe yourself, what would they be?"

Drawing in a breath, Miranda maintained her gaze on the Koosh ball in her lap. "So, I would have to say: quirky, hard-working, and loyal." She exhaled slowly before adding another thought. "And also anxious, self-conscious, and awkward. For now."

"How was this conversation similar to or different from other conversations you've had with psychologists or therapists?"

"So, today, your questions helped me open up and tell you things in detail. I did not feel rushed. You really listened. And you brought up new ways to look at things that made sense to me. So, mostly different from other experiences with therapists."

"Good to know. Thank you for your observations. Here's the last question. What is a key takeaway for you from our conversation today?"

Miranda drew in a signature breath while she gathered her thoughts. She slowly exhaled before she spoke. "So, context and routine make all the difference. And there's nothing wrong with having a different rhythm."

Miranda's autism diagnostic summary and her Brain Style Profile

How do we summarize our explanation of Miranda's autism diagnosis at this later stage in life? Let's read a description of her autism story that starts with summarizing her lived experience to contextualize the diagnosis for the reader. After the context is established, the reader has a reference point to take in the autism diagnosis. Miranda has a written description she can take in and incorporate into her personal story.

Summary

Miranda presented as a highly intelligent, articulate, and thoughtful adult who cares passionately about her work and the people she loves. She has a long-standing struggle with managing intense feelings of anxiety and depression, and has had exposure to challenging relationships and situations at various points throughout her life. Diagnostically, her emotional regulation challenges have historically been understood as a function of anxiety and depression rather than having her anxiety and depression understood as a by-product of her underlying neuro-developmental differences. Throughout this diagnostic process, Miranda consistently presented with the dichotomy of a debilitating interior negative narrative contrasted with a routine of masking and deflecting from that internal experience to focus on the needs and problems of others. She displayed a pattern of heightened reactivity to sensory stressors, and this combined with the confusion she experiences in relation to social communication leaves her feeling stressed and destabilized a great deal of the time. This is apparent in her ongoing pattern of predisposition to being flooded with feelings of anger or anxiety, her struggles with managing sensory input, and her having to manage her interior negative narrative while managing the mask of presenting to others without disclosing the depth and breadth of her interior struggles. This pattern of internal narrative and external behavioral, emotional, and communication differences is best understood as a function of Miranda's previously undiagnosed autism spectrum brain style differences. Highly competent and verbally fluent women with underlying autism spectrum brain style differences often have their autism spectrum differences overlooked, as they mask effectively and their anxiety and depression are attributed to stressors and trauma. Miranda displays a long-standing social, emotional, communication, and sensory pattern of behavior and development that represents an intersection between her autism spectrum brain style and the resulting destabilization or trauma resulting from the internalization of her differences. It is important to note that although Miranda has experienced some emotionally challenging events over the course of her life, her internalization of stressors into a negative self-narrative and her ongoing struggles with managing emotional and behavioral regulation are suggestive of neurodivergent development in addition to her trauma history.

Miranda displayed a profile of behaviors consistent with a diagnosis of Autism Spectrum Disorder (Level 1 for Social Communication; Level 1 for Restricted, Repetitive Behaviors) 299.00, F84.0, without intellectual impairment, without language impairment, and with another known medical condition (Generalized Anxiety Disorder [DSM-5 200.02; ICD-10 F41.]).

In the area of social communication, without supports in place, Miranda displays challenges in social communication that cause noticeable distress for her. Miranda struggles at times in her ability to participate in shared conversational exchanges with others. Her tolerance for incoming language demands is notably lower than her drive to initiate communication related to her preferred areas of interest. Miranda becomes somewhat stressed and reactive when communication demands are placed on her, as evidenced by her behavior of retreating from the source of demands.

In the area of restricted, repetitive behaviors, Miranda's inflexibility of behavior, reactivity to incoming demands, and her sensory sensitivities appear frequently enough to be obvious to the casual observer and interfere at times with her functioning in a variety of contexts. Miranda experiences distress or difficulty managing her need for predictability, limiting social interactions with others, and regulating her agitation and anxiety levels.

That brings us to the end of Miranda's autism story for now. You may find that you've recognized aspects of Miranda's story in the older adults you've assessed and supported in your clinical practice. Miranda's Brain Style Profile is outlined in Boxes 3.4, 3.5, and 3.6. Her pattern of strengths and differences is characteristic of many highly verbally fluent autistic adults who receive their diagnosis later in life. At the same time, her singular profile reveals her individual, nuanced, and unique story. We'll revisit Miranda and link her Brain Style Profile to positive course corrections supports in Part II of this book.

Box 3.4 Miranda's Brain Style Profile

Language and Communication

Strengths

Highly verbally fluent and applies her skills in her library science work

Asks thoughtful and compelling questions and works diligently to apply ideas and information

Thinks about and describes details well

Enjoys participating in conversations with others with familiar contexts related to her library science work and shared interests in dogs and music

Has developed an excellent strategy of repeating what others say to clarify meaning when in conversations with others

Differences

Conversations are often organized around presenting facts and details about events in a narrative

Hard work for Miranda to simultaneously take in information from her conversational partner and manage coordinated use of unspoken communication features such as eye gaze and gestures

Experiences hesitancy when she has to process incoming information and respond to her conversational partner

---

In social conversations, struggles with listening to conversational partner and experiences anxiety while focused on formulating her response to conversational content

In social situations, Miranda is often dependent on her conversational partner for the conversational flow

In social conversations, Miranda often experiences uncertainty about the intent and meaning of what others say and worries about misinterpreting conversational perspectives

Displays a low threshold for managing sustained back-and-forth exchanges regardless of context or topic, but does better at sustaining conversations related to helping her students organize and complete research projects

Fatigued by the process she undergoes of carefully processing input and formulating her responses in a real-time conversational exchange

Has developed an internal narrative centered on negative beliefs about herself while masking those thoughts and beliefs when interacting with others

---

Box 3.5 Miranda's Brain Style Profile

Social Relationships and Emotions

Strengths

Maintains a consistently serious, thoughtful, and calm demeanor

Connected with her husband, work colleagues, and students, and has established unique and positive relationships within the boundaries of each type of relationship

Genuinely enjoys helping others and experiencing successful outcomes with goal-directed projects

Can identify and describe basic feelings and their link to situations

Cares deeply about others

Enjoys the structure of family and non-work time when the sensory aspects are manageable and when the events are part of an expected routine

Thoughtfully prepares for social demands and responds well to others even when she experiences internal stress and distress regarding her understanding of the nuances involved in everyday social exchange

Dedicated to better understanding herself and others

Differences

Displays and recognizes her low threshold for managing incoming social demands

Hard work for Miranda to interpret social communication and the intent of others, leading to the internal routine of extensively replaying and second-guessing her responses and the responses of others after participating in social exchanges

Has long-standing struggles with intense feelings of anxiety and depression connected to the divide between her external behavior patterns and her internal experience of stress and uncertainty about her social exchange capabilities

Miranda's highly developed masking skills result in a notable gap between how she presents herself to others in social exchanges, and how she experiences uncertainty and distress regarding social interactions with others, leading to internal feelings of otherness, isolation, anxiety, and negative thinking

Internalizes and expresses deep worries and anticipates negative outcomes

Struggles with managing her ongoing internal experiences of anxiety, fatigue, and agitation in response to daily stressors

---

Box 3.6 Miranda's Brain Style Profile

Sensory Use and Interests

Strengths

Careful and systematic thinker who has a strong drive to learn and apply skills and information

Has pursued advanced training and gained expertise in her chosen field of library science and has maintained a long-term and well-esteemed work life

Attends to visual details and retains information well when encoded visually

Has developed a range of age-appropriate interests and genuinely enjoys engaging in those activities, including reading, music, pet activities, and researching topics of interest

Enjoys learning about and retains detailed knowledge of facts, data, and information

Creates and follows visual schedules and routines

Focuses on systematic ways to approach and solve challenges, and excels in developing organizational systems for research and work projects for herself and her students

Recognizes her need for reduced stimulation sensory regrouping times to gain the energy to manage interactive and environmental demands

Does best when she can engage in sequential processing of information and sequential completion of tasks

Has identified and applies her sensory self-soothing routines, including sitting with a dog in her lap to regulate by rhythmically stroking the soft fur, structuring her environment to minimize clutter and create a predictable visual field, wearing clothing that falls in the range she has identified as providing positive sensory input, and managing the type and degree of ambient sound

Differences

Has pronounced sensory sensitivities to incoming sounds, smells, and textures that are unsettling to her and are sources of internal stress and distress

Challenging for Miranda to flexibly shift her thinking when she becomes anxious or agitated (perceives something as unfair or that others are not listening to her or understanding her)

Displays a pattern of inflexible thinking that affects her ability to shift perspectives in relation to how she views herself and her circumstances

Requires purposeful focusing to recognize inflexible thinking and behavior patterns and to introduce regulation and brain resetting routines

Engages in a pattern of distinctive body movements and mannerisms, including averting her eye gaze when in conversations with others, taking in and exhaling breath while absorbing information from her conversational partner, maintaining a static body posture, engaging in gentle body rocking, and seeking out soft textures to create self-soothing input and routines

Managing a lifelong autism diagnosis in the adult years

The sample cases of Morgan and Miranda focused on how you might go about assessing and supporting verbally fluent adults in the process of exploring their initial autism diagnosis using the neuro-informed framework. What about working with adults who have a long-standing autism diagnosis as they navigate their adult years? Before we leave the world of assessing and supporting autistic adults, let's discuss ways in which you might apply the sensory-based perspective and Brain Style Profile to an autistic adult with an early and lifelong diagnosis.

Adults with an autism diagnosis from early childhood often develop spoken language at a later than expected age. Over half the children who are not yet using spoken language at age five years go on to develop basic spoken language by adulthood (Maltman et al., 2021). Basic spoken language, or emerging verbal fluency, can be described as the adult using single-word and phrase speech to communicate their wants, needs, and interests in a way that is understood by others in their life. Autistic adults with emerging verbal fluency require substantial supports, including living with caregivers, most often parents or other family members. If your clinical practice includes this population of adults, your work involves supporting the autistic adult along with the adult's caregivers and family members. Families caring for an autistic adult often experience isolation and chronically high levels of stress and anxiety that affect their health-related quality of life (Herrema et al., 2017; Duckert et al., 2023). Common worries include supporting the autistic adult family member in finding meaningful work or activities (Shattuck et al., 2012; Taylor et al., 2014), finding compatible social pathways (Orsmond et al., 2013), and managing activities of daily living with a degree of autonomy and independence (Auld et al., 2022). Competitive employment rates for autistic adults are significantly lower than for the general population, as up to 70% of autistic adults are reported as being outside of the workforce throughout their lives (Hickey et al., 2024).

This isolation and lack of community resources place stress on all family members, and the family may reach out to you for support at different points in the autistic adult's lifespan. Common themes include finding ways to increase the adult's autonomous engagement in activities of daily living, helping with mood regulation and the accompanying dysregulated behavior routines, and developing a plan to help the autistic adult expand their time and energy into engagement in activities beyond their involvement in self-directed activities related to the adult's areas of preferred interest. As parents age along with their adult autistic child, their worries about ongoing care become magnified. Many autistic adults depend on family members for support throughout their lives (Forbes et al., 2023).

The narrative for families caring for an adult autistic relative often includes not only the experience of isolation but also a sense of timelessness and fatigue. Things have been this way seemingly always, and it can be difficult to imagine that change is possible. Much of your supportive work with autistic adults and their families centers around helping the autistic adult explore their identity in a more positive and fully realized way. The first step in helping the autistic adult and their family members make this shift in redefining the autistic narrative is to include a strengths-based conversation. Let's look at how that unfolds with Matt, a 31-year-old autistic man, and his father, Matt's primary caregiver.

Matt's MIGDAS-2 updated diagnostic conversation

Matt's father requested a consultation evaluation to provide an updated profile of Matt's autism spectrum brain style differences, and discuss recommended supports for Matt for his continued development of independent management of his daily living and life skills. His father stated that his goals for Matt as Matt continues to progress though adulthood include the following: to gain the necessary skills to pursue gainful employment, to be able to live by himself or with a roommate, and to communicate better about his wants and needs.

Matt was initially given a diagnosis of autism as a young child. He received specialized educational services throughout his school years. Matt transitioned into a vocational day training program for developmentally disabled adults. The focus of the program was to provide support in the areas of activities of daily living, job skills, and social activities. Matt's father had obtained legal guardianship for his adult son and they lived together.

When asked what activities Matt enjoyed doing in his free time, his father stated that Matt's preferred activities included playing *Super Mario* video games and watching You Tube videos related to the Nintendo game universe. He noted that Matt has a strong preference for spending time alone, but added that from time to time his son spontaneously looked for his father to share a funny video clip. Strengths for Matt noted by his father included Matt's generally congenial and good-natured demeanor and his ability to apply his attention to details and love of routines to independently use his alarm to wake in the morning and prepare for his weekday schedule of attending his adult program. Differences for Matt described by his father included Matt's pronounced sensory preferences and sensitivities. He highlighted Matt's strong preference for organizing his time around solitary exploration of his interests, with an emphasis on paying close attention to visual details and a drive to repeatedly examine details related to his beloved video characters. His father mentioned an additional example of his son's attention to visual details as well. He noted that Matt routinely inspected his socks for any signs of holes or imperfections, and when he spotted a small variation, he immediately threw the pair away. Matt's deeply entrenched pattern of specific sensory sensitivities was an area in which Matt's father sought guidance. Foremost on his father's list was his son's aversion to water touching his head and to the sensation of toothbrush bristles that resulted in Matt's vigorous resistance to engage in daily hygiene routines. Matt also resisted attempts to establish a physical movement or exercise routine, and due to this combined with his limited range of food preferences (specific meats, starches, and canned green beans), his father expressed concern for Matt's long-term health and well-being. Socially, Matt's father noted that his adult son experienced pronounced anxiety in response to changes in his expected routine and to being in environments where his sensory threshold for auditory and olfactory input were breached. This included his heightened anxiety in the face of encouragement to try new foods, and when small changes in his daily routine were suggested or introduced.

When asked to describe how Matt expressed anger or agitation, and situations that trigger those reactions, his father stated that Matt's main trigger was the area of how chores are being done. He added that when agitated, Matt engaged in a pattern of yelling, crying, burying his face in his hands, and lying on the floor. He added that the process of Matt resetting his regulation level often took a combination of time paired with a withdrawal of input or demands.

When asked to pick three words or qualities that best describe Matt, his father stated that Matt was sweet-natured, innocent, and showed a low motivation to participate in tasks that were outside of his self-directed areas of preferred interest, namely, chores, exercising, and participating in social activities.

Matt's MIGDAS-2 diagnostic conversation summary

Matt, a sturdily built man wearing a baseball cap and T-shirt that both featured Nintendo figures, participated in the MIGDAS-2 sensory-based interview conversation. He explored various sensory fidgets throughout the meeting, with a particular interest in manipulating the range of magnet building pieces (X-ball; Ball of Whacks). Let's read his diagnostic interview summary to reveal his adult brain style story of strengths and differences.

Language and Communication

Matt's Language and Communication profile showed the pattern of differences typically seen in adults with Autism Spectrum Disorder, Level

2 to 3, requiring substantial to very substantial support. Matt displayed some areas of distinctive strengths as well as distinctive differences. Strengths for Matt included his basic but solid language skills, both in terms of his ability to understand and to use language to communicate his interests and needs. He responded to questions in a thoughtful way, and addressed his responses directly to the listener. Matt displayed several notable and significant differences in the area of Language and Communication. He spoke with a stilted, fast-paced, staccato, and unvarying cadence. Matt's spontaneous communications included rote and scripted use of language. For example, the way Matt communicated that his threshold for managing incoming language demands from his conversational partner was to use the repeating phrase: "I'm getting dizzy." When prompted to ask a question of this psychologist, Matt was unable to formulate a question. However, when he was provided with binary choices, he consistently provided thoughtful answers. When Matt was able to anchor his language with a visual framework, he was better able to expand on his use of language, For example, when asked to talk about a funny YouTube video he had watched, Matt was able to name the characters involved (Mario, Luigi, and Yoshi) and to describe the sequence of the physical moves each character made in a video he enjoyed. He became notably more alert, engaged, and slightly more verbally fluent when discussing his areas of preferred interest, or when responding to prompts to list the steps in his daily routines. Matt noted that processing incoming language is hard work for him and he fatigues relatively quickly when having to engage in protracted back-and-forth conversations. In addition to repeating the phrase: "I'm getting dizzy" to signal that he was finding it taxing to continue participating in a conversational exchange, Matt also displayed some mildly agitated behavior, intensified his focus on constructing the magnet puzzles he was manipulating, and moved away from the source of demands to place completed magnet puzzles in a neat line on a bookshelf. Matt's ability to use joint attention social communication functions, including eye gaze, changes in facial expression, and gestures, was somewhat limited, as was his ability to take in social communication joint attention cues from his conversational partner.

This pattern of Language and Communication strengths and differences is characteristic of autistic adults with basic language and communication skills.

Social Relationships and Emotional Responses

As is oftentimes the case for autistic adults, Matt has a desire for social relationships with others but struggles with his ability to understand, use, and respond to social exchanges. Areas of strength for Matt include his good-natured, pleasant, and agreeable demeanor. He has established and maintains a close and loving relationship with his father, and has established and maintains positive relationships with his adult peers and support staff. Matt was polite, engaged, and responsive to this psychologist throughout the interview process. He displayed a sense of humor, and a genuine enjoyment in sharing his worldview and interests with others, including sharing time with this psychologist when he was invited to show and tell her about his beloved Super Mario characters. Matt recalled this psychologist's name, and at the end of the session, when she told him how nice it was to meet Matt, he replied: "Nice to meet you too, Marilyn!" Matt used eye contact on several occasions during the session to communicate his endorsement of the descriptions this psychologist provided about Matt's brain style and suggested supports. In the area of emotional responses, Matt displayed an emerging awareness of a range of emotions and an emerging ability to identify emotional states in himself. Differences in Matt's Social Relationships and Emotions included his dependence on his conversational partner to prompt social topics and to keep the social conversation going when the topic expanded beyond Matt's areas of preferred interest. When asked to talk about his friends in his day program, Matt stated: "No friends." When queried about times he had experienced specific emotions, Matt stated that he feels lonely at times. Matt noted that his preference is to spend time alone, and described his alone time as relaxing. Matt responded with visible anxiety and agitation when suggested adjustments in his daily living skills routines were discussed with him. However, it was apparent that Matt was listening carefully, and considering options rather than rejecting ideas solely because they signified a change for him. Matt was particularly attentive to suggestions made by this psychologist after she provided an understanding of the sensory aspects of Matt's experiences. For example, when Matt was prompted to talk about washing his hair and brushing his teeth, he actively participated by responding to questions to target the specific sensory aspects of the activity that were bothersome to him. He expressed his preferences and was able to state that changes were difficult for him, but he would consider adding incremental changes.

Matt displayed a pattern of differences in the areas of social relationships and emotional responses that is characteristic of the autistic adult brain style pattern of strengths and differences.

Sensory Use and Interests

Matt displayed a pattern of sensory differences that is commonly seen in adults with autism spectrum brain style differences. Strengths for

Matt in the area of Sensory Use and Interests include his drive to create and maintain predictable routines. He has established independent routines for starting and ending his day, pays close attention to time and is punctual with appointments. His father reported that Matt generally anticipates and participates in his scheduled activities, and as long as he can anticipate the transition, Matt is willing to shift from his self-directed, sensory-based solitary agenda to participate in structured activities with others. Matt is a visual thinker, who seeks out routines and activities that involve sequences to follow, contain visual manipulatives, and have low-load language and low-load social demands. Following predictable routines helps Matt organize and regulate his behavior.

Differences for Matt in the area of Sensory Use and Interests include his low threshold for managing incoming demands (verbal, social) that creates a drive for solitary enactment of his preferred and familiar self-directed routines. Participating in activities with others is hard work for Matt, and he requires time to regroup and reset his brain with solitary and familiar routines after he has expended the effort required to engage socially with others, communicate with others, and follow the agenda set by others. By report and direct observation, Matt displays sensitivities to incoming sounds, including verbal input. He displayed some inflexibility in his ability to alter established routines, most notably in the sensory-driven areas of bathing, food, and exercise. During the interview session, Matt engaged in some repetitive behaviors to organize and regulate, including focusing on objects while he manipulated them without flexibly shifting his focus from the objects to his conversational partner, mild body tensing, close visual inspection of objects, and categorizing and lining up objects provided to him as part of the diagnostic interview process.

Matt's pattern of differences in the area of Sensory Use and Interests is characteristic of autistic adults with straightforward and fundamental language and communication skills.

Matt's MIGDAS-2 overall Pattern of Observations, currently and by history, was consistent with his long-standing autism diagnosis.

This revealing of Matt's autism story in this way points the reader toward an appreciation of his strengths first, and then his differences. Describing how Matt engages with the world provides the structure that will lead to the development of positive supports that are a match for his unique and singular life story. As you read Matt's Brain Style Profile in Boxes 3.7, 3.8 and 3.9, think about adults you know and how you can apply the descriptors to support their understanding of their adult brain style pattern of strengths and differences. We'll look at a few key supports for Matt when we revisit his story in Part II.

Box 3.7 Matt's Brain Style Profile

Language and Communication

Strengths

Has developed solid basic language skills

Enjoys initiating conversations with others about his areas of interest

Has a fundamental understanding of language, especially when it is paired with visual contextual cues

Does best with language when he is provided with binary choices instead of being asked open-ended questions

Communicates his wants and needs when his threshold for managing incoming language demands has not been surpassed

Differences

Speaks with a distinctive stilted, staccato, and fast-paced style

Processing incoming language is hard work for his brain, and he requires additional time to formulate his response to incoming queries and comments

Nonverbal communication functions not always integrated with verbal communication (eye contact, gestures, facial expressions)

Box 3.8 Matt's Brain Style Profile

Social Relationships and Emotions

Strengths

Connected with his father and enjoys doing activities together

Is establishing connections with his adult peers in his day program

On his initiation, genuinely enjoys it when others share in his interests

Has a sense of humor and enjoys it when others appreciate his perspective

Responsive to others in the work setting when they initiate brief social interactions

Can identify and describe basic feelings and their link to situations

Manages his anxiety and agitation by retreating from the source of demands and engaging in familiar self-directed, visually based routines

Differences

Low threshold for incoming social demands

Limited repertoire of coping strategies to manage his reactivity to unexpected outcomes when engaged in social exchanges with others

Matt's stress and distress responses are triggered by incoming demands, including unexpected changes in his expected routines and sensory input to which he has a sensitivity (smells, sounds, unexpected visual details)

Reactive routines include heightened anxiety or agitation and accompanying behaviors

Challenging for Matt to reset his regulation level when his reactivity is triggered

---

Box 3.9 Matt's Brain Style Profile

Sensory Use and Interests

Strengths

Visual thinker who does best with visual contextual cues, predictable routines, and can engage well in tasks that involve the manipulation of objects or materials

Has developed independent interests and genuinely enjoys engaging in those activities (gaming, watching YouTube videos, searching for collectibles on the Internet)

Enjoys establishing and maintaining predictable routines

Works cooperatively with others within his established and expected routines

Differences

Relatively low threshold for incoming demands (sensory, social communication, flexibly shifting from his agenda to follow the agenda of others)

Adheres to routines and finds changes in his routine to be distressing and unsettling

> Has established some binary thinking paradigms that limit his ability to think flexibly
>
> Engages in some recurrent body movements and mannerisms that serve the function of regulating his system, including close visual inspection of preferred objects or games, and retreating from the source of language and social demands

As you develop and expand your adult autism assessment skills, familiarizing yourself with neuro-affirming assessment tools and resources (Monteiro & Stegall, 2018; Hartman et al., 2023) is fundamentally important. Equally important is practicing your application of these skills as you support the lived experiences of the autistic adults in your clinical practice.

Over the last three chapters, we have focused on understanding the autistic Brain Style Profile across the lifespan. Now let's turn our focus to linking the individual's Brain Style Profile to a compelling way to think, talk, and write about positive supports. We'll talk about ways to support the autistic story in Part II.

References

Bell, D. C. (2023). Neurodiversity in the general practice workforce. *InnovAiT.* 16(9):450–455. doi: 10.1177/17557380231179742

Constantino, J. N., & Gruber, C. P. (2012). *Social Responsiveness Scale-Second Edition (SRS-2)*. Torrance, CA: Western Psychological Services.

Cooper, K., Russell, A. J., Lei, J., & Smith, L. G. (2023). The impact of a positive autism identity and autistic community solidarity on social anxiety and mental health in autistic young people. *Autism.* Apr;27(3):848–857. doi: 10.1177/13623613221118351. PMID: 36062470; PMCID: PMC10074754.

Dückert, S., Bart, S., Gewohn, P., König, H., Schöttle, D., Konnopka, A., Rahlff, P., Erik, F., Vogeley, K., Schulz, H., David, N., & Peth, J. (2023). Health-related quality of life in family caregivers of autistic adults. *Front Psychiatry.* Dec 18;14:1290407. doi: 10.3389/fpsyt.2023.1290407. PMID: 38193135; PMCID: PMC10773769.

Forbes, G., Kent, R., Charman, T., Baird, G., Pickles, A., & Simonoff, E. (2023). How do autistic people fare in adult life and can we predict it from childhood? *Autism Res.* Feb;16(2):458–473. doi: 10.1002/aur.2868. PMID: 36519265; PMCID: PMC10947100.

Fusar-Poli, L., Brondino, N., Politi, P., & Aguglia, E. (2022). Missed diagnoses and misdiagnoses of adults with autism spectrum disorder. *Eur Arch Psychiatry Clin Neurosci.* Mar;272(2):187–198. doi: 10.1007/s00406-020-01189-w. PMID: 32892291; PMCID: PMC8866369.

Gratton, F. V., Strang, J. F., Song, M., Cooper, K., Kallitsounaki, A., Lai, M. C., Lawson, W., van der Miesen, A. I. R., & Wimms, H. E. (2023). The intersection of autism and transgender and nonbinary identities: Community and academic dialogue on research and advocacy. *Autism Adulthood*. Jun 1;5(2):112–124. doi: 10.1089/aut.2023.0042. PMID: 37346986; PMCID: PMC10280197.

Hartman, D., O'Donnell-Killen, T., Doyle, J.K., Kavanaugh, M., Day, A., and Azevedo, J. (2023). *The Adult Autism Assessment Handbook; A Neurodiversity Affirmative Approach*. London: Jessica Kingsley Publisher.

Herrema, R., Garland, D., Osborne, M., Freeston, M., Honey, E., & Rodgers, J. (2017). Mental wellbeing of family members of autistic adults. *J Autism Dev Disord*. Nov;47(11):3589–3599. doi: 10.1007/s10803-017-3269-z. PMID: 28861652; PMCID: PMC5633644.

Hickey, E. J., DaWalt, L. S., Hong, J., Taylor, J. L., & Mailick, M. R. (2024). Trajectories of competitive employment of autistic adults through late midlife. *Healthcare (Basel)*. Jan 20;12(2):265. doi: 10.3390/healthcare12020265. PMID: 38275545; PMCID: PMC10815573.

Hull, L., Mandy, W., Lai, M.-C., Baron-Cohen, S., Allison, C., Smith, P., & Petrides, K. V. (2020). Development and validation of the Camouflaging Autistic Traits Questionnaire (CAT-Q). *J Autism Dev Disorders*. 49(3):819–833. https://doi.org/10.1007/s10803-018-3792-6

Jadav, N., & Bal, V. H. (2022). Associations between co-occurring conditions and age of autism diagnosis: Implications for mental health training and adult autism research. *Autism Res*. 15(11):2112–2125. https://doi.org/10.1002/aur.2808

Kentrou, V,. Livingston, L.A., Grove, R., Hoekstra, R. A., & Begeer, S. (2024). Perceived misdiagnosis of psychiatric conditions in autistic adults. *eClinicalMedicine*. 71: 102586. doi: 10.106/j.eclinm.2024.102586

Lau-Zhu, A., Fritz, A., & McLoughlin, G. (2019). Overlaps and distinctions between attention deficit/hyperactivity disorder and autism spectrum disorder in young adulthood: Systematic review and guiding framework for EEG-imaging research. *Neurosci Biobehav Rev*. Jan;96:93–115. doi: 10.1016/j.neubiorev.2018.10.009. PMID: 30367918; PMCID: PMC6331660.

Maltman, N., DaWalt, L. S., Hong, J., & Mailick, M. (2021). Brief report: Socioeconomic factors associated with minimally verbal status in individuals with ASD. *J Autism Dev Disord*. Jun;51(6):2139–2145. doi: 10.1007/s10803-020-04646-6. PMID: 32914289; PMCID: PMC7943642.

McCrossin, R. (2022). Finding the true number of females with autistic spectrum disorder by estimating the biases in initial recognition and clinical diagnosis. *Children (Basel)*. Feb 17;9(2):272. doi: 10.3390/children9020272. PMID: 35204992; PMCID: PMC8870038.

Monteiro, M., & Stegall, S. (2018). *Monteiro Interview Guidelines for Diagnosing the Autism Spectrum, Second Edition*. Torrance, CA: WPS Publishing.

Orsmond, G. I., Shattuck, P. T., Cooper, B. P., Sterzing, P. R., Anderson, K. A. (2013). Social participation among young adults with an autism spectrum disorder. *J Autism Dev Disord*. Nov;43(11):2710–9. doi: 10.1007/s10803-013-1833-8. PMID: 23615687; PMCID: PMC3795788.

Shattuck, P. T., Narendorf, S. C., Cooper, B., Sterzing, P. R., Wagner, M., Taylor, J. L. (2012). Postsecondary education and employment among youth with an autism spectrum disorder. *Pediatrics*. Jun;129(6):1042–9. doi: 10.1542/peds.2011-2864. PMID: 22585766; PMCID: PMC3362908.

Shaw, S. C. K., Fossi, A., Carravallah, L. A., Rabenstein, K., Ross, W., & Doherty, M. (2023). The experiences of autistic doctors: A cross-sectional study. *Front Psychiatry*. Jul 18;14:1160994. doi: 10.3389/fpsyt.2023.1160994. PMID: 37533891; PMCID: PMC10393275.

Stokes, G. R. (2018). A quantitative analysis of mental health among sexual and gender minority groups in ASD. *J Autism Dev Disord*. Jun;48(6):2052–2063. PMID: 29362955.

Taylor, J. L., Smith, L. E., & Mailick, M. R. (2014). Engagement in vocational activities promotes behavioral development for adults with autism spectrum disorders *J Autism Dev Disord*. Jun;44(6):1447–60. doi: 10.1007/s10803-013-2010-9. PMID: 24287880; PMCID: PMC4024367.

Warrier, V., Greenberg, D. M., Weir, E, Buckingham, C., Smith, P., Lai, M. C., Allison, C., & Baron-Cohen, S. (2020). Elevated rates of autism, other neurodevelopmental and psychiatric diagnoses, and autistic traits in transgender and gender-diverse individuals. *Nat Commun*. Aug 7;11(1):3959. PMID: 32770077; PMCID: PMC7415151.

Welsh, P., Hawker, D., Horne, K., Little, L., Muggleton, J., Henshaw, E., Hutchinson, J., & Nicholls, A. (2022). Neurodiversity is not just for those we work with. *Psychologist*. 35:2.

Part II

Laying the foundation

Linking the Brain Style Profile to positive supports

As a clinician, how do you approach the process of identifying supports? In this section, we'll turn our attention to a way to think, talk, and write about positive supports that are a fit for the individual's autistic Brain Style Profile of strengths and differences. We 'll start by establishing a context for *why* we are recommending specific supports. When we establish a context, we can partner effectively with individuals and their families to help each person self-determine specific supports that are the best fit for them. We'll discuss how to organize the way in which we place suggested supports into a systematic framework so the person's support story is an extension of their autism story.

When we are able to describe the individual's complex, nuanced, and singular autism story, we help that person and their family become powerful advocates, advancing the understanding of the person's perspective and worldview. When we are able to describe a rationale for positive supports that are a fit for the individual's unique autism profile, a similar process occurs. We help the person and their family tell the story of not only *what* supports would be helpful but also *why* those supports are necessary. In telling the story about necessary positive supports in an accessible way we participate in a powerful shift in the narrative that promotes a greater understanding of and respect for the individual's autistic brain style. This in turn leads to an increased motivation for others in the autistic person's life to appreciate different perspectives and to examine "course corrections" they can make. It becomes a shared and collaborative process and also an inclusive process. Everyone looks at their participation and makes adjustments accordingly.

To create a context for positive supports, let's revisit our Descriptive Triangle and rename the central concept to reflect key areas of support. This sets the foundation for identifying essential areas that are in sync with the autistic pattern of brain style strengths and differences. The Descriptive Triangle process of revealing the key areas of support is depicted below in a series of progressive triangles.

DOI: 10.4324/9781003532576-6

The Descriptive Triangle for Key Areas of Support

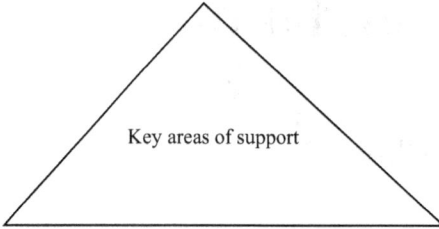

Source: © Marilyn J. Monteiro, PhD.

We'll start with the first of the three key areas of support and place that at the top of our triangle: Organizational supports. Organizational supports align with Language and Communication differences.

Organizational

(Language and Communication)

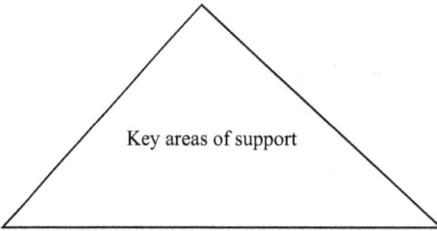

Source: © Marilyn J. Monteiro, PhD.

Now we can describe the rationale for why organizational supports are essential supports for the autistic brain style and the accompanying Language and Communication differences. The rationale provides the context for understanding the *why* behind this key area of suggested supports. When the context of why is clear, the recommended supports tell a compelling story.

Let's set the context for organizational supports by describing the two central autistic language and communication patterns of differences that affect the individual's need for organizational supports. The first pattern centers on understanding that Language and Communication differences affect the way in which the autism spectrum brain takes in information. Specifically, processing incoming language and managing verbal directives are sources of stress that lead to fatigue as the individual's threshold for taking in information is surpassed. Even individuals with high levels of verbal fluency become reactive or distressed when they are required to manage too much verbal input. The second pattern concerns recognizing that the autism spectrum brain organizes and regulates best when the individual can see and respond to visual contextual cues. Even when individuals are highly verbally fluent, the use of visual contextual cues supports the individual's ability to take in information and organize a response to that information. In other words, the autistic brain takes in information more efficiently when the individual has a visual context and routines in place to support the auditory input of spoken language.

When we lay the foundation of describing the recognizable autistic process involved in managing incoming language and communication demands we are ready to link that description to specific positive supports. For example, for a young child who is not yet using spoken language, the visual contextual cues provided by creating and using a dynamic, interactive visual communication schedule logically follows the understanding of the child's autistic Language and Communication differences. For a verbally fluent adult, a transition routine that signals the context for the incoming communication demand allows the adult to flexibly shift and prepare for the incoming information. Across age and ability levels, an essential support for establishing contextual cues and routines includes the use of physical proximity paired with a transition routine that is a fit for the specific individual. Organizational supports also encompass the areas of initiating and completing goal-directed activities. Goal-directed activities cover the scope from learning tasks for young children to school work for children to study skills and work skills for adolescents and adults across the lifespan.

The second key area of support aligns with Social Relationships and Emotional Responses and we'll call those supports Social Knowledge and Self-Determination.

Organizational

(Language and Communication)

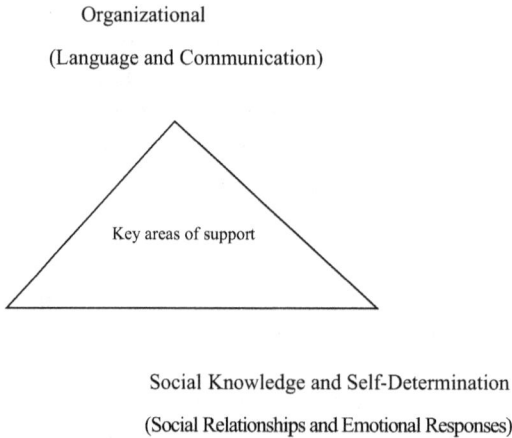

Key areas of support

Social Knowledge and Self-Determination

(Social Relationships and Emotional Responses)

Source: © Marilyn J. Monteiro, PhD.

Let's set the context for social knowledge and self-determination supports by describing the key patterns of social relationship autistic differences. The autism spectrum brain organizes around object-focused and topic-focused routines and narratives. In other words, the autistic individual creates and maintains routines related to their areas of interest, often with a strength of placing details within a topic-focused schematic context. This serves the function of reducing internal stress and distress, as object-focused and topic-focused routines can be self-initiated, have predictable elements, and minimize the unpredictability inherent in social exchanges with others. This difference results in the individual's social narratives of self and others becoming less developed than their topic-focused or object-focused narratives. Social exchanges commonly contain a key element of social narrative use and recognition. This difference in narrative focus increases the autistic individual's level of stress and distress in social exchanges with others, as the autistic brain has to work hard to recognize, interpret, and respond to social communication cues.

In the realm of Social Relationships, the autistic individual experiences stress and oftentimes a lack of success in two entry points regarding social overtures. The first entry point occurs when the individual struggles to manage *social overtures from others*. Interpreting the context set by others, organizing a response, coordinating that response and extending a shared exchange are all parts of the stress involved in any social encounter. The second entry point is the experience the individual has when *their social overtures* to share their object or topic-focused interests are not understood or shared by the person with whom they are making the object-focused social overture. Over time, the individual's experience sets up a narrative of a lack of success in managing incoming social overtures, and a lack of success in using their object-focused social overtures. This leads to an internalized negative narrative. "There's something wrong with me"; "I don't want to go there/do that" are themes that come from trying to establish a context for why things are not working. Autistic individuals have a drive to share their interests and to connect with others. When there is a pattern of being out of sync with others in daily social exchanges, distress and an internal negative self-narrative become amplified.

Friendships and genuine connections are an important part of the human experience for everyone. Understanding each autistic person's way of connecting with others forms the entry point for partnering to craft positive social supports. Describing the individual's lived experience patterns sets the context for understanding the autistic perspective. Specific supports can then be discussed and developed with each person (Bedard & Hecker, 2020; Monteiro, 2021; Monteiro, 2021). Positive supports include using the individual's strengths in recognizing patterns and developing routines to create social narratives, along with supporting self-determined decisions around finding compatible social pathways.

To complete our triangle of key areas of support, we'll discuss the third area in which we need to set a context for supports. The area of exploring and developing regulation supports is linked to the brain style pattern of strengths and differences in the area Sensory Use and Interests.

The Descriptive Triangle for Key Areas of Support

Organizational

(Language and Communication)

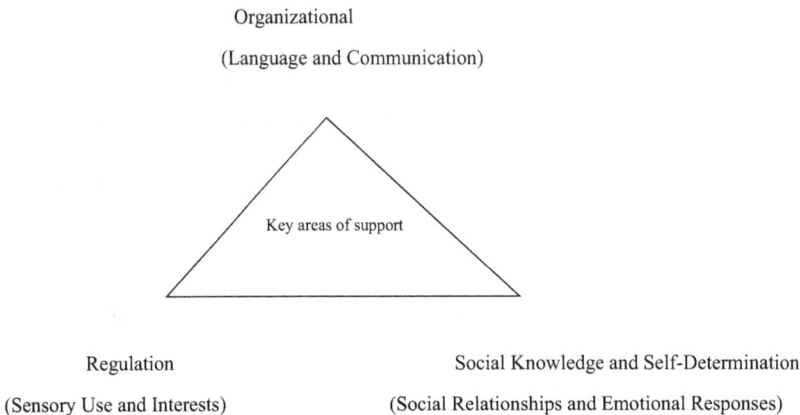

Key areas of support

Regulation   Social Knowledge and Self-Determination

(Sensory Use and Interests)   (Social Relationships and Emotional Responses)

Source: © Marilyn J. Monteiro, PhD.

Emotional regulation and its counterpart, emotional dysregulation, are closely linked to the individual's singular and distinctive autistic brain style pattern of sensory preferences and sensitivities. When the binary autism brain switches from thinking to reacting, or from a state of regulation to dysregulation, the individual experiences a profoundly destabilizing and distressing routine. The destabilizing switch is instantly recognizable to the individual, and oftentimes also to others around them. Because the sensory-based triggers for the disruption are outside of the control of the individual, their recognition of the switch is paired with a cascading or spiraling emotional sequence. The *reactive brain routine* that results can be described as the sequence of emotions, words, and actions the individual experiences and enacts when in a dysregulated state. These routines are often deeply embedded, that is to say, they have occurred in the same way many, many times in response to dysregulation triggers. Recognizing the sensory sensitivities component at the center of emotional dysregulation routines is essential to understanding the types of supports the person needs to better understand and manage their destabilizing emotional experiences. This understanding of the sensory component places the focus on supports that help the individual develop their ability to monitor their regulation level and create brain reset routines to enact before their threshold for managing input has been surpassed and their reactive brain routines have been triggered. Once the individual's reactive brain routines are triggered, incoming demands and input add to the stress level and often prolong or exacerbate the dysregulation episode before the individual is able to reset their regulation level and regain their emotionally balanced state.

Understandably, revisiting reactive brain routines after they occur can be distressing to the individual. When the brain switches from thinking to reacting, the individual's entire system is communicating, essentially, the following message about managing incoming information and sensory input: TOO MUCH!!!! If we place our focus on supports for the individual after brain reactivity and dysregulation have been triggered, we will be less helpful than if we focus on exploring the form and function of brain *regulation* routines. This shift in focus from deconstructing the details related to brain dysregulation to exploring the form and function of routines that regulate the individual's system leads us to identifying proactive brain regulation supports. Now we have a context to explore positive supports, including emotional regulation scales. We can work with the individual to identify brain reset routines to craft regulation supports and routines that are the best fit for their individual style, age, and ability level. We can link the person's areas of preferred interest to the idea of proactive brain reset routines. The development of individualized and visual regulation measures supports the individual's ability to identify, self-monitor, and self-regulate before making the switch from their thinking to their reacting brain.

The contents of this section of the book are intended to provide you with a way to consider contextualizing or organizing your positive support recommendations for individuals and families with whom you work and support. This organizational system and the description of specific positive supports are based on decades of feedback working with autistic individuals, their families, and their educational teams. Consider this visual framework for suggested supports as a starting point for the way in which you think, talk, and write about supports for autistic individuals in your practice. Then add the wisdom you've gained from your experience and incorporate these suggestions into your narrative practice.

Please note that the specific positive supports described in this section of the book can be beneficial for many individuals but are often essential for individuals with autism spectrum brain style differences. You may find that you recommend a support that is not described in this book, as each clinician brings their own history and experience to their clinical practice. If you bring additional suggestions to your reading of this section of the book, by all means, integrate your suggestions into the context provided here.

When we link the descriptive profile of the individual to a systematic framework of positive support we lay the groundwork for positive change. Let's begin by exploring ways to support the autistic story for young children across levels of verbal fluency.

References

Bedard, R., & Hecker, L. (2020). *A Spectrum of Solutions for Clients with Autism*. New York: Routledge Taylor & Francis.

Monteiro, M. (2021). Narrative therapy and the autism spectrum: a model for clinicians. *Hum Syst*. :1–15. doi: 10.1177/263440412110 49763

Monteiro, M. (2021). Individualizing the autism assessment process: A framework for school psychologists. *Psychology in the Schools*, 1–13. https://doi.org/ 10.1002/pits.22624

4   Support the story

Young children across levels of verbal fluency – Maya and Maxwell

When the parents and caregivers of young autistic children partner with clinicians like yourself to develop a positive support plan for the child, the work you do together profoundly affects the daily life and development of the child and the family. The child's Brain Style Profile provides the family with a strengths-based and accessible way to understand the young child's worldview. Pairing that profile of the child's pattern of strengths and differences with a positive support plan provides the foundation for everyone in the family to begin to shift their lived experience narrative from powerless to capable (Monteiro, 2016).

You'll recall Maya and her Brain Style Profile of strengths and differences from Chapter 1. In this chapter, Maya's suggested supports and strategies provide her parents and caregivers with an accessible way to identify practical ways to support her individualized profile of communication, social, and sensory differences. This narrative framework of describing positive supports provides parents and caregivers with specific and feasible strategies, while placing the suggested supports into a context of why they would be a good fit for the child.

In the report excerpt provided below, Maya is described as a child with areas of strength along with distinctive brain style differences. The narrative emphasizes her strengths and describes the conditions under which, as a young child who is not yet consistently using spoken language, Maya is the most organized and responsive. This lays the foundation to list organizational, social, and regulation supports for her that emphasize the use of visual contextual cues and routines.

Her areas of preferred interest, including characters from her beloved *Pokoyo* program, letters, numbers, and maraca shaker eggs, are referenced as sensory entry points to incorporate into her positive support routines.

As you read Maya's suggested supports and strategies and the description of the *why* each support is being recommended, think about how you

DOI: 10.4324/9781003532576-7

might use a similar way of describing positive supports for the young autistic children in your clinical practice.

Suggested supports and strategies for Maya

Maya is a happy, positive, gentle-natured, and appealing 3 year, 2-month-old girl who displayed areas of strength in addition to some distinctive brain style differences. Both by report and demonstrated during this consultation evaluation, Maya did best when incoming language and social demands were linked with visual contextual cues, and when language and social demands were linked with opportunities for shared exploration of interesting sensory-based materials. Maya showed an interest in exploring a range of materials during the consultation evaluation, although she consistently used the novel materials to create routines that were self-directed rather than shared with a play partner.

*Maya would benefit from specific, systematic supports to help her development in the areas of **organization** routines and the development of her **social play skills** and her **self-determination narrative**. Maya would also benefit from the development of emotional **regulation** routines.*

- *In the area of **organization**, including organization and use of functional language skills, Maya would benefit from the following:*

  o *Maya is a visual, three-dimensional learner who organizes by focusing on objects of interest in her surroundings. To help her expand her ability to anticipate and follow routines, manage changes in her routine, and shift from her agenda to the agenda of others, she would benefit from the systematic use of visual schedules. A visual schedule that includes the dynamic and interactive component of Maya being guided to match representational objects or pictures as part of her transition time routine will work well for her. Pairing the use of the representation matching objects or pictures with verbal labeling ("Bath time") will support Maya as she expands her ability to anticipate and verbally label activities throughout her day. Her parents already have a well-established and consistent daily routine for Maya, so adding this visual and tactile component will support Maya's development in the areas of anticipation of routines and of labeling actions with words. The visual objects and/or picture communication routine serves the function of "showing" Maya the routine while prompting the adults to pair verbal directives and labeling with objects. This is a perfect* fit for Maya's object-focused exploration of the world. Hearing the labeling language while seeing the representational object will help Maya expand her verbal communication skills repertoire.

o Showing while telling is an important building block for communication skills and flexibility for Maya. Including visual representational objects or pictures that can be matched at the location of each daily activity is a great place to start in helping Maya make the association between objects, words, and activities, and to increase her spontaneous use of communication to request and label. For example, matching rubber duckies for bathtime and a toothbrush for hygiene routines will work well for Maya, while providing her parents with objects to prompt "showing while telling. This will support Maya in her ability to build brain flexibility and organizational skills. Formalizing the process of using visual prompts is an important fit for Maya's learning style.

o Maya is not yet consistently anticipating and following adult-directed learning routines. She would benefit from the introduction of a visually structured work system. Setting up developmental tasks for Maya, such as color matching, inset puzzles with shapes, and so on, in containers to the left of her work space, and providing short, repeating sessions with her to pattern the routine of taking the first of three work materials out of a container (bin or bags), working on the task from start to finish, even if hand-over-hand guidance is initially required, and dropping the completed task (inset puzzle, folder with Velcro to attach matching items) into the "finish" basket to the right of her work space upon completion of the activity creates a routine for her. Setting up a sequence of "work/break/work/break," where Maya begins to anticipate "how much" work is required and "how long" she will be expected to follow directions, and following each brief work session with a high-preference "break" or activity, such as opening a container that holds special maraca eggs or nesting toys or Pocoyo-themed books and objects. Showing Maya a container to drop the preferred objects into at the end of the brief sensory-focused break, followed by the action of opening a container with "work" materials creates a transition routine between low-demand and higher demand activities and routines. As Maya begins to anticipate and internalize this routine, her brain develops flexibility to anticipate and make the shift from her agenda to following the agenda of others.

o To introduce the work/break/work/break routine at home, Maya's mother might use a floor mat, blanket, or small table to signal "work" time. Maya can then visually associate time on the mat or blanket with guided playtime, as opposed to free playtime when *she is not in the designated work area. The use of containers, simple "put in" tasks, with developmental materials such as inset puzzles, pegboards, nesting toys, and so on, paired with the use of a "finish" basket will help Maya anticipate, organize, and expand her use of goal-directed play with developmental toys and materials. It will also provide opportunities to shape social play elements such as taking turns and sharing objects.*

- *In the area of **social skills and self-determination narrative**, Maya would benefit from the following:*

   o *Maya has loving relationships with her parents, but has not yet developed the ability to consistently understand and respond to her social and play partners. She is beginning to show an interest in turning the pages of books and consistently seeks out cuddle time with her parents. She also enjoys screen time with electronics involving letters and numbers and her beloved Pokoyo characters. Maya would benefit from the introduction of visual social books or social stories that use photos to match, and photos paired with simple sentences in the first person to help build Maya's narrative about herself and her life (sample topic for social storybook would be: "Me and my family," with photos to match while hearing the verbal labeling of each family member. This can be set up electronically on a device such as an iPad, and Maya can swipe each page as her parents read the caption to her and touch the photos. Adding photos of Maya engaged in preferred activities with family members, and when she is with her therapists and peers will be helpful for her social narrative development as well.*

   o *Currently, Maya has a repertoire of play interests but has not yet developed the repertoire of skills required to participate in shared exchanges with a play partner. She would benefit from direct teaching of the component skills involved in shared play with others. For example, pairing the "clean-up" song with the routine of holding a container and modeling picking up objects will help Maya better organize her play and participate in a shared activity. Practicing turn-taking with a cause-and-effect developmental object, such as a spinning light-up toy or maraca egg shaker, and having brief, repeating sessions of exchanging the object between play partners, is an excellent way to introduce the concepts of shared play and taking turns.*

   o *In the area of supporting Maya's developing self-determination, the introduction of visual communication supports provides a systematic way for Maya to clearly communicate her wants and needs. Her parents and caregivers are encouraged to pay close*

*attention to opportunities to receive and respect Maya's commu-
nication regarding her wishes and intentions. In other words, the
use of visual communication routines provides opportunities for
Maya not only to respond to incoming requests and directives but
also for her to more clearly express her self-determined wants and
needs in a way that can be better understood and responded to by
the important people in her world.*

- *In the area of **regulation** routines, Maya would benefit from the
following:*

   o *Maya showed a pattern of reacting to incoming demands by
   moving away from the source of demands. She is not yet able
   to predictably anticipate "how much" and "how long" demands
   will occur, adding to her hesitancy and resistance to incoming
   requests or demands. Maya is still developing the skills of anticipation and prediction of start-to-finish with developmental
   tasks. The combined use of dynamic, interactive visual schedule
   supports and the use of "first/then" rapid cycle work/break/work/
   break routines to establish a cycle of Maya's ability to sustain her
   engagement with tasks she is directed by others to complete,
   interspersed with opportunities to retreat and regroup with solitary or sensory-based routines where she can explore the sensory properties of materials without the structure of guiding her to
   engage in goal-directed play, will help Maya better recognize and
   respond to adult prompts.*

   o *Maya is already using a routine of retreating from stressors by
   seeking out sensory, object-focused regrouping breaks when
   incoming language, social, and work demands exceed her capacity to engage with and respond to others instead of becoming
   agitated, and distressed. At the same time, it is currently challenging for Maya to shift flexibly from her sensory-based play to
   follow directives and social overtures from others. As she enters
   into formal, structured therapy interventions and in her preschool
   setting, establishing systematic sensory regrouping breaks planned
   into her day in a proactive way will support Maya as she practices
   self-regulation across settings. It will also lead to increasing her
   threshold for incoming demands while increasing her ability to
   flexibly shift from her agenda to the agenda of others.*

The written narrative describing the positive supports in a contextualized
way provides a reference point for the family and other caregivers to
adjust and reframe the way in which they approach daily routines as they

see things from the child's sensory-based perspective. They can explore the ways in which visual supports are a better fit for both the child and themselves.

Without an organized context to support communication and other organizational routines, parents and caregivers often experience a high level of stress and fatigue in everyday life. Even though they are working hard to engage the child and support the child's development, there is a sense of working hard without the corresponding positive outcomes. In my work with parents, we often discuss the question: Who is working harder, you or your child? This leads to an exploration of the established routines of the parent relying on their most efficient means of communication (spoken language, often without proximity or other visual cues), and how that cancels out the most efficient means of communication for their child (proximity, paired with a transition routine to allow the shift of agendas, and pairing the spoken request with visual contextual cues). The shift from powerless to capable starts with the "course correction" of adjusting communication to fit the child's brain style patterns of strengths and differences. As described in Maya's summary, the course corrections center on contextualizing incoming language and engineering the environment to provide visual routines.

How would the suggested positive supports differ for a verbally fluent young child? The emphasis for younger children who are verbally fluent includes ways to provide a clearer context for incoming information to reduce the child's experience of emotional reactivity. Verbally fluent autistic children use their spontaneous spoken language to label and describe. In other words, they are already using their self-initiated spoken language to show while telling, as they are best able to organize, retrieve, and use their language when they have a visual context. This connection forms the basis of helping adults in the young child's world understand the importance of "showing while telling" as the foundation for their communication with the verbally fluent child. "Showing while telling," or providing visual contextual cues paired with spoken language, is the most efficient way for the young verbally fluent child to flexibly shift their focus and take in information from others. It follows that if the child is able to more efficiently take in information from others, the child's capacity for managing stress and distress will increase as well. In turn, organizational and communication supports are essential building blocks to support emotional regulation and stability.

Let's revisit Maxwell from Chapter 1 and explore how his three areas of positive supports fit together with his autism spectrum Brain Style Profile. As you recall, Maxwell's passionate areas of interest included dinosaurs and building with Legos and other materials. He showed a well-established pattern of narrating his play and exploration of materials along with genuine enjoyment when others followed his lead while he played. He also showed the pattern of hard work for his brain to flexibly shift and respond to his conversational or play partner. His brain flexibility differences were closely linked to his low threshold for incoming demands and his resulting rapid shifting from his thinking to his reacting brain. The sample report provided below is one way to incorporate Maxwell's pattern of strengths and differences into his recommended supports in the three key areas. Because organization and regulation are intertwined areas of challenge for Maxwell, the sequence of suggested supports includes a focus on those two areas first, and then on social knowledge and self-determination supports. In Maxwell's narrative report, suggestions are included for his anticipated school-based support team, as his parents were preparing for Maxwell's transition to primary school after his fifth birthday.

Suggested supports and strategies for Maxwell

Maxwell is an intelligent, outgoing, and somewhat serious 4 year, 10-month-old boy who organized and used his language best with this psychologist when Maxwell was initiating directions and statements related to his play, and when the play materials or his conversational partner provided visual context cues. His reactivity in response to demands is best understood as a response to surpassing his threshold for incoming language, social, sensory, or work demands. Maxwell's reactive behavior routines are well established, and he would benefit from structured supports that take his complex brain style (intelligent and able to learn information, paired with his sensory and social communication differences) into consideration.

*Maxwell would benefit from specific, systematic interventions to help him in the areas of **organization** and **regulation** of his behavior. Maxwell would also benefit from the development of his **social knowledge** and his **self-determination** narrative.*

*In the area of **organization**, currently, because Maxwell has well-developed language skills, the adults mostly rely on verbal prompts and explanations to guide Maxwell through daily transitions. However, this reliance on spoken language directives is fatiguing for Maxwell and he oftentimes responds with resistance, agitation, or distress. At home currently, and as he enters the faster paced and more demanding environment of primary school in the coming year, relying on verbal directives will most likely exacerbate his existing pattern of reactivity in response to verbal input.*

When Maxwell becomes fatigued with processing incoming verbal information, his subsequent pattern of shutting down or reacting to the demands with his dysregulated behavior routines makes it challenging for him to reset his regulation level and follow the flow of events around him.

Adults in his world benefit from understanding the well-developed strengths for Maxwell's brain as he consistently seeks out patterns and routines. The use of visual supports paired with verbal input will significantly reduce his stress level, as the verbal directives are placed within an instantly recognizable pattern or context.

Maxwell's brain is also best able to organize and regulate when he self-initiates routines and activities. As adults understand this pattern, they can include a routine of placing Maxwell in charge of checking his schedule, using checklists, and visually anticipating a sequence of "first/ then" throughout his day. Maxwell can then be prompted to "tell" and "show" the adult the steps involved in the organized behavior during transitions, a distinctively different experience from his current experience of reactivity when asked to follow verbal directives.

Maxwell would benefit from the following:

- Develop a visual schedule that includes a dynamic and interactive component (check boxes off as part of his transition time routine; linked with a visual depiction of a preferred area of interest, such as mini dinosaur figures following a path through key aspects of each activity or setting). This will be helpful in supporting Maxwell's ability to move himself through the independent process of completing daily routines at home and later at school while providing the adult with the visual supports to prompt Maxwell to check what comes next instead of having Maxwell maintain his current prompt dependency on the adult to tell Maxwell each step while he becomes resistant and dysregulated.

- Consider establishing a transition routine to help Maxwell develop the ability to flexibly shift his attention and focus from his sensory-driven internal agenda to prepare for receiving input from others. The use of an object or verbal routine paired with physical proximity will provide Maxwell with the incoming signals communicating that it is time to shift from his agenda and prepare to receive input. For Maxwell, the use of a particular dinosaur figure designated as his "messenger" and a verbal routine with an agreed-upon word ("Ready?", "Question coming in. Ready?", or something along those lines) provides the support and scaffolding he requires to shift from his agenda and prepare to take in information. As the adult establishes proximity and, without talking, waits for Maxwell to register their presence, they provide him with the time he needs to shift his focus. The exchange of the three-dimensional dinosaur figure establishes the visual context for Maxwell to orient toward his conversational partner and prepare to receive input. The question-and-answer routine further establishes the shift. When the adult then gives a simple directive or asks a question, Maxwell experiences success. When the adult receives the dinosaur figure back again, Maxwell has a context for understanding the exchange is over until the next time. Repeated cycles of this routine help Maxwell replace his current experience of distress and resistance to incoming demands with a success loop.

- Implement a routine where the adults talk less, and show while telling using visual supports (visual and interactive schedule, "first/then" card, job cards, T-chart for words and actions). Reducing verbal directions and verbal input is critical, as Maxwell demonstrates a low threshold for incoming language demands.
- At home and subsequently at school, the use of visual systems will help him take in the context of requests and the scope of demands. The use of containers, labels, and other organizational structures will help Maxwell better anticipate the scope and sequence of everyday tasks and participate in activities that require him to follow directions and engage in activities outside of his selected and preferred routines. Establishing the transition routine of taking materials out of containers and placing them into containers at the start and end of everyday routines helps Maxwell maintain a sense of predictability and control across work tasks.
- To help Maxwell build his threshold for following an agenda set by others, he would benefit from coming into repeated contact with a cycle or routine of "work" (demands imposed on him) and "breaks" (self-selected sensory-driven routines and activities). Pairing the cycle of work/break with his visual schedule and helping Maxwell notice when his brain and body are getting energy from his breaks and from getting his work done, are all components that establish a meaningful context for demands for him.

In the area of **regulation**, Maxwell frequently experiences agitation and distress regarding language, social, sensory, and environmental demands. Providing visual tools to help Maxwell learn to self-monitor and apply self-regulation routines will be very helpful for him. The use of proactive brain reset routines is strongly encouraged, as Maxwell needs to experience being able to begin to be overwhelmed, and then doing an activity that regulates and restores his energy level to replace his current routine of becoming overwhelmed and reacting, or withdrawing and following his own agenda instead of following verbal choices set by adults. The use of a visual "work/break" schematic will help Maxwell better anticipate and connect the value of having expected times to engage in preferred activities, helping him sustain his efforts and engagement with tasks that require managing incoming information. Currently Maxwell's parents are consistently using the reduced stimulation brain reset routine. They are encouraged to add the suggested supports below, and to introduce the language of "reset my brain" with Maxwell. He likes to know how things work, and providing him with an understanding of what is happening when his brain goes from thinking to reacting, and having visually accessible lists of brain reset activities and routines will be meaningful and impactful for Maxwell.

Maxwell would benefit from the following:

- Put together a self-regulation, visual scale, developed with Maxwell, to help him identify the words, actions, and feeling states he associates with each level of regulation, with Levels 1–3 being the target range and Levels 4 and 5 identified as the "reacting" levels; paired with an area of visual interest or metaphor, such as dinosaurs that are happy and playing and dinosaurs that are tired and grumpy, or battery levels, or any number of visual metaphors that resonate with him. Pair the metaphor with words describing the experience he is having at each level. For example: Level 1 = My brain and body are calm and working together, my brain is thinking about things I like, I can find my words to talk to others, I can move my body, look at things I enjoy seeing, and do activities I like, such as building, playing, and naming things; Level 3 = My brain and body are feeling stressed, and I need to take a brain reset break doing something from my Brain Reset Menu list, I am talking loudly, I am having trouble focusing on what others are saying or doing, and my body wants to move away from other people or to shout and cry just like a baby T-Rex who is getting hungry and mad; Levels 4 and 5 = TOO MUCH!!!! My brain and body are stressed, I need to take a break from all the listening and following directions, I cannot keep listening and talking to others, it is hard for me to use my words, so I need to take a break and use my hands with building or working with something I like.
- Pair his visual self-regulation scale with prompts throughout the day to check in with the visual scale describing his words, actions, and emotions, and rating: "How am I doing?" to establish a proactive routine of self-monitoring and self-regulation.
- Include a high density of labeling his regulation levels with him when he is in a regulated state (Levels 1–3). This means looking for frequent opportunities to support Maxwell in noticing when his brain and body are staying calm and are working together.
- Include the development of a "brain reset menu" of activities and materials that can by cycled through during the day. The use of containers for his sensory stress kit, for example, provides an

organized routine for Maxwell to anticipate and follow to practice self-regulation.

- *Provide systematic brain reset/sensory regrouping breaks planned into his day in a proactive way; link the use of these breaks with his self-monitoring of his regulation scale.*
- *Use "words and actions" T-charts to identify and build adaptive replacement behavior routines.*
- *Introduce the concept of "train my brain" to teach adaptive coping skills routines.*
- *Consider the proactive use of a reduced stimulation learning setting as part of Maxwell's sensory regrouping brain reset tool kit. Designating low stimulation retreat areas for Maxwell at home and in the classroom and at school will be helpful.*

*In the area of **social knowledge** and **self-determination** narrative, Maxwell is a child who is outgoing, affectionate, and creative in his play and exploration of the world around him. He seeks out others to share his interests, and struggles with closing the gap between his desire for social connections and his brain's ability to notice and respond to social cues from his social and play partners. Maxwell struggles with understanding the perspective of others when he assumes the role of telling others what to do instead of sharing a conversation or play routine with them. Maxwell has not yet developed the ability to use his well-developed language skills to talk about himself or his feelings in a detailed, self-aware way. In social interactions with peers, Maxwell has verbalized to his parents that he experiences that others do not want to play with him. Providing Maxwell with systematic visual supports and coaching for social skills and social routines will help him develop a positive and alternative narrative about himself in relation to others.*

Maxwell would benefit from the following:

- *Develop a notebook about Maxwell that contains all his tools.*
    - o *Include his personal narrative in the notebook, built with him over time, with his Brain Style Profile, narrative about himself and his life, and his skills, talents, and goals; include "5 things my teacher needs to know about me" that highlights his strengths, interests, and differences.*
    - o *Include coaching to identify social aspects of his friends and classmates and age-appropriate ways to engage socially with peers.*

- *Systematically use visual social scripts, comic strip conversations, and step-by-step visual maps to help Maxwell better anticipate social routines and to teach Maxwell social exchan ge and social communication routines with peers. For example, create a step-by-step visual map for "Find a friend at recess," and coach Maxwell to review the steps prior to recess (for example, From a list of choices, pick a friend; pick an activity; pick the words and actions to start the play.).*
- *Use T-chart discrimination sheets to help Maxwell identify his current, reactive words and actions, and contrast those visually with the adaptive replacement alternatives ("Words and actions I used to use" versus "Words and actions I use now that I am almost five years old").*
- *Systematically use visual supports to increase Maxwell's vocabulary to identify and express his emotions.*
- *Consider providing Maxwell with direct teaching of social and social conversation skills through social skills or social language groups. Shape his use of prosocial skills by creating videos as he practices social skills in small groups and at home.*
- *To increase his awareness of his voice volume, use a visual scale with a movable brad for each level of volume.*

There are countless other ways to describe supports for young children, and you are encouraged to adapt and configure the way in which you describe and discuss recommended supports. Although a review of published materials is beyond the scope of this book, you are encouraged to explore the many published materials that guide clinicians through the use of visual supports (Mesibov et. al, 2004; Sussman & Lewis, 2012; Eckenrode et. al, 2013), social knowledge and self-determination supports (Hodgdon, 2023); and regulation supports for young autistic children (Young, 2004; Buron & Curtis, 2021). As you review materials, you are encouraged to think about their application to specific young children and their families in your clinical practice.

The context provided by the Descriptive Triangle helps parents and caregivers with a plan and practical guidelines that support their child's autism story. The support story begins by linking their child's pattern of strengths and differences in development to concrete strategies and supports. The plan provides them first with the rationale for the supports that would be helpful and then with specific suggestions for changes in the way the child's organizational, social relationship, and regulation needs are understood. The written document with this personalized information provides parents and caregivers of young children with their child's unique story, along with ways to support that story.

Now that we've explored supporting the story of young autistic children and their families, let's discuss supporting the story of children and adolescents.

References

Buron, K. D., & Curtis, M. (2021). *The Incredible 5-poin Scale: Assisting Students in Understanding Social Interactions and Managing their Emotional Responses*. Minnesota: Kari Dunn Buron.

Eckenrode, L., Fennell, P., & Hearsey, K. (2013). *Tasks Galore*. Raleigh, North Carolina: Tasks Galore Publishing.

Hodgdon, L. (2023). *Visual Strategies for Improving Communication: Practical Supports for Autism Spectrum Disorders*. Troy, Michigan: QuirkRoberts Press.

Mesibov, G. B., Shea, V., & Schoplet, E (2004). *The TEACCH Approach to Autism Spectrum Disorders*. Virginia: Springer Publications.

Monteiro, M. (2016). *Family Therapy and the Autism Spectrum: Autism Conversations in Narrative Practice*. New York: Routledge Taylor & Francis.

Sussman, F., & Lewis, R. B. (2012). *More than Words: A Parent's Guide to Building Interaction and Language Skills for Children with Autism Spectrum Disorder or Social Communication Difficulties*. Ontario, Canada: Hanen Centre Press.

Young, M. (2024). *Autism Emotional Regulation Tips for Parents*. New York: McNally Jackson Books.

5 Support the story

Children and adolescents – Malik and Marissa

As autistic children enter school, their lives becomes increasingly more complex. That added complexity often comes with the lived experience of stress in response to life events, along with the development of resiliency in facing daily challenges (Greenlee et al., 2024). The sensory demands on the child's system are multifaceted and can be experienced by the child as relentless, as most of the child's day centers around following the agenda of others. There is little time to recharge their system through immersion in their beloved routines that center on their preferred activities and interests. The rush to get ready for school in the morning, the bombardment of sensory input throughout the school day, and the seemingly never-ending verbal demands to complete work and move from one activity to the next build up and constantly threaten to overwhelm the child's threshold for managing incoming demands. On top of these factors, the child also has to manage the labyrinth of navigating through social exchanges with their peers. The autistic child is often highly vulnerable in social relationships during school-age years, as peers are more likely to target them for bullying and harassment (Chen & Schwartz, 2012; Morales-Hidalgo et al., 2024). For many autistic children, this adverse childhood social experience adds to their general sense of a lack of predictable stability in their daily life. Because the autistic child has to expend a great deal of their energy to manage these daily sensory and social demands, they often experience social isolation, chronic stress, anxiety, depression, and exhaustion. The cost is high but is also oftentimes hidden. When the autistic child or adolescent has strong language and cognitive abilities and has not received a formal diagnosis, the expectation that they will be able to adapt and manage alongside their peers is held firmly in place. Even when the autistic child has been identified as eligible for specialized school supports, their daily school experience is often fraught with stressors. For many autistic children, this experience of stressors and their impact on the child's sense of well-being intensifies during their adolescent years.

DOI: 10.4324/9781003532576-8

It is within this context that parents seek out support from clinicians like yourself to better understand their complex child. The work you do as you partner with children, adolescents, and their families can make a profound difference in the way in which they navigate through the home and school demands of childhood and adolescence. Linking a neuro-informed understanding of the autistic child's or adolescent's story to concrete ways to support their story, provides the autistic child and their family with a context and tools to bolster the child's social and emotional development. The accessible and descriptive positive supports framework we'll be discussing here also gives parents the context they need to advocate for their child's school accommodations and modifications. It helps the child's teachers better understand and support the child in the school setting.

Here are words we want to hear from teachers:

Before your team helped me understand Malik's autistic brain style, I thought he was being willful and defiant. Understanding how his brain experiences sensory overload changed everything in the classroom. I see things from his perspective now and use a different approach that works for both of us.

Supporting Malik's autism story

The remark above from Malik's teacher leads us to our discussion of key supports for Malik's autism story. As we explore his support story, imagine yourself applying the rationale for and description of his recommended strategies to children in your clinical practice. Malik's complex behavioral profile included attention and focusing differences and generalized anxiety patterns, along with his autism spectrum brain style pattern of strengths and differences. His recommended supports reflect the need to support his executive functioning brain processes differences (Barkley, 2020). Malik, as is the case for many autistic children, faced daily struggles in the area of brain flexibility, including applying adaptable thinking abilities along with planning and reasoning skills. He also needed supports to help him manage his differences in the areas of working memory, problem-solving skills, and the application of reasoning strategies. Finally, Malik needed supports in the area of inhibition control, including managing his reactions to input and applying self-monitoring and self-regulation routines.

Organizational supports for Malik include the reminder for the adults in his world that the use of visual supports paired with verbal directives and input are necessary to increase his ability to take in information, manage transitions and develop stamina to sustain his work efforts. In the excerpt below, you will recognize specific visually organized support systems to incorporate into Malik's school and home routines that are essential for verbally fluent autistic children and that you may already find yourself recommending for the children in your clinical practice. Here we place those recommended supports into a context. Clearly communicating the link between Malik's autistic communication differences and the need for visual supports sets the context for adults to change the way in which they understand Malik's verbal fluency. Changing the perspective to include an understanding of the verbally fluent child's autistic pattern of strengths (self-initiated, contextualized use of language) and differences (responding to incoming language demands) guides the adults in the child's world to understand the need for visual contextualization of incoming language demands. We begin by describing this key set of communication patterns.

Suggested organizational supports and strategies for Malik

In the area of organization, Malik is a highly visual learner who encodes language best when verbal information is paired with visual contextual cues. He would benefit at school and at home during transition times by having adults partner with him to develop visual checklists and directives to replace and/or support their use of verbal questions and multistep directives. Malik would respond less reactively if he were given verbal directives paired with visual prompts (show while telling). This pairing will increase Malik's capacity to take in and follow verbal multistep directions. Checklists that are dynamic and interactive will work best, and will prepare Malik to manage the step-by-step routines he will need to accomplish daily tasks independently when he makes the transition through pre-adolescence over the next few years.

Now that we've set the context for *why* supports are necessary, we are ready to identify specific visual organizational supports.

Malik would benefit from the following visual organizational supports:

- *Help him develop and use visual schedules and routines across settings that lay out the steps involved in classwork and homework assignments with boxes to check as each step is completed*
- *Visual schedules that include the dynamic and interactive component of, for example, checking boxes off as part of his transition time routine will work well for him, as Malik will experience the organizing routine of preparing for the shift from one activity to the next*
- *Malik will benefit from the use of an organizational notebook for his schedules, checklists, and assignments by subject matter and category (to be completed; to be turned in) with systematic adult coaching to master the routine of using it throughout the day*

- *Consider organizing Malik's work with visual step-by-step maps, especially when writing assignments are given, as Malik struggles with his ability to get started and complete written assignments; this visual structure will support him well, as it gives him a visual context to follow*
- *Establish a transition routine of taking materials out of containers and placing them into containers at the start and end of tasks; this will help Malik maintain a sense of predictability and control across work tasks*
- *Consider adding bins or drawers to his desk area in the classroom so that he can be prompted to keep his materials in a readily accessible and visually labeled place*
- *Malik would also benefit from homework sessions organized around a visually linked work/break/work/break cycle that allows Malik to experience increased flexibility in successfully shifting between his agenda and the agenda of others, and provides Malik with the experience of working and restoring his energy level in cycles that do not include depleting his resources*

Because Malik has handwriting or dysgraphia differences, teaching him keyboarding skills was also recommended. Because Malik sought out physical movement and input, alternative seating arrangements are suggested as well.

- *Begin developing keyboarding as an alternative to handwriting*
- *Consider providing alternative seating arrangements, such as a yoga ball chair, bean bag chair, or standing table, to provide Malik with movement opportunities and body regulation routines while working in class*

Malik's *Regulation support* needs: developing his personalized regulation scale

As we revisit Malik's regulation differences, we have an opportunity to explore how to structure the process of creating an individualized regulation scale with a child who struggles with the destabilizing binary brain experience of shifting rapidly from their thinking/regulated brain to their reacting/dysregulated brain. Let's sit in on the conversation with Malik that extends the dialogue about Malik's use of a word meme ("Meep") as a sign that his brain and system are switching from their regulated to dysregulated state. We contextualized his routine with the descriptive metaphor of a glitch: "Maybe your brain has hit a glitch and needs to reset." Malik showed his connection with the glitch metaphor when he named it his

"Meep glitch." In this extended conversation, we lay the foundation for developing Malik's regulation scale.

"So, Malik, may I show you a way to understand what happens when your brain has a glitch?" I provided Malik with an introductory context for our conversation with the visual cue of holding up my small notepad and pencil. Malik took this in and waited attentively.

I wrote the numbers 1, 2, 3, 4, and 5 across the top of the page and drew a line under the numbers. Malik looked at the numbers and as he watched, I drew a line from the top to the bottom of the page between the numbers 3 and 4. The regulation narrative is depicted below in a series of progressive scales so you can follow along with the process of revealing Malik's regulation narrative with him.

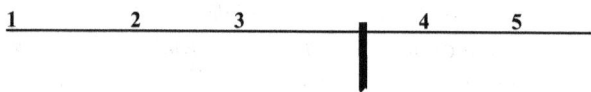

1	2	3		4	5

Source: © Marilyn J. Monteiro, PhD.

"So, Malik, let's think of this as a way to show how your brain goes from thinking to reacting." I wrote the words above each side of the T-chart. Malik showed that he was with me as he watched the page.

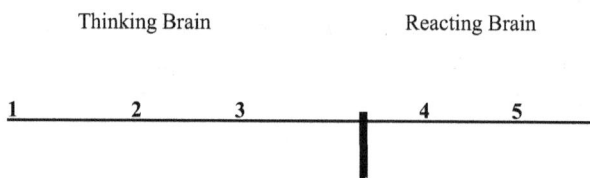

Thinking Brain   Reacting Brain

1	2	3		4	5

Source: © Marilyn J. Monteiro, PhD.

"When you are in your thinking brain, things are good, right?" Malik nodded in agreement.

"We can talk about that as being at a level 1: My brain and body are calm and working together. Things are good." I wrote those words under number 1 as Malik watched.

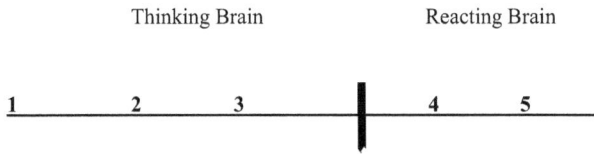

Thinking Brain   Reacting Brain

1   2   3 | 4   5

My brain and body are calm and

working together. Things are good.

Source: © Marilyn J. Monteiro, PhD.

"Let's think about what is happening when things are good for you. Things are good for you when you are doing the things you love, like playing *Minecraft*, building with Legos, playing your keyboard. Correct?" Malik's head bobbed up and down as he looked at the page.

"Let's look at what those things have in common." I wrote a list under number 1 while naming the list to Malik. "They are things that your brain and body love to do and they give you energy…they are *your* interests… and when you do them, it blocks out bothersome things around you, giving you a break from stress." Again Malik followed the writing on the page and waited for me to continue.

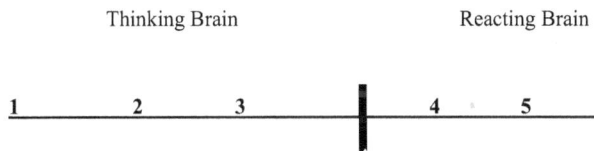

Thinking Brain   Reacting Brain

1   2   3 | 4   5

My brain and body are calm and

working together. Things are good.

Minecraft, Legos, music: when I

do the things I love, I gain energy

and take a stress break

Source: © Marilyn J. Monteiro, PhD.

"Am I describing it right?" I asked, and waited for Malik to respond.

He bounced up and down gently in his perched position. "Yes, yes, and yes!" he declared.

"Now let's talk about what starts to happen when your brain are body are getting stressed." I wrote those words on the page under number 3.

"Meep glitch!" Malik reminded me of the way we had previously described when his brain and body start to experience stress.

"Thank you, Malik! We absolutely need to add that to describe your brain and body stress experience." I added his phrasing to the page. He signaled his approval with his intense continued focus on the evolving chart on the page.

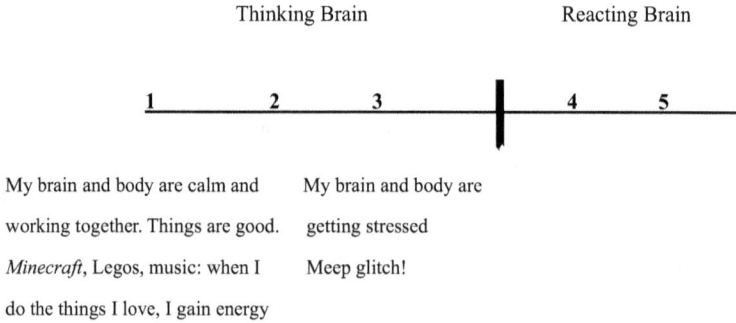

Thinking Brain   Reacting Brain

1 _____ 2 _____ 3 _____ | _____ 4 _____ 5

My brain and body are calm and   My brain and body are

working together. Things are good.   getting stressed

Minecraft, Legos, music: when I   Meep glitch!

do the things I love, I gain energy

Source: © Marilyn J. Monteiro, PhD.

"This is where things get tricky for your brain and body, Malik. Your brain doesn't really have a plan or system in place yet to help you reset and fix the glitch. The glitch mostly happens when your parents or teacher ask you to do something and you have to stop doing what you love. Your brain pattern is to jump the line..." I took my pencil and had it jump over the line from underneath the number 3 to between numbers 4 and 5. "...and before you know it, you have made the switch from your thinking brain to your reacting brain." I wrote the words TOO MUCH!!! on the right hand side of the chart.

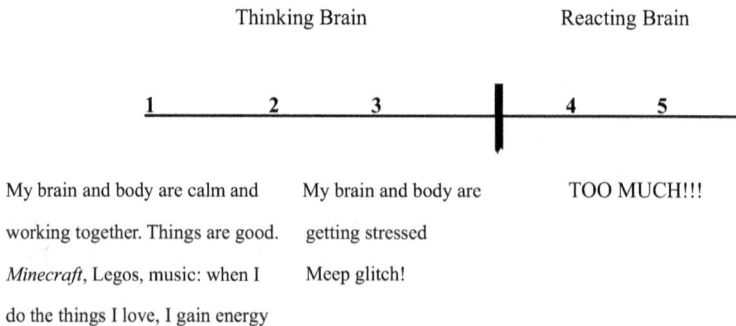

Thinking Brain   Reacting Brain

1 _____ 2 _____ 3 _____ | _____ 4 _____ 5

My brain and body are calm and   My brain and body are   TOO MUCH!!!

working together. Things are good.   getting stressed

Minecraft, Legos, music: when I   Meep glitch!

do the things I love, I gain energy

Source: © Marilyn J. Monteiro, PhD.

"What are your thoughts about how I described that jump, Malik?" Malik wordlessly made a thumbs up gesture.

"Thank you, Malik, for that confirmation. There is another thing that is happening when your brain and body make the jump from thinking to reacting that would be helpful for us to notice. You are a boy whose brain does an excellent job of creating routines. You notice details and get creative all the time when you are doing the things you love and are able to follow your familiar routines: toggling between creative and survival mode in *Minecraft*, building things, coding things. Your brain likes routines. Am I describing your brain experience about right?" Malik nodded.

"So, of course, your brain and body follow a *routine* when you have a glitch and jump the line." I paused for a moment as this idea was absorbed by Malik. I took my pencil and drew several lines with arrows crossing from the thinking to the reacting sides of the chart as a way to visually depict the binary process of dysregulation Malik was experiencing as his deeply embedded reactive behavior routine.

Thinking Brain   Reacting Brain

1   2   3 | 4   5

My brain and body are calm and   My brain and body are   TOO MUCH!!!

working together. Things are good.   getting stressed

Minecraft, Legos, music: when I   Meep glitch

do the things I love, I gain energy

→

→

→

Source: © Marilyn J. Monteiro, PhD.

"The better we are able to recognize and describe the words and actions that signal that TOO MUCH is going on for your system, the better we will be at changing your reactive routine and replacing it with a way to reset your brain before your system jumps the line." I wrote the words Brain Reset Break! on the page under number 3. I added the initials BRB.

	Thinking Brain		Reacting Brain	
1	2	3	4	5

My brain and body are calm and working together. Things are good.

Minecraft, Legos, music: when I do the things I love, I gain energy

My brain and body are getting stressed

Meep glitch

Brain Reset Break! BRB

TOO MUCH!!!

→

→

→

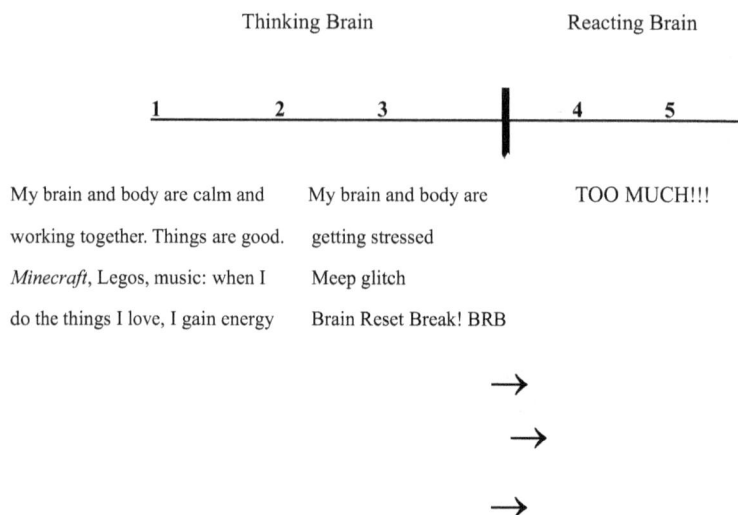

Source: © Marilyn J. Monteiro, PhD.

Malik clearly followed the visual contextualization of his familiar experience of his brain "jumping the line" from thinking to reacting. I knew he was taking in the brain reset break idea when he spontaneously made his next comment.

"Hey! BRB is something I can say to people: Be Right Back!" He popped up to a standing position and walked to the other side of the room, giving a backward wave with one hand as he demonstrated saying "BRB" and exiting the scene.

"I love it, Malik! BRB can replace 'Meep' as your clearer way to communicate that you are getting stressed and need to take a brain reset break. Let's see how we can show what happens to your system when you are able to change your routine from jumping the line to resetting your thinking brain level." Malik strode across the room and resumed his perched stance near the document.

I continued. "When you use your BRB routines, Malik, you are training your brain to switch out the jumping the line reacting routine with a routine that keeps your brain and body on the thinking side of the line. I added a few reverse arrows to make this point.

Thinking Brain   Reacting Brain

1	2	3		4	5

My brain and body are calm and   My brain and body are   TOO MUCH!!!

working together. Things are good.   getting stressed

Minecraft, Legos, music: when I   Meep glitch

do the things I love, I gain energy   Brain Reset Break! BRB

$\rightarrow$

$\rightarrow$

$\rightarrow$

↵

↵

↵

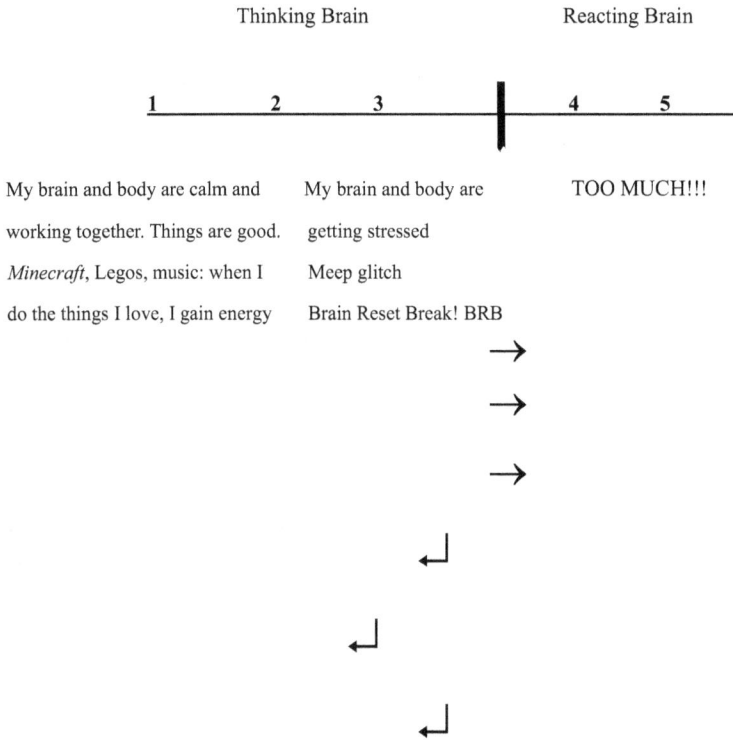

Source: © Marilyn J. Monteiro, PhD.

"So, Malik, we just worked together to create a diagram that shows what happens to your brain and body when it is calm and gaining energy, and when your system gets stressed and you switch from thinking to reacting mode. I labeled the chart "Malik's Brain Reset Plan" and handed it to him. He reached out and immediately held it in front of him as he examined it further.

"This is the starting point for the plan to help you replace your old reactive routine with your new thinking brain routine. It will be a lot of work, but will make things better too. What do you think about working on developing this plan together?"

"Good plan." Malik's two words spoke volumes.

"I have a suggestion for what the next step is in our plan, Malik. Would you like to hear it?" He nodded.

"Now we have to make this your *personal* plan and brain scale. We need a metaphor or theme that is your idea so you can show people what your level is even when you are at a level 5 and have lost your words to express yourself. You have so many interests that whatever you pick will be great. Sometimes people use *Minecraft* characters that match each level, or *Super Mario* characters, or weather patterns, or batteries. The next step is for you to take this home and think about your theme and pick your images to show above each number or level."

"Interesting...I could use the bosses in ascending order of difficulty to beat...or maybe use the five modes...I do jump the line sometimes with hardcore mode..." Malik's musings showed he was committed to the task of personalizing his scale and making it his own.

"Can't wait to see what you come up with, Malik. We'll also work together to create your list of brain reset activities, or you could say, create a brain reset menu, sort of like a *Minecraft* game menu. The list will include routines you can practice to reset your level and can be used at school as well as at home."

Malik took this idea in and quickly replied, "That will be good."

We went on in future meetings to extend Malik's understanding of and ability to create regulation routines. You can adopt the regulation scale model to support children and adolescents as you guide them through an understanding of the rationale behind creating visual regulation supports in your clinical practice. Box 5.1 lays out the basic structure that you can adapt and use in the important work you do supporting autistic children and adolescents as they learn to add self-monitoring and self-regulation of their brain and system to their daily routines.

Box 5.1 Autism spectrum brain style differences: a framework for providing positive behavior supports

Regulation Supports

The Binary Brain

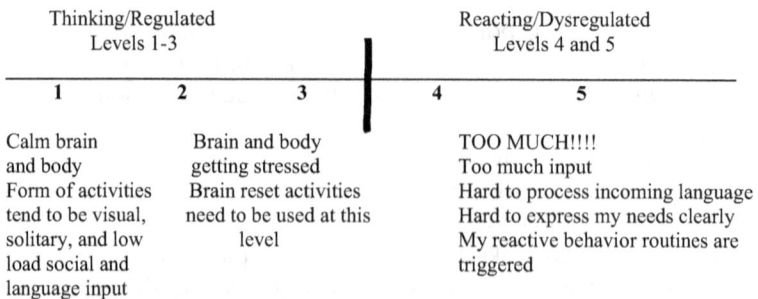

Thinking/Regulated Levels 1-3			Reacting/Dysregulated Levels 4 and 5	
1	2	3	4	5
Calm brain and body	Brain and body getting stressed		TOO MUCH!!!!	
Form of activities tend to be visual, solitary, and low load social and language input	Brain reset activities need to be used at this level		Too much input Hard to process incoming language Hard to express my needs clearly My reactive behavior routines are triggered	

- Select a metaphor with the individual to create a visual reference for the scale (images related to preferred topic work well)
- Identify the words, actions, and feelings associated with each level
- Identify the activities associated with Level 1
- Describe the *form* of the activities associated with Level 1 (solitary, low-load social demands, low-load social communications demands, high-load visual, spatial thinking opportunities, reduced stimulation setting)
- Create a brain reset menu of activities that can be practiced at Level 3 to reset the brain and maintain a regulated emotional state
- Practicing this proactive brain reset routine replaces the counter-productive routine of being triggered into a reactive state

What about social knowledge and self-determination supports for children like Malik? In this section on suggested supports, there are two main themes that are important to emphasize. The first is the idea of providing the child with a systematic way to identify and tell their personal story. When the supports come from the foundation of exploring the child's singular story of their interests, preferences, strengths, and differences, we are helping others in the child's world understand and appreciate the child's worldview and perspective. The development of social behaviors and routines becomes a collaborative process instead of a list of required skills acquisition for the neurodivergent child. Here the theme is supporting the child in revealing and telling their lived experience story through the development of their narrative notebook. This in turn leads to the development of tools to support the child's management of their brain style differences, to experience success in navigating through the complex social world during childhood and adolescence, and to discover compatible social connections.

The second idea that is an outgrowth of systematically exploring the child's story involves creating pathways to support and respect the individual's self-determination. Partnering directly with the child to develop their notebook containing their narrative and tools provides the child with an avenue for exploring and expressing their individual personhood. The suggested tool of creating a list of "Five things my teacher needs to know about me" is designed to provide a path for the child to form meaningful connections with the adults in their school life and advocate for the supports they need.

Let's read what Malik's social knowledge and self-determination suggested supports look like. You can then apply Malik's suggested supports to children with whom you work in your clinical practice.

Malik's social knowledge and self-determination supports

In the area of social knowledge acquisition and his self-determination narrative, Malik would benefit from the following:

- *Provide counseling supports for Malik that specifically address his Brain Style Profile of strengths and differences to help him develop a social self-narrative with a positive and empowered understanding of his brain style and tools that will help him manage his differences, and increase his emotional vocabulary though the use of visually structured counseling supports.*
- *Develop a notebook about Malik that contains all his tools; reference his notebook frequently at school, at home, and in counseling to support his acquisition of skills and his awareness of his application of positive strategies.*
- *Include his personal narrative in the notebook, built with him over time, with his Brain Style Profile, narrative about himself and his life, and his skills, talents, and goals; include information about his interests, ways to regulate, and things he's learned about how to manage his reactivity to be in sync with his age and ability level.*
- *As the social world of peer interactions becomes more complex during pre-adolescence and beyond, Malik would benefit from direct coaching in the development of his awareness of his needs and perspective, as well as the perspective of others and how to best manage social situations. This includes helping Malik explore self-determined pathways for compatible social connections with his peers. The systematic use of visual contextual supports such as visual social scripts, comic strip conversations, and step-by-step visual maps will help Malik recognize and anticipate social routines along with identifying adaptive replacement routines that will work well for him in his peer relationships (for example, replacing Malik's current routine of leaving group discussions with routine things he can say and do to participate in a different way that works for him in relation to his peers).*
- *Use visual protocols to help Malik build his flexibility and prosocial behavior repertoire when working or socializing collaboratively with peers (a visual "spin the spinner" with choices for words and action choices to engage a peer during group projects and games, for example; have those choices replace Malik's current repertoire of behavior routines of refusing to participate, criticizing or correcting peers, or leaving the group meeting in a dysregulated state).*
- *As Malik identifies social areas that are a source of stress for him, directly coach and teach specific social routines using visual supports to help Malik better anticipate and recognize when to apply his adaptive*

and age-congruent social communication routines with peers. For example, work with Malik to develop words and actions for Malik to use with peers during games and to teach flexible thinking routines when Malik perceives others as not following the rules.

- *Include a list of "Five things my teachers need to know about me" to help Malik prepare for advocating for his needs with his teachers; arrange for a meeting with his teachers for Malik to discuss the list of strengths and areas of needed supports (for example: I learn best when teachers show me what they mean when they give me directions and when I have a visual checklist to follow; I need regular, short breaks during the day in a quiet place to reset my brain and system; writing assignments work best for me when I can follow a story map and use a keyboard).*

The suggested supports listed above provide a way to help the adults in the child's world genuinely understand the child's nuanced worldview and how their worldview informs the need for positive supports. When you provide an organized document that tells the *why* and the *what* about positive supports for organization, regulation, and social knowledge/self-determination, you create the foundation for individualizing the support process for each child and their family.

Supporting the adolescent autistic story

How do the positive support recommendations change when the focus is on supporting the adolescent autistic story? Let's revisit Marisa and her story.

Marisa's story mirrors the life experience of many girls who receive their initial autism diagnosis during their adolescent years. Academically, Marissa was a highly capable student who internalized the impact that managing daily assignments and academic deadlines had on her anxiety and stress level. In the classroom, her teachers experienced Marissa as a quiet and capable student whom they did not get to know very well, as she generally kept to herself. Her avoidance of her peers was apparent in her routine of being the first one to leave class and rush through the hallway to her next class, and her use of her sketchbook or other books to focus on during social downtime. The idea that Marisa might have autistic sensory sensitivities that affected her ability to manage school demands was not under consideration, as the impact of her sensory sensitivities was literally camouflaged or hidden from view—unless one looked more closely.

Closer inspection of Marissa's lived experience revealed an autistic story familiar to those of you who have explored the diagnosis with autistic adolescent girls in your clinical practices. In the classroom, managing the sensory input created by peers moving, talking, and laughing while the teacher delivered instruction was a constant source of stress and fatigue for Marisa that aggregated across the course of the school day. It took all of her energy to take in information about class assignments, and she often experienced confusion paired with a reticence to initiate asking her teachers for clarification. This pattern was accompanied by Marisa's unrecognized differences in her ability to initiate requests for help or clarification. Her teachers were willing to help, but it was up to Marisa to approach them and make the request. By the end of the day, once she was at home, Marisa had to work through her distress and confusion before she was able to start on her assignments. Only at home did her distress and confusion burst through in the form of crying jags and of experiencing high levels of anxiety and agitation. When Marisa was able to understand these patterns as reactive behavior routines in response to her sensory overload, new options for managing her stress level emerged. These options could then be discussed and placed into Marisa's organizational and regulation supports.

Marisa's organizational supports

To help Marisa better understand the need for organizational supports, we started by identifying her strengths and differences in the area of communication.

"Marisa, let's explore ways to reduce your levels of stress and distress in response to school assignments so you will have a plan in place to support your brain style in school now, and then later when you move on to your university studies."

Marisa listened attentively. I had given her a notepad and pencil as we started this conversation and encouraged her to write the main points as we explored them, using a section to make her list of strengths and one for listing her differences. This documentation process provides the adolescent with a visual context that facilitates their absorption and retention of the information about their brain style patterns. As the adolescent uses their own words to construct their list of strengths and differences, they experience that absorption and retention process. For Marisa, we discussed the importance of her development of a way to think and talk about her brain style in positive, descriptive terms. As the chronicler of her Brain Style Profile of strengths and differences, Marisa applied her own language to tell the story in her own words.

"Let's start by revisiting your brain style strengths in the area of Language and Communication. Your understanding of language and your ability to communicate complex ideas is highly developed, and you are able to apply those talents when your system is not in a state of stress or agitation. Does that describe your experience of your language strengths and abilities?"

Marisa took this in and replied, "Yes. Especially the part about applying skills when I am not stressed." She took a moment to write her interpretation of this description under the heading of "Strengths" on her paper. When she finished writing, I invited her to share her narrative description.

Marisa readily shared her written summary. "I wrote: 'Love exploring words and language and ideas; enjoy learning new things; get blocked from my talents when I get stressed.'"

"Beautifully said, Marisa. With those language and communication strengths in mind, it would be helpful to highlight a key difference in your brain style that can lead to your experience of stress and distress in the classroom."

I paused as Marisa took this in and then continued, "You've talked about the fact that you recognize when you need clarification and that is a definite strength for you." I paused while Marisa wrote, "Know when I need help or clarification" under strengths.

"A key difference that we've been exploring together is how your brain manages the challenge of *initiating* or *starting* things. We've talked about how it is hard work for your brain to open the door to help and support by initiating or making the request for clarification or help."

Under "Differences" Marisa wrote, "Really hard to ask for help when I need it; initiating asking for help/clarification hard work for me."

She read her evolving narrative as she wrote it, clearly making it her own.

I continued. "Let's highlight one additional strength and then link your strengths and differences to a support plan, shall we?"

Marisa nodded in agreement as she looked at her expanding list.

"The first of two additional strengths we've discussed is your awareness that knowing ahead of time what the plan is and having the plan in writing helps you anticipate and prepare for success. In other words, knowing the plan and seeing the plan in writing helps your brain and system *organize* and *anticipate* demands."

Marisa wrote: "Having a plan in writing helps me organize and get started with work demands."

I amplified the connection she made after she read her statement aloud. "Marisa, I love the way you linked how having a plan in writing helps you both organize *and* get started or initiate getting your work done."

Marisa was now fully engaged in the process of exploring how her system responded to demands. And when she was fully engaged and had a context for the conversation, she began initiating and sharing her observations. "You know, I do better with starting things when my teachers or parents help me by giving me a frame of reference. You know, like when they start the conversation by telling me what they want to talk about." She paused thoughtfully before she continued with her thoughts. "It's also helpful when they help me list out the small steps that lead to completing the task...cleaning my room, organizing a science project..."

"Oh, I really like that observation, Marisa. A frame of reference is a context, right? When you have a frame of reference, it helps you take in the content of the conversation. When you are able to take in the information, you can organize a plan. When the adults pair the context or frame of reference with helping you list out steps, that provides the scaffolding your brain needs to access your talents and abilities."

Marisa nodded as she wrote: "Adults help by giving me a frame of reference/context and listing small steps to get me started and I take it from there; scaffold = support."

"You know, Marisa, in this conversation that is exactly what just happened. You were given a frame of reference and coaching on small steps for this task, and then you were able to get started and use your talents and abilities. Just now, you began to initiate or start on your own by offering up an observation about yourself. Well done."

I then connected the observations of her strengths and differences to a commonly recommended school accommodation. "At school, to help scaffold and support your development of starting or initiating when you recognize you need help or clarification, you now have a way to advocate for setting up check-in times with your teachers for clarification and questions. If a time is in your schedule, it becomes part of an expected plan. Expected plans are a great fit for your brain style."

Marisa wrote: "Planned check-in times for clarification and questions."

"Marisa, you've also talked about how tiring and challenging it is for you to manage the classroom cross-talk while you are trying to take in what the teacher is covering during class periods. Another accommodation for you might be to have your teachers understand your need to block out all of that sensory input by having a seat always available to you that is front and center to the class instruction. That accommodation is often referred to as 'preferential seating.'"

Marisa wrote: "Preferential seating/block out distractions/noise and crosstalk; tiring and stressful."

We continued in this way to put together Marisa's organizational supports in her own words. The process was one of self-determination, and led us to discussing supports for her in the area of self-determination and social knowledge.

Marisa's social knowledge and self-determination supports

In the area of self-determination supports, we discussed distilling Marisa's list of strengths, differences, and accommodations into a list of "Five things my teachers need to know about me." Creating a list like that supports the adolescent in preparing to have self-advocacy conversations with the adults in their school and work lives. This tool helps the adolescent experience the important age-congruent developmental shift from prompt-dependency to autonomy. Instead of relying on parents to explain what they need, they have a structure in place that supports them in identifying and describing their needs directly with teachers in school. These discussions lead to the teaming between the adolescent and their teachers in crafting supports and accommodations together. Both the adolescent and the teacher commit to understanding the adolescent's strengths and differences, and to making course corrections in the ways they work together for successful outcomes. As you read Marisa's list of five things her teachers need to know about her, think about how you can apply this framework and tool to support the autistic adolescents in your clinical practice.

5 things my teachers need to know about me:

1. *I am a student who is eager to learn and take my education seriously*
2. *I sometimes hesitate to ask for clarification and help, and do best when we have a planned check-in time for me to meet with you to review the frame of reference for assignments and list necessary steps in a written plan*
3. *During class periods, it is helpful if you initiate checking in with me from time to time instead of waiting for me to do so because I struggle with reaching out for help*
4. *Managing multiple sensory aspects of the classroom such as noise levels and social bantering is tiring for my system, and I do best with taking in information if I am seated close to the instructor and to the visual information provided during lectures and direct teaching times*
5. *I am a careful thinker, so it sometimes takes me a minute or two after you ask a question for me to answer; I am listening even if I'm not looking at you*

This tool can be used across ages and ability levels by adjusting the language level and introducing visual depictions for younger children and changing the framework for adults to reflect "Five things my employer needs to know about me."

In the area of social knowledge supports, adolescents like Marisa benefit from access to coaching or counseling supports. Merely listing the need for counseling supports, however, leaves out the rationale or context for the specific types of supports the autistic adolescent needs. How do you contextualize the rationale for the specific types of counseling supports that are the best fit for the autistic adolescent?

For the autistic adolescent, organizing counseling conversations around supporting the understanding of their profile of strengths and differences creates a context for understanding and expressing their singular worldview.

Let's read how this recommended support can be written for Marissa and by extension, for adolescents in your practice.

In the area of self-determination and social knowledge supports, Marisa is seeking a meaningful way to understand her divergent thinking and development, and to internalize her differences in a positive rather than a negative or discouraging framework. She would benefit from counseling and coaching to develop her understanding of her distinctive brain style pattern of strengths and differences. Marisa is a student who is goal-directed, and she expends a great deal of energy to complete her work accurately and to gain positive feedback from her teachers and from her grades. Coaching or counseling to help her identify her brain style strengths and differences will help Marisa set goals regarding the supports she needs not only to be successful with her academics but also to be successful in managing her internal stress level.

- *Counseling that supports Marisa in her development of her social narrative would be highly beneficial. Marisa enjoys drawing and writing in the anime style and follows the narrative stories in the* Magic Girl *genre that encompass themes of the transformative power of discovering gifts and talents, the experience of being an outsider in a group, and the commitment to values around social justice and kindness. She would benefit from linking her knowledge of character development in the stories she enjoys to identifying character types in her peers. These connections can then be linked to her discernment of peers to approach and respond to as she expands her repertoire of engaging in social exchanges with her classmates. Using her interest in and abilities in the area of anime culture and art to construct meaningful visual social skills prompts for adaptive routines will help Marisa explore positive behaviors and positive outcomes in her development of self-determination skills as well as in expanding her skill sets when engaging in interactions with others. The exploration of her area of preferred interest in anime characters provides a powerful way to help Marisa expand her development of social narrative awareness and to provide social narrative coaching and support.*
- *Exploring compatible social pathways is a discussion that flows naturally from discussions around her interest in anime. For Marisa, participating in school social groups organized around her interests in art and anime provides an entry point for her to expand her social engagement with her peers.*
- *Because Marisa is faced with a number of social group activities that are part of her secondary school experience, counseling supports can help her explore ways to manage those social and sensory demands. For example, having a routine in which she anticipates participating*

in social events with one peer or a small group, instead of or within larger group activities would give Marisa the context she needs to manage her level of participation in school events. Developing coping strategies and routines to structure her participation in stressful social events would provide important social supports for Marisa. For example, coaching Marisa to develop an entry and exit plan when she participates in large group social events and have the option to opt out and substitute other activities when she identifies that the sensory demands of the event or setting may exceed her capabilities, is a way to help Marisa self-determine ways to successfully navigate social demands.

- *The development of a notebook for Marisa to use as her personal repository for information and support tools would work well for her. Including her personal narrative in the notebook, built together with her over time, with her Brain Style Profile, narrative about herself and her life, and her skills, talents, and goals, would be beneficial for Marisa.*
- *Counseling supports can also be used to help Marisa develop her emotional vocabulary and to establish adaptive replacement routines so she can learn to manage her emotional reactivity in ways that build her confidence in her ability to manage and regulate successfully. This will reduce her overall anxiety level and build her positive narrative regarding herself and her abilities.*
- *Marisa would benefit from counseling supports to discuss how and under what conditions she wants to choose to disclose her autism diagnosis. Coaching for Marisa in this area might include helping her identify what her teachers need to know about her learning style, and providing Marisa with effective ways to advocate for her needs in the classroom by telling her teachers about her learning style ("Five things my teachers need to know about me.").*

Marisa's regulation supports

A key focus for autistic adolescents in the area of regulation supports centers on providing a context for understanding how their sensory preferences and sensitivities affect mood and system regulation. For Marisa, as is often-times the experience for autistic adolescents, access to extended time in a reduced stimulation environment is a fundamental need for system regulation and energy restoration. Coaching and counseling supports that help the autistic adolescent identify the key aspects of their sensory regulation needs provide the starting point for developing regulation supports they can turn to in daily life. In other words, starting with the identification of the person's sensory needs and preferences provides a way to explore and discuss the development and use of routines that are a fit for their needs.

For Marisa, her identification of the restorative function of time alone in a quiet setting where she focused on self-selected visual input was the starting point for her development of regulation supports. This identification of the conditions under which she gains restorative energy led to the development of routines, plans, and strategies she could use to self-monitor, self-regulate, and reset her brain and system. By definition, the absence of opportunities to engage in restorative sensory routines can be linked to the experience of stress, anxiety, agitation, and fatigue. Putting those two concepts together leads to supporting the adolescent in identifying and advocating for the supports they need to increase their regulation levels and resiliency in response to sensory and environmental stressors.

"Marisa, now that you've made the association between having restorative quiet time and how that affects your anxiety and stress levels, let's explore practical ways to insert sensory regulation reset breaks into your school day. Let's start by identifying the settings at school that provide you with what your system needs."

"Oh, that's easy to identify. Definitely the library. I go there to avoid the cafeteria and commons area where it is always chaotic and loud." She hesitated before adding a second setting. "I have a standing offer to take a break anytime and go to the counselor's office area, but I haven't actually used that option. I didn't really know how to explain why I would be showing up there, but now I do. I am comfortable telling the counselor I need a reset break from all of the sensory input."

"So, Marisa, it sounds like changing your understanding of how sensory aspects of your environment affect what happens to your system and your ability to stay regulated, is helping you identify settings you can use to take reset breaks and restore your energy level during the school day. And now you have a way to ask for what you need and to explain those needs to your teachers and school counselor. Am I describing that correctly?"

"For sure. I feel like I have a plan to use."

"And as we've discussed before, your brain and system do best when you have a context for understanding what is happening to you, paired with a plan of action and strategies. We'll continue to work together to identify more details related to settings and situations that help your system stay regulated, along with better understanding the details of what goes into the experience of becoming overwhelmed and distressed."

We went on to discuss how Marisa might gather information about aspects of her school environment that were regulating for her, and contrast those with aspects that were dysregulating and sources of stress and distress. This process of coaching the adolescent to gather detailed information about patterns embedded in their daily experiences empowers them to more clearly understand and describe their lived experiences. This self-awareness leads to self-advocacy for what they need. For Marisa, we

discussed her development of her regulation metric, using the same structure you've seen applied with Malik earlier in this chapter.

Within the context of understanding the sensory components of Marisa's
system regulation supports, we also identified an associated area for counseling assistance and coaching: Marisa's development of her vocabulary to
describe her emotional states. The process of coaching Marisa as she developed
her emotional vocabulary led directly to identifying the narrative routine she
used internally when her system was in a state of dysregulation. As is the
case for many autistic adolescents who struggle with emotional dysregulation
linked to sensory overload, Marissa had a deeply embedded routine of telling
herself what was wrong with her. When the negative thoughts and feelings
are reframed as routines, the next step is coaching the adolescent to replace
their negative self-narrative with a strengths-based descriptive narrative that
focuses on naming the emotions, the conditions that triggered the emotions,
and the strategies she could use to reset her system.

Marisa's deeply embedded dysregulation routine included her telling herself that she was worthless and defective. Let's read how Marisa was coached
to replace her negative routine with the empowering and adaptive routine.

"Marisa, thank you for telling me the things you tell yourself when you
become stressed and anxious. Now that you have a better understanding of
how your system dysregulation gets triggered, let's explore replacing the old
way of reacting with a new way. When you tell yourself negative things about
yourself, does it add to or reduce your anxious and distressed feelings?"

"Makes it worse," Marisa confirmed.

"But it's a routine, and one that you've had in place for a long time. So
let's talk about creating a replacement routine of things you can practice
telling yourself that may be helpful. It's important that the replacement
things you tell yourself describe what is happening instead of shaming you.
What are your thoughts about replacing the old routine?"

Marisa considered this. "Not sure what I would tell myself differently. It's
pretty much an automatic thing now."

"Yes, you've been telling yourself the negative story about yourself for
a long time. So let's see if some of the ways of describing your sensory
experience sound like things you could tell yourself that resonate as true
to your situation. Would you prefer writing the contrasting things to say, or
would you prefer that I write them?"

I asked Marisa the binary question to give her the choice to write her
negative thoughts herself, or to have me do it for her. She asked me to write
while she listened.

I drew a T on a notepad and wrote "Old words and actions" on the left
side of the T, and "New words and actions" on the right side.

"Let's start with describing the new words for your replacement routine.
The words need to describe what is happening to you; they are the effect of

your circumstances. Let's try this: "When I start to feel anxious and want to withdraw from a situation, that feeling is telling me important information. It's telling me that I am experiencing sensory overload and that it's time to focus on and use my plan to regulate my sensory system. I soothe myself by reminding myself that I will feel better after I use my brain reset tools and routines." I wrote the statements on the right hand side of the T chart. "Your thoughts about the new statements?"

"Good. Different from what I usually tell myself."

"Now, let's write the statements you most frequently tell yourself when your system gets dysregulated."

Marisa hesitated for a moment before she spoke. In a quiet voice she said her negative words aloud. "Worthless. Defective. Crazy."

"It's hard to say those aloud, Marisa. I really admire you for doing this." I wrote: " 'I tell myself I am worthless, defective, crazy. I want to shut down and disappear. That's the old routine, When I use those words and that routine, I feel worse. My goal is to notice when I start to use the old routine and practice using the new routine.' How does that sound, Marisa?"

"Good."

"So here is the page with the reframe on it. If you don't mind, please take a moment to practice saying the reframe aloud."

Marisa nodded and took a moment before she used her voice to make the empowering statement.

"Thank you for doing that. Would you tell me how saying those words was the same or different from when you named your old ways of talking to yourself?"

"Better."

We went on to craft the brain reset words and actions Marisa would begin to practice using at school and at home. Before leaving the meeting, Marisa placed the T chart in her notebook, along with her other documents and tools.

Additional supports

Of course, there are many additional ways you can list resources and recommend supports for the children and adolescents in your clinical practice. The goal here is to provide you with a way to organize and contextualize the supports you recommend, and to do so in a strengths-based way. You are encouraged to explore the many published materials that guide clinicians through the use of visual supports (Earles-Vollrath et al., 2018), social knowledge and self-determination supports (Winner, 2020, 2021), and regulation supports for autistic children and adolescents (Smith & Griffin, 2017; Wrobel, 2017). As you review materials, you are encouraged to think about their application to the specific children, adolescents, and their families in your clinical practice.

Through your work with autistic children and their families, you may also have developed additional organizational tools, social knowledge and self-determination strategies, and regulation supports. You are encouraged to link them to the framework and context for understanding the autism worldview so both the autistic child or adolescent and the adults in their world increase their understanding of the child's story and how they can best partner with the child to support their story.

That brings us to looking at ways to support the adult story. Let's explore how this might look in our next chapter.

References

Barkley, R. A. (2020). *Executive Functions: What They Are, How They Work, and Why They Evolved*. New York: Guilford Press.

Black, M. H., Kuzminski, R., Wang, J., Lee, C., Hafidzuddin, S., & McGarry, S. (2024). Experiences of friendships for individuals on the autism spectrum: A scoping review. *Rev J Autism Dev Disord*. 11:184–209. https://doi.org/10.1007/s40489-022-00332-8

Chen, P.-Y., & Schwartz, I. S. (2012). Bullying and victimization experiences of students with autism spectrum disorders in elementary schools. *Focus Autism Deve Dis*. 27(4):200–212. https://doi.org/10.1177/1088357612459556

Earles-Vollrath, T. L., Tapscott Cook, K., Kemper, T. G., & Ganz, J. B. (2018). *Visual Supports*. Austin, Texas: Pro-Ed Publisher.

Greenlee, J. L., Putney, J. M., Hickey, E., Winter, M. A., & Hartley, S. L. (2024). An exploratory study of resilience to stressful life events in autistic children. *Res Autism Spectr Disord*. 114. https://doi.org/10.1016/j.rasd.2024.102371

Kemp, J., Mitchelson, M., & Wise, S. J. (2024). *The Neurodivergence Skills Workbook for Autism and ADHD: Cultivate Self-compassion, Love Authentically, and be your own Advocate*. Oakland, California: New Harbinger Press.

Morales-Hidalgo, P., Voltas, N., & Canals, J. (2024). Self-perceived bullying victimization in pre-adolescents on the autism spectrum: EPINED study. *Autism*. https://doi.org/10.1177/13623613241244875

Smith, B., & Griffin, L. (2017). *Executive Function series set of 10 storybooks*. Boys Town, Nebraska: Boys Town Press.

Winner, M. G., & Crooke, P. (2020). *You are a Social Detective! Explaining Social Thinking to Kids*. Santa Clara, California: Social Thinking Press.

Winner, M. G., & Crooke, P. (2021). *Socially Curious and Curiously Social: A Social Thinking Guidebook for Bright Teens and Young Adults*. Santa Clara, California: Social Thinking Press.

Wrobel, M. (2017). *Taking Care of Myself2: For Teenagers and Young Adults with Autism*. Arlington, Texas: Future Horizons Publisher.

6 Support the story

Adults across the lifespan – Morgan, Miranda, and Matt

How does the approach to supporting the adult's autism story differ from the ways in which we've explored supports for children and adolescents? Just as we've seen as we've looked at ways to support the autistic story in children and adolescents, supporting the adult autistic story centers on helping the adult identify organizational, social knowledge, and regulation supports that are a fit for their needs. We start with partnering with the adult to help them identify their priorities. What would they like to change, or not change? What is their perspective on how they think, talk, and communicate with others about their autistic identity? Throughout this book we've focused on using a neuro-informed approach to provide each autistic child, adolescent, or adult with the shared experience of being accepted and understood by their clinician while gaining new ways to understand their unique pattern of brain style strengths and differences. With adults, that shared experience provides the entry point for focused discussions to help the adult identify, develop, and prioritize individualized ways to support their complex, unique, and singular life story.

There will be adults in your clinical practice who come to mind as we revisit Morgan, Miranda, and Matt in this chapter. The suggested supports outlined for each of the three autistic adults here can be readily adapted and applied to the important work you do. If you are reading this chapter, you are most likely a clinician who has experience and training in a range of therapy techniques and approaches, many of which have been shown to be helpful and applicable in therapy work with autistic adults (Moore et al., 2024). You are encouraged to adapt and apply those skills in your work with autistic adults. The focus here is on ways to connect the adult's autistic Brain Style Profile to the supports they self-determine as priorities to improve their quality of life in meaningful ways.

DOI: 10.4324/9781003532576-9

Supporting Morgan's autism story

As you recall, Morgan was a young adult whose personal identity was already emerging to include her gender expression and her identification of her areas of preferred interest. She was well on her path toward matching her understanding of herself and her interests with compatible social pathways to form meaningful relationships and connections with others outside of her immediate family. Morgan also showed an awareness of her attention and focusing differences, and of her emotional regulation differences, along with recognizing and acknowledging her cognitive and skills-based competencies. With that in mind, let's read a summary of Morgan's suggested supports across the three key areas.

Morgan's suggested supports and recommendations

Morgan would benefit from individual counseling and support from a specialist familiar with autism spectrum brain style differences in twice-exceptional young adults who also have attention and focusing differences. As Morgan prepares to make the transition to college and to independent adult living, she would benefit from the following recommendations in the areas of developing her organizational supports, social knowledge and self-determination supports, and regulation supports.

Organizational supports

Although Morgan has a strong drive for autonomy and has goals for independent living, she currently relies on others to prompt her to prioritize and complete adult activities of daily living. Morgan would benefit from the following organizational supports as she prepares for independent adult life and as she makes the transition into her university studies program.

- *At home, Morgan self-determined the following organizational support goals:*
  - *Set up checklists and visual systems to increase her autonomy in completing daily self-care routines*
  - *Work with her counselor to systematically increase her autonomy in the areas of adult daily living (shopping, cooking, budgeting expenses)*
- *At her university, through her university support center for students with disabilities, Morgan noted that she would benefit from starting*

the school year with weekly or twice-weekly meetings with a counselor to help her develop and consistently use the following:

  o *Having an organizational system for managing academic demands and deadlines*
  o *Planning for study times and locations*
  o *Understanding and establishing sensory brain reset breaks to shape sustained work production and output*

• *Morgan also identified that she would benefit from working with a college counselor to review her Brain Style Profile of strengths and differences, and to develop a list of "5 things my professors or instructors need to know about me." Developing this list and setting up a time with each professor or instructor to discuss strengths and differences will provide Morgan with practice and experience in the areas of self-determination and self-advocacy. Morgan identified the following accommodations she would benefit from in the university setting:*

  o *Preferential seating*
  o *Agreement with her instructors to stand and take short breaks during lectures as needed*
  o *Access to lecture notes to review before and after class*
  o *Assistance with note taking during class*
  o *Test taking in a quiet and small group setting*

Social knowledge and self-determination supports

Morgan has a well-developed understanding and appreciation of her complex and multifaceted identity as a young adult. Through her areas of interest she has found compatible social pathways and has developed a core group of supportive peers. She and her parents have worked diligently to provide Morgan with a path toward independent adult living, and her parents support Morgan's emerging autonomy and self-determination goals and priorities. As a young neurodivergent adult, Morgan noted that she would benefit from counseling supports to help her navigate through social situations she will encounter in her university and employment settings. Working with Morgan individually and within a family context is encouraged, as this will help both Morgan and her family support system gain understanding and tools related to Morgan's distinctive worldview and needs, and help her continue to strengthen her self-determination goals for her adult life path.

- *Morgan stated that she is seeking individual therapy to help her continue in her development of her understanding of her strengths and differences and apply that knowledge to her self-determination of her social and personal goals and priorities. This includes supporting Morgan as she develops her personal narrative and defines how she can self-advocate for her needs across the settings of university, work, home, and social relationships in her adult life.*
- *Morgan identified that her parents would benefit from gaining a better understanding of Morgan's complex and multifaceted brain style pattern of strengths and differences, including her autism spectrum differences. They already display a nuanced understanding of Morgan, and are an important and consistent source of support for her. Helping them place this diagnosis into a functional context would be helpful for Morgan and her parents.*
- *Morgan observed that she seeks out information independently regarding a range of topics and stated that she would benefit from exploring additional information about how autism spectrum brain style differences affect young adults in particular. Resources were suggested as sources of information for Morgan to explore, along with referrals to young adult neurodivergent groups.*

Regulation supports

- *Morgan identified that she has a lifelong pattern of struggling with her emotional regulation, most notably experienced as her anxiety response to stressors. She noted that her recent understanding of the autistic sensory component that factors into the triggering of her anxious emotional state has led to an interest in working with her counselor to explore strategies to manage and plan proactively for environmental and sensory stressors. Morgan noted that she would benefit from coaching to help her better understand her brain's strength of creating and maintaining patterns and routines. Specifically, she expressed an interest in better understanding her current deeply embedded routine of internalizing and repeating negative statements about herself, and in receiving guidance on how to generate and internalize the use of adaptive replacement words and actions linked to self-soothing and regulation of her system.*
- *We discussed how Morgan would benefit from the use of visual regulation supports in the form of T-charts comparing and contrasting her old and new routines when her anxiety is triggered, and a regulation self-monitoring visual schematic that she designs and endorses using her artistic talents and perspective. As Morgan begins to increase her*

skills in the areas of self-monitoring and self-regulation of her emotional state, she would benefit from the use of the metrics of frequency, duration, intensity, and peculiarity (as defined by how out of sync her emotional state and self-narrative are in relation to the circumstances) to measure incremental progress.

- *Morgan has already identified and integrated the use of the sensory regulation strategies of interspersing high-load stimulation activities (time with others; time completing required tasks) with restorative low-load stimulation activities (solitary time spent engaged in high-interest activities). At the present time, Morgan has noted that she finds the transition back into required activities to be a challenging one, resulting in postponement of necessary tasks and prolonged extensions of her solitary time. She would benefit from working with her counselor to develop and practice the routine of switching between low-load and high-load environments to reduce her current prolonged avoidance routines.*

- *Morgan is committed to using multimodal ways of supporting her complex brain style and behavioral profile, and noted that she would benefit from continued consultation with her attending physician to assess and manage medications related to her attention and focusing needs and her anxiety. She added that understanding her complex Brain Style Profile, including her autism spectrum differences are important new information to discuss with the physician managing her medication supports.*

When reading Morgan's supports, you may have noted that whenever possible, the narrative includes the self-determination theme. The suggested supports are organized into the now familiar three categories. Each set of recommended supports includes a statement about Morgan choosing or endorsing the support. This distinction is important, as it communicates to the autistic adult that the recommended supports are priorities they self-determined in partnership with their neuro-informed clinician.

Miranda's suggested supports

What do supports look like for adults who are exploring their autistic identity in midlife? For adults like Miranda who have found their vocation and have established a primary relationship, it may appear that there is no obvious need for supports. The metric to apply to determine the need for supports in the areas of organization, self-knowledge and self-determination, and regulation is a simple one. Supports are needed when the adult is experiencing chronic stress and distress related to their ability to cope with and manage daily stressors. The identification of supports that are a fit for the adult's autistic brain style pattern of strengths and differences can make a profound difference in the adult's quality of life. As we explore Miranda's suggested supports, think about ways you might adapt her recommendations to fit the needs of the autistic adults in your clinical practice.

Miranda's autism support story starts with helping her connect the three areas of organization, regulation, and social knowledge. Two key narrative shifts occurred for Miranda when she received her autism diagnosis. The first was when she made the connection that in the absence of a context to make sense out of social communication exchanges, she filled the gap with her internal negative narrative to create a *predictable routine*. This gave her a context to understand the destabilizing and exhausting emotional cycle she aptly named "the aftermath." The second was in connecting her iden- tified strength (her ability to create and maintain predictable routines that served the function of helping her organize and regulate her system) to apply that strength to create an *adaptive replacement routine* for her current "aftermath" routine. As you recall, Miranda described the connection in this way: "So, maybe I can figure out a way to switch out 'the aftermath' with 'the reset.' "

These connections provide the context for the following suggested organizational and regulation supports:

- *Support Miranda in the development of her internal narrative routines from her current negative self-narrative to the posi- tive narrative replacement routines that include descriptive and self-soothing statements. Use visual depictions comparing and contrasting narrative routines that fall into "the aftermath" category with the replacement narrative routines that fall into "the reset" cat- egory. Support Miranda in identifying and describing the emotions connected with each routine.*
- *To help Miranda contextualize why she developed and maintained the negative narrative routines, remind her that the negative narrative routines were adaptive for her at one time in the absence of a context to understand and cope with social communication demands. The negative narrative routines are now a source of stress, distress, and emotional destabilization, and she has the context to develop and use positive replacement internal narratives.*
- *Help Miranda identify routine prompts, phrases, and strategies she can use as a routine in social conversations when she is unclear about the context for the conversation ("That's interesting. Could you say it again in a slightly different way?" "How can I be helpful?" "Tell me more." "Give me a minute and I'll get back with you." "I'm not familiar with that. Would you explain what you mean?").*

- *Support Miranda in identifying the form of brain reset breaks she can use throughout the day. Exploring the form includes helping her name the dimensions of the setting along with the specific activities she engages in to reset her brain and system. Encourage Miranda to create her "reset" list with a space for her to note her regulation level before and after each reset cycle.*
- *Explore ways she can set up intentional and proactive brain reset breaks during her workday, along with the narrative statements she can routinely use to communicate her intentions to her colleagues and students.*

Miranda showed self-determination for change for many years as she worked diligently in therapy to change the course of her social and emotional life experiences. In the absence of the autistic context for understanding the interplay between her social communication and her sensory profile of strengths and differences, she relied on masking and internalizing her confusion and distress as a coping tool. For Miranda's social knowledge and self-determination supports, two key themes were important to highlight. The first centers around encouraging Miranda to work closely with a clinician who is knowledgeable about the adult autistic brain style. In partnership with her neuro-informed clinician, Miranda could be guided to recraft her personal narrative in positive, empowering terms. She would be able to explore and develop ways to describe her Brain Style Profile of strengths and differences and to self-determine how she wanted to communicate this information to the people in her life. Miranda could also be given trusted resources not only to learn more about autistic adults and their experiences but also to connect with other neurodivergent individuals with whom she would be able to express herself without censor. She would be able to hear and absorb the lived experiences of others and connect with them as she hears familiar experiences in their stories.

The second theme centers around making adjustments in her primary relationship. With adults like Miranda, framing the process of adjusting perspectives and communication patterns in a primary relationship as small but important *course corrections* can be powerful. This allows for the integration of the autistic narrative into the dynamic between partners in a positive way. Comparing and contrasting brain styles between partners is an inclusive and equalizing experience. The most efficient way for one person to communicate their needs may be entirely different from the way their partner logically structures their communication. The intent of each person's behavior can be clarified instead of inferred when styles are compared and contrasted in this way. When the sensory dimensions that affect the autistic adult's behavior patterns are highlighted and explored, and the autistic person experiences being truly understood by their partner, they in turn can take in information about their partner's perspective and needs. When the autistic strengths-based narrative is introduced into a relationship, the fundamental dynamics shift for many couples. Change becomes a collaborative process. Course corrections make that change possible and manageable (Monteiro, 2020).

This provides the context for Miranda's suggested supports for social knowledge and self-determination:

- *Miranda expressed interest in participating in ongoing counseling with a clinician experienced in the area of understanding the autistic adult brain style and masking to support her exploration of adaptive communication and sensory strategies to use in the work and home settings. Topics include exploring her Brain Style Profile that highlights her distinctive pattern of strengths and differences in the areas of Language and Communication, Social Relationships and Emotions, and Sensory Use and Interests. This provides the starting point for Miranda to integrate her autistic brain style narrative into how she thinks about herself and communicates about herself with others. Other topics Miranda expressed an interest in exploring in counseling include Miranda creating positive behavior routines to reduce her stress level in daily interactions with others. For example, she might develop routine ways to ask for the context in conversations when she is uncertain and set up proactive sensory breaks and routines throughout the day to increase her ability to stay regulated and less stressed throughout the workday.*
- *Miranda is beginning to recognize the pattern of an increase in her stress level when she makes the transition from one setting to another in daily life. Most notably, the transition from work to home at the end of the day was identified as a transition time that would benefit from the development of a proactive replacement routine. She expressed a goal of developing a positive transition routine so that that upon returning home from work, she will be better able to stay regulated and change the patterns of interaction with her partner to develop reliably positive outcomes.*
- *Miranda and her husband are committed to learning new ways to understand one another and communicate more effectively as they learn to understand how Miranda's brain style pattern of strengths and differences informs not only how she communicates but how she takes in information from her communication partner. They would benefit from participation in couples counseling with a clinician experienced in working with neurodivergent adults. A clinician would be helpful in providing guidance for Miranda and her husband to explore positive perspective sharing and engagement in the*

process of each partner participating in course corrections in their understanding of their partner and their words and action patterns of exchanges within the relationship.

In your clinical practice, you are encouraged to adapt and add suggested supports that are a fit for the individuals with whom you work. You may want to add specific therapy approaches you recommend along with books or community resources related to autism and adulthood. There is an ever expanding library of narratives related to autism and adulthood (Silberman, 2016; Kemp et al., 2024).This includes books related to lived experience (Nerenberg, 2021; Prizant & Fields-Meyer, 2022; Schembari, 2024), unmasking (Price, 2022; Oliver, 2024), and sensory self-care (Garvey, 2023). Supporting the adult's autism story includes staying current and knowledgeable about books and resources along with good clinical skills. Miranda's support story provides one way to organize the process to support you as you work with the adults in your clinical practice.

Matt's suggested supports

Matt's autism story contained elements that you most certainly will recognize in many of the adults with emerging language skills that you support in your clinical practice. Supporting their stories starts with appreciating their life experiences related to their routines and engagement with their beloved areas of preferred interest and placing that narrative front and center in your recommendations. Starting with what works for the adult instead of emphasizing their areas of struggle leads to creative ways to support growth and adult life skills development. For Matt, this meant starting with appreciating two aspects of his lived experience. The first was recognizing his good-natured demeanor and noticing that when Matt could rely on expected predictable routines, he was able to sustain his regulated brain and system and his easy-going outlook on life. The second was exploring the form and function of his preferred and beloved area of interest. Together, these formed the rhythm of Matt's daily life. As you read Matt's recommended supports, you'll see these two key features described and connected with ways to support his adult journey of gaining autonomy, mastering skills, and stepping into his own story.

Summary recommendations for Matt

The following supports are recommended for Matt in the areas of organizational skills, regulation skills, and social skills/self-determination skills:
    In the area of organizational skills, Matt would benefit from the following supports:

- *Matt's autism spectrum differences affect his ability to process incoming language and respond to verbal directives, and his threshold for managing incoming verbal demands is often quite low. The stressors involved in managing incoming language demands leads to Matt's experience of anxiety and agitation. Matt communicates his level of distress by engaging in a routine of withdrawing from the exchange and moving away from the source of demands. He is a highly visual learner who enjoys predictable outcomes and enacting familiar routines. Matt would benefit from the use of visual step-by-step checklists and visual directions to support his participation in household chores and routines. "Showing" Matt the list of tasks, or the steps involved in a task or chore, rather than relying solely on verbal prompts and reminders, will help Matt better anticipate demands, participate in completing non-preferred tasks and activities, and expand his repertoire of independent routines. Visual lists, step-by-step visual schematics, and visual calendars serve the function of communicating to Matt: "how much," "how long, and "when" non-preferred tasks will be in his schedule. They also provide him with a visual representation of "first/then." That is to say, he can better anticipate and visually see the link between doing the non-preferred activity followed by his preferred, solitary, sensory-driven routines.*

- *Having an interactive component to Matt's visual supports is important, as he will engage with his lists in a way that provides him with step-by-step visual confirmation of moving toward completion of a routine. Matt's enduring enthusiasm for characters in the Nintendo world, and specifically the Super Mario world, provide a natural visual way for Matt to link, for example, choosing a character to move through the completion of a task or a routine. When this routine was discussed with Matt, he selected Mario as his character to walk through his daily schedule. As he started the sequence, he exclaimed Mario's signature phrase ("Here we go!"). He wanted to add a picture of Bowser, the boss character Mario tries to defeat in the games, at the end of the checklist sequence. As we went through the sequence together, Matt moved his Mario figure through each step. At the end of the sequence, he plucked Bowser off of the list, replacing him with Mario, and exclaiming: "So long-a, Bowser!" Working closely with Matt in this way as he goes through the process of character selection and of connecting the use of that character to a sequence of his own behavior, provides a natural way to support Matt's increasing independence. He will experience self-determination in choosing the characters, and at the end of a successful sequence of task completion, he has a narrative to share about his accomplishments.*

- *Matt would benefit from direct teaching or coaching on how to support his organizational and planning skills in the areas of daily living skills through the use of visual checklists and supports. Linking the development and use of his organizational and planning systems with a narrative book of photos and text describing his experiences will add to Matt's repertoire of sharing his story to others*

In the area of regulation skills, Matt would benefit from the following supports:

- *Matt is developing an awareness of his emotions and emotional triggers. He would benefit from counseling supports to develop adaptive coping skills when he becomes emotionally dysregulated, and to support the development of flexible thinking. This is essential to help Matt begin to set behavior and life goals that fall outside of his currently established routines and comfort level.*
- *Visual supports, including working with Matt to develop a visual self-regulation scale; identifying words, actions, feelings; and having a regulation plan, would be helpful for Matt.*
- *To help Matt expand his currently established routines regarding bathing, food, and exercise, the use of predictable, incremental, and visually defined steps is recommended as a good fit for his brain style. For example, in the area of bathing and washing his hair, we discussed the following incremental adjustments to his current routine:*
  - o *Try on and select a pair of water-resistant goggles to wear when his father washes his hair*
  - o *Visually list on a weekly calendar the days designated as hair washing day so Matt can better anticipate the upcoming event*
  - o *Gradually shift the focus from having his father wash his hair to Matt washing his hair*
  - o *Use a sponge attached to a brush to promote Matt's scrubbing his body, including his back, legs, and feet*

- *To promote Matt's expansion of food choices, visually depict a designated day and meal when a new food will be introduced, and set up the contingency that on that day and for that meal only, Matt will eat one or more bites of the non-preferred food before eating a preferred food. Use visual checklists to set up meal planning and preparation for Matt, with his input, for one meal a week. Provide binary choices rather than open-ended choices regarding meal choices.*
- *To promote Matt's development of exercise routines, he would benefit from visual supports to help him see "how much" and "how long."*

Matt self-determined that he preferred walking indoors to other forms of physical movement for exercise. We discussed setting a goal to walk on the treadmill he had at home, but use a countdown timer instead of having Matt see the time increasing, as the increasing time creates anxiety and triggers his escape and avoidance behaviors. Having conversations with Matt where he watches brief video clips showing various forms of exercise will work well for Matt to help him expand his knowledge about possible options and to self-determine options he might be interested in exploring. As with the use of a tread-mill, Matt will do best if the time and schedule for the exercise activity are included in his weekly visual calendar of events.

In the area of social skills/self-determination skills, Matt would benefit from the following supports:

- *Although Matt has established clear preferences, interests, and abilities, he has not yet developed the social narrative to talk or think about himself. He would benefit from working with a counselor or therapist on developing a book about himself, his interests, his abilities, his life, and his goals for the future. Created over time, the visual book format (either physically or electronically) will support Matt in thinking about and appreciating his life story. It will also provide a supportive way for Matt to share his life story with others.*
- *Matt will most certainly benefit from continued participation in his current programs, including his social skills group.*

There are many, many more ways adults experience the world through their unique autistic point of view, but we will stop here for now. Take the structure and language provided here and integrate it into your own training and experience as you support the stories for the autistic adults in your clinical practice. Reveal their story and support their story. The autistic adults who experience your neuro-informed approach will appreciate your efforts and most definitely benefit from your guidance and support.

References

Garvey, N. (2023). *Looking After Your Autistic Self: A Personalized Self-care Approach to Managing your Sensory and Emotional Wellbeing*. London: Jessica Kingsley Press.

Kemp, J., Mitchelson, M, & Wise, S. J. (2024). *The Neurodivergence Skills Workbook for Autism and ADHD: Cultivate Self-compassion, Live Authentically, and Be Your Own Advocate*. Oakland, California: New Harbinger Press.

Monteiro, M. (2020). The power of the autism narrative. In Bedard, R, and Hecker, L. (Eds), *A Spectrum of Solutions for Clients with Autism: Treatment for Adolescents and Adults*. New York: Routledge.

Moore, L., Larkin, F., & Foley, S. (2024). Mental health professionals' experiences of adapting mental health interventions for autistic adults: A systematic review and thematic synthesis. *J Autism Dev Disord*. 54: 2484–2501. https://doi.org/10.1007/s10803-023-06006-6

Nerenberg, J. (2021). *Divergent Mind: Thriving in a World that wasn't Designed for You*. New York: HarperOne Press.

Oliver, E. (2024). *The ADHD and Autism Unmasking Workbook*. www.emilyoliverauthor.com

Price, D. (2022). *Unmasking Autism: Discovering the New Faces of Neurodiversity*. Harmony Press.

Prizant, B. M. & Fields-Meyer, T. (2022). *Uniquely Human: Updated and Expanded: A Different Way of Seeing Autism*. New York: Simon and Schuster.

Schembari, M. (2024). *A Little Less Broken: How and Autism Diagnosis Final Made Me Whole*. New York: Flatiron Books.

Silberman, S. (2016). *Neurotribes: The Legacy of Autism and the Future of Neurodiversity*. New York: Avery Press.

A final conversation and glossary of descriptive terms

Before we end our time together, I wanted to provide you with a glossary of the neuro-affirming language terms you've encountered throughout this book. As you begin to change the way in which you think, talk, and write about the autistic brain style pattern of strengths and differences in your clinical practice, there is work involved in paying attention to the words you use. Are you describing observable patterns that the individuals with whom you work can either confirm or clarify as being consistent with their lived experiences? Read the descriptive language provided below as well as throughout the book. Absorb it. Then make it your own and incorporate it into your individual communication style. Apply the descriptive language in your work with autistic individuals in your clinical practice.

Thank you for sharing your time with me as you read this book. And thank you for the important work you do supporting autistic individuals and their families in your clinical practice. The work you do changes lives. Please take in and apply this neuro-informed and positive way to think, talk, and write about the autistic lived experience. The individuals who seek you out for guidance and support will benefit so very much.

Glossary of descriptive terms

Block out incoming sources of stress: This term refers to a key function of sensory-based activities and routines for the individual. When the individual is engaged in self-initiated preferred activities, they experience a reprieve from incoming demands as they block out incoming sources of stress.

Body proximity: This term reminds clinicians to pay attention to body proximity, as movement has meaning. A pattern of meaningful movement to recognize is one in which the child stays in the area close to the adult when object-focused and sensory play are shared, but moves away from the adult when language and social overtures are made. In conversations, the individual becomes notably alert and engaged when sharing topics of preferred interest, with a corresponding withdrawal of engagement during social communication overtures and topic exploration. These patterns can be noted with the child's parents for confirmation or clarification, and with the verbally fluent individual to confirm or clarify their experience.

Brain reset breaks and activities: This term describes the process of identifying the specific environments and sensory routines that serve the function of organizing and regulating the individual's brain and system. These can then be linked to the creation of brain reset breaks or routines that the individual can practice using in a proactive way to build resiliency and regulation. Proactive use of brain reset breaks includes self-monitoring and employing a brief sensory reset break routine before returning to a nonpreferred task or activity. The goal is for the individual to increase and sustain their regulated state. This process of increasing the individual's ability to stay regulated not only reduces their destabilized brain state but also raises their threshold for managing incoming demands.

Brain Style Profile: The author's structured way to provide each individual's profile of strengths and differences in the three key areas of the Descriptive Triangle using strengths-based descriptive language.

Careful thinker: This describes the process for individuals who require additional time to process incoming language demands and to organize, retrieve, and use their language in response to input.

Complex developmental and behavioral profile: The author's suggested way to set the context for describing the profile for individuals who are living with multiple areas of neurodivergence.

Context and visual contextual cues: This term is used to highlight the importance of contextualization for the autistic individual to take in information, process that information, and organize their response to the information. Contextual cues are routines that provide the context for the individual and allow for the flexible transition in focus to take in incoming information. Visual contextual cues "show" the context, while the person "tells" the information or request.

Course corrections: This term can be used when the clinician is helping individuals and their family members explore incremental and practical shifts they can consider making in their communication, social, and emotional patterns of responding and enacting routines.

Create and maintain predictable routines: The individual organizes and regulates their brain and system through a process of forming and enacting systematic patterns of behavior. The individual's routines are distinctive in that they are self-initiated, provide a familiar and recognizable context, are a source of system regulation, and provide a reprieve from the hard work of responding to incoming demands.

Descriptive Triangle: The author's visual framework for thinking, talking, and writing about the individual's autistic Brain Style Profile of strengths and differences across age and ability levels in three key areas: Language and Communication, Social Relationships and Emotions, and Sensory Use and Interests.

Emerging skills: Emerging skills are skills the individual is beginning to acquire but has not reached the point at which they can readily access and apply those skills. An example of an emerging spoken language skill is a child who spontaneously labels visual aspects of objects of interest but is not yet responding to prompts from others to do so.

Extension: This refers to the conditions under which the individual extends their communication or play routines. The clinician is looking for a notable difference between the individual's spontaneous use of extension with self-initiated topics and play and their increase in prompt dependency, and limited extension when the topic or play are initiated by the clinician.

Flexibly shift from their agenda to follow the agenda of others: This reminds the clinician to explore the degree to which the individual experiences stress when their system is required to shift flexibly from their self-initiated, contextualized routines to incoming communication directives, social overtures, and transitions from self-initiated activities, to follow a schedule of events or agenda set by others.

Form: This term reminds the clinician to describe the sensory aspects of behavior patterns. The form of the individual's area of preferred interest refers to the sensory and brain dimensions in use during their exploration of preferred activities. Building with Legos, for example, can be described by the form of a visual, tactile, creative, three-dimensional, problem-solving, goal-directed activity. The form of the activity can then be linked directly to brain processes, such as visuospatial processing.

Function: This term reminds the clinician to look for patterns of functionality in the individual's creation and maintenance of predictable routines. The three functions that can be confirmed or clarified during the autism assessment process are as follows: the activity provides a sense of organization for the individual's brain and system; the activity is experienced as a source of regulation and self-soothing for the individual's brain and system; and the individual experiences a reprieve from managing incoming demands as they block out incoming sources of stress.

Hard work for the brain: This describes the individual's experience of managing incoming demands, as engaging in interactive exchanges requires work for the individual's brain and system. The hard work refers to the individual's required efforts of switching from their agenda to take in the context and respond to the agenda of others. The demands for brain flexibility and management of unpredictable input are experienced as the draining of energy and as potential sources of system stress and distress.

High threshold for sustaining engagement with areas of preferred interest: This refers to the individual's experience of a higher than expected need to access and engage in sustained focus on their areas of preferred interest. The high threshold need is important to understand, as it highlights the lived experience of the sensory aspects that drive the need to engage in preferred routines along with their restorative function.

Incoming demands: This term is used to distinguish the lived experience difference for the individual when responding to or managing incoming information. Incoming information can be defined as a source of demand for the individual's brain and system, creating stress. Any input that is not self-initiated is a source of incoming demands. This refers to the hard work for the individual's brain and system when they are required to flexibly shift their focus to take in information. Incoming demands refer to input that requires the individual to take in and respond to information while determining the context for that information, including communication, social, sensory, transition, and nonpreferred activities input. Sources of incoming demands include communication overtures from others, changes in expected routines, interruptions that require flexible shifting from the individual's sensory-driven agenda to follow the agenda of others, and sensory input.

Initiation: This term reminds the clinician to look for patterns that characterize the conditions under which the individual initiates or starts communication, social engagement, or play with another person. Key patterns include initiation linked to the individual's areas of preferred interest for which they have a context that provides access to a fluid process of organizing, retrieving, and using language and object-focused play routines that also contain accessible and familiar elements.

Limited to no verbal fluency: The child, adolescent, or adult is not yet using spoken language or is emerging in their ability to use spoken language, but is not yet using that language to participate in shared spoken exchanges with others. However, the individual uses and responds to visually contextualized information to some degree.

Low load language activities and demands: Identifying activities that are restorative for the individual oftentimes includes recognizing the reprieve provided to that individual's brain and system when they are able to engage in activities and demands in which the expectation is to experience limited interactive or incoming social language demands. Reading preferred books, for example, is a low load language activity because the individual gets a reprieve from the hard work of managing incoming language demands.

Low threshold for managing incoming demands: This refers to the individual's experience of living with a lower than expected ability to take in and manage incoming demands throughout the day. The threshold is a moving one and depends on the individual's available mental, physical, and emotional resources along with the frequency, duration, and intensity of the expected demands.

Mirroring: The clinician enters into the interaction with a neurodivergent individual with the mindful intention of respectfully taking that individual's perspective. An authentic shared experience occurs when the clinician adjusts their behavior and communication style to align themselves to be in sync with the way in which the neurodivergent individual communicates their way of being in the world.

Nonspeaking shared exchange: This term provides the clinician with a way to describe the medical term "nonverbal joint attention." Further descriptors include differences in the individual's use of and response to eye gaze, changes in facial expression, use of gestures, and body orientation toward and in response to the conversational or play partner.

Not yet using spoken language: This is a descriptive way to distinguish when the individual is not yet speaking, while acknowledging their developing use of nonspeaking language and communication abilities.

Organize: This refers to the identification of activities and routines that serve the function of providing the individual with a context and a sense of understanding and anticipating meaningful experiences and routines.

Patterns of strengths and differences: The identification of the individual's distinctive patterns of strengths and differences in the three areas of Language and Communication, Social Relationships and Emotions, and Sensory Use and Interests. Differences are characterized as neurodivergent ways of experiencing and responding to communication, social, and sensory needs, input, and demands.

Preferred or passionate areas of interest: Identifying and describing the individual's areas of preferred or passionate interest provide the entry point for exploring their brain style strengths and understanding their autistic sensory entry point. Preferred interests are ones that are self-initiated and provide a context for the experience. Exploring the form of the individual's preferred interests leads to supporting the individual's understanding of their preferred interest routines and ways those interests may provide compatible social pathways with others.

Reactive behavior routines: The sequence of emotions, words, and actions the individual experiences and enacts when their brain and system switch from a regulated to a dysregulated state.

Recurrent and distinctive body movements and mannerism: The individual's notable patterns of creating and maintaining predictable routines that organize around their body movements and mannerisms. These patterns serve a self-soothing and self-regulation function.

Regulate: This term reminds the clinician to explore and describe activities, patterns, and routines that the individual experiences as sources of self-soothing and regulation of their brain and system.

Self-initiated: The use of this term is linked to the understanding that self-initiated communication, activities, routines, and actions are predictable and a source of organization and regulation for the individual. This contrasts with the hard work involved when the individual has to shift their focus to manage incoming demands and information.

Sensory Use and Interests: This provides clinicians with a descriptive renaming of the medical terms of restricted interests and repetitive behaviors. Sensory use can be defined in terms of the individual's distinctive pattern of preferences and sensitivities. This information directly links up with the exploration of sensory brain reset routines the individual can develop and use to organize and regulate their system and to block out incoming sources of stress. Naming the individual's areas of preferred interests leads directly to the identification of the form of those interests and their connection with the individual's brain style pattern of strengths and differences. This information leads to the development of visually and contextually based supports and strategies that are a fit for the individual's autistic brain style.

Shared exchanges: This term reminds the clinician to recognize the autistic pattern of differences in the verbally fluent individual's ability to *simultaneously* organize, retrieve, and use their language, while using and responding to spoken and unspoken communication features with a conversational partner. The pattern of autistic differences in shared exchanges with children who are not yet using spoken language emerges when the clinician uses social play overtures.

Social overture: This term helps the clinician distinguish between expected ways to start a shared exchange and the autistic social overture of making a social connection through the sensory entry point of invitations to talk about topics of interest for which the individual has a readily accessible context or object-focused play.

Sources of stress and distress: This refers to the identification of the starting points that define when the individual switches from their regulated to dysregulated state. The sources can be environmental, interpersonal, or a combination of identifiable incoming demands.

Thinking versus reacting brain: This refers to the binary experience of switching from a regulated to a dysregulated emotional and behavioral state. Characterizing the individual's words and actions associated with their thinking/regulated brain and body can then be contrasted with the words and actions associated with their reacting/dysregulated brain and system.

Verbally fluent: Individuals who have well-developed language skills, including spoken language and the ability to understand and apply language concepts.

Visual contextual cues: This refers to providing the individual with a readily accessible context for taking in information from other people, resulting in the individual's ability to access their language and regulated response to the incoming information. Visual contextual cues can range from pairing spoken language requests with visual supports to creating visual routines to facilitate transitions from the individual's focus on their agenda to prepare to take in information from another person. For example, pairing physical proximity with a routine way to structure the incoming information ("pause button"; verbally stating the context for the upcoming information) is a way to create a visual contextual routine.

Vocalizes to communicate and express emotions: This phrase reminds the clinician to emphasize the communicative function of the child's vocalizations. For the autistic child's Language and Communication Brain Style Profile, a strength to note is often the child's use of vocalizations to communicate and express emotions, including delight and protest. At the same time, a notable difference for the child includes the observation that the child is *not yet directing their vocalizations toward a listener or conversational partner.*

Worldview: This term encourages clinicians to appreciate and share the singular perspective and lived experience of the autistic individual as they guide the person through the autism assessment and support process.

Index

For Product Safety Concerns and Information please contact our EU
representative GPSR@taylorandfrancis.com
Taylor & Francis Verlag GmbH, Kaufingerstraße 24, 80331 München, Germany

www.ingramcontent.com/pod-product-compliance
Lightning Source LLC
Chambersburg PA
CBHW070324270326
41926CB00017B/3742